S0-AYH-513

THE POLITICS OF DIVINATION

THE

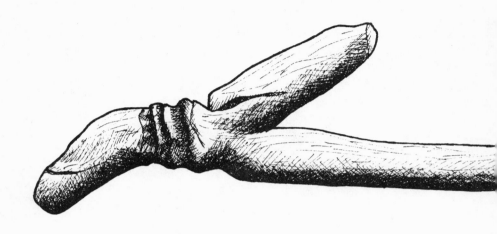

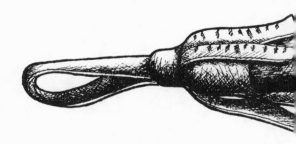

UNIVERSITY OF CALIFORNIA Berkeley Los Angeles London

POLITICS OF DIVINATION

A Processual View of Reactions to Illness and
Deviance among the Sisala of Northern Ghana

Eugene L. Mendonsa

FERNALD LIBRARY
COLBY-SAWYER COLLEGE
NEW LONDON, N.H. 03257

DT
510.43
S57
M46

6/83 Finnegan 25.65

91117

University of California Press
Berkeley and Los Angeles, California

University of California Press, Ltd.
London, England

Copyright © 1982 by The Regents of the University of California

Library of Congress Cataloging in Publication Data

Mendonsa, Eugene L.
  The politics of divination.

  Bibliography: p. 245
  1. Sisala (African people)—Social life and
customs. 2. Sisala (African people)—Medicine.
3. Divination—Ghana—Case studies. I. Title.
DT510.43.S57M46   1982   966.7   81-16400
ISBN 0-520-04594-7   AACR2

Printed in the United States of America

1   2   3   4   5   6   7   8   9

Designed by Linda M. Robertson

*To Merlin Myers, who started
me on the path . . .*

Contents

Preface

This book represents a shift in my thinking. When I began my career as an anthropologist, I studied both sociology and social anthropology. In the latter discipline I was introduced to the subject matter by a gifted teacher, Merlin G. Myers, who had completed his doctorate at Cambridge University. Through him I learned of Durkheim, Radcliffe-Brown, Malinowski, and many others. Through other sociology professors I learned about consensus theorists too—for example, Talcott Parsons—but I also came into contact with the writings of such men as George Homans, Kurt Lewin, C. Wright Mills, C. H. Cooley, George H. Mead, W. I. Thomas, Max Weber, and Karl Marx. Most of these scholars were introduced to me by two sociology professors, Genevieve DeHoyos and James Duke, to whom I will forever be grateful.

When I myself attended Cambridge University for postgraduate studies, I had expected to find structural-functionalism, or consensus theory, alive and well, but it was on the wane. Instead of a Kuhnian mature paradigm, I was exposed to a variety of competing models. The influences of Levi-Strauss and Leach were strong, as was the more sociohistorical comparative view of Jack Goody, a strong influence on me and a good friend to whom I am very grateful. Network theory was also being talked about, especially since John Barnes had just come to Cambridge as the head of the newly founded sociology department. Visitors from America were also discussing such seemingly exotic subdisciplines as cognitive anthropology and componential analysis. It was an exciting time in my life intellectually, but I could not clearly see much connection among many of these points of view.

My adviser, Prof. Meyer Fortes, who was also a warm and helpful friend to me and who has my heartfelt thanks, had suggested upon my arrival that I spend some time in the Haddon Anthropology Library reading the articles of the last ten years (1960—1970) in the major anthropology journals. This exercise, while seen as profitable by me now, did not at the time serve to proffer the idea of theoretical unity within the field of anthropology.

Then came the fieldwork. I had originally intended to do it in Portugal but switched to Uganda because of the wealth of African resources at Cambridge. The takeover by Idi Amin, however, put an end to that plan. I began to look around for another African field site and was put on to the Sisala at the suggestion of Esther Newcomb Goody, to whom I am thankful for that idea and for all her help during my Cambridge years.

I had planned to do the normal one- to two-year field trip, return, and write-up, but circumstances caused me to return in the spring of 1972 after only nine months in the field. On the basis of that fieldwork, I wrote my thesis on divination. I was unable to return to the field until the summer of 1975, when I followed up on the cases I had come to know about previously. Thus, circumstances forced me into making an extended case analysis; this was not an intended plan. Teaching responsibilities meant that I could spend only three months among the Sisala on this trip, and my third trip did not come until two years later, when I also spent the summer in Ghana. During these years I was teaching and writing about the Sisala and working over my field notes and the divinatory cases with which I had become familiar.

When I came to teach at the University of California, Los Angeles, in 1976, I began to go back to interests aroused by my earlier exposure to symbolic interactionism and cognitive studies. I reread Blumer as well as many cognitive anthropologists. I gave a series of graduate seminars on these subjects and profited greatly from the lively discussions of my graduate students, to whom I would like to provide a collective thank-you. A highlight of one such seminar was a guest lecture kindly given by my colleague from the sociology department, Harold Garfinkel. This contact led me to read the ethnomethodologists. Around this same time Sally Falk Moore joined our department, and I greatly benefited from exposure to her ideas and writings on law and social process, a debt that will be evident upon the reading of this book. Through her influence I read more deeply in the recent literature coming out of Gluckman's influence at Manchester. I was also influenced by the visit of Bruce Kapferer, who led some stimulating discussions about transactional analysis and ritual healing.

The shift in my thinking has resulted from my personal history of interactions with a variety of persons and schools of thought. During these years I became aware of a gap between, on the one hand, theories that talked about the subjective nature of man and his action within limited social fields, and, on the other, theories that talked about large-scale structures or macro-historical shifts. I came to see the need to link the two levels of analysis, and I came to view social process as the key bridging concept, though in the back of my mind was the remark of one prominent Cambridge anthropologist, who warned me that "this idea of process is a very dangerous concept." Perhaps it is.

Sally Moore (1978:42–43) notes that social process refers to changes in individual situations and changes in culture. I assume that the two are linked, though I have not yet fully developed ways of doing so, and I see this as a major task for anthropology. *Process* is used to describe universal contexts of social contact, such as cooperation or competition; or to describe a series of events that recur in a specific institutional context, such as plea bargaining or the politics of divination; or, finally, to describe the types of circumstances that lead to such results as urbanization, industrialization, and lineage fission. All three ways of looking at process have two common elements: they are based on observations made over time, and they concern the movements in the fortunes and relationships of individuals. Such processes may influence and alter socio-cultural formations. This book is a tentative step in the direction of understanding how we can account for the presence of both order and change in society. I only hope that this effort will be of some benefit to others also engaged in this quest.

Throughout this work I have tried to follow the orthography of R. Blass's *Sisaala-English/English-Sisaala Dictionary*. She, however, uses many diacritical marks that could not be used in this publication. I have for the most part conformed to her orthography in spelling, with one or two exceptions; for example, she spells the name of the group "Sisaala," and I stay with the spelling as it appears in the ethnography already published.

I am indebted to many people for helping me directly or indirectly along the way, some of whom I have already mentioned. I would like to make special thanks to Sally Falk Moore, Robert Edgerton, John Kennedy, Tim Earle and Nancy Levine, all of whom kindly took time from busy schedules to read and comment on earlier drafts of this book. Their comments enhanced the book, and any errors or shortcomings are mine. Special mention also goes to my three principal field assistants, the late Marifa Kanton, Bubachebe Yeliwiejang, and Nenkentie Fuojang, as well as to the chiefs of Tumu and Bujan, who kindly and freely helped me a great deal. I would like to thank the fine ethnomusicologist Mary Seavoy, who, while studying Sisala music, helped me in times of sickness and need.

A special mention goes to Martha Chaves Mendonsa and to my children, Matthew and Melissa, who endured much hardship and deprivation on my account. Also, a note of thanks to Sandy and Freida Stewart for their kindness to me while in Cambridge.

Finally, I would like to acknowledge the financial support of the electors of the Anthony Wilken Studentship at Cambridge University, the Smuts Fund, the British Universities Student Travel Association, the Academic Senate of the University of California, and Wolfson College at Cambridge University.

1
Introduction

I This book is about the exercise of power through divinatory means in Sisala-land, northern Ghana. In the normal religious process of divining, participants manipulate the institutional structure to attempt to coerce others. Divination is used to seek redress of misfortune. As this is done, the reality of the social order is recreated and affirmed in the minds of ritual participants. This search results in the labeling of a deviant, who must perform an expiatory rite to redress his wrongdoing. As participants struggle to label another or avoid being labeled, their definitions of self, social order, and the relation between them is molded. This symbolic management and control of social reality through the divinatory process periodically provides social power and a means of reaffirming and altering the social order.

Politics refers to the distribution, maintenance, and exercise of power within social groups. The politics of divination occur between segments within the lineage and between kin units within the larger descent group. Here I will concentrate on conflict between authorities and subordinates in intralineage relations. Within the lineage system, especially among members of the economically corporate and residentially based lineage, elders use divination to control the behavior of subordinates, who may become labeled as deviants by these means. Thus, relations within domestic groups in Sisala society have a power component. I will show that dominant members of the lineage have ritual means at their disposal for political control of subordinates. These rites are supposed to provide elders with social power to counteract the natural physical power of the younger generation. They do not always do so, but as

1

elders and subordinates struggle to settle disputes within the divinatory process, they reaffirm and remold their society.

This book is an effort, first, to integrate actual ethnographic data on disputes with the literature on symbolic interaction and the labeling theory of deviance, and, second, to help us comprehend the utilitarian aspects of the ritual institutions used to settle disputes. My research revealed cases of conflict and dispute in a West African tribal setting which may further our understanding of man as actor and man as one whose life is patterned by a priori structures. At the most general level, this work is concerned with the ever-changing relationship between social life and its cultural representation. The latter appears as an ideal model of society—how things should be. The former is the flux of everyday life situations as they are experienced by members of society. While the ideal model changes in response to material and social factors, it also influences them. This model exists at any given moment as the mental representations of the members of society and the cultural codes, to the extent that they are represented outside the minds and memories of people. As such, it is a structural moment in time. I assume that this ideal model undergoes subtle changes as it is passed from generation to generation, but it also undergoes changes each time it is reinterpreted through divination and other ritual performances. These rituals involve the reaffirmation of the moral imperatives of the mythical past, and as such, they are institutionalization processes, but they also involve the exercise of power, the manipulation of symbols, and deviation from cultural ideals.

If moral imperatives exist and the resulting pattern of behavior does not conform exactly to them, then we need to analyze the processes that mediate between them. Viewing man as actor, we can see that these processes involve a series of decisions and operations leading to an end or ends. How do goal-oriented operations link individual acts to symbolic formations? In other words, what are the operations that result in observed social patterns? In this book I intend to show that the divinatory process is one such link. It performs a connective function in that it permits willful individuals to negotiate and to recreate their social order as they attempt to explain misfortune, cure illness, and redress impaired social relations. Since they all work within the framework of a shared cultural system and since they communicate with each other about things, the result of their interaction is not random or chaotic.

When we better understand action as it occurs within such institutional contexts as divination, we will better understand social organization and the links between action and pattern. I will show, for example, how the cosmology and disease etiology of the Sisala and their institution of divination provide a structured framework within which elders and subordinates settle disputes. As deviants are labeled and charged with the responsibility for family misfortune, their behavior has intended and unintended consequences for the social order. Really, this is the key theoretical question facing social anthropology: Can we develop a theory that takes into account the intentions of actors and the unintended consequences of their intended behavior? And, more specifically, does action within divination restore impaired social relations? For how long? What percentage of cases have this result? If impaired social relations are not repaired, what happens? Does divination act as a bypass device—in other words, does it allow disputants to bypass imperfections in the social order in order to arrive at a specific solution to an immediate problem?

This work also seeks to clarify the processes by which the social order emerges and is maintained as men use symbols to interact with each other. It provides empirical data and a theoretical perspective indicating that the social order has a negotiated character. Specifically, it shows that within the divinatory process in Sisala-land disputes are settled according to rules, but people use rules creatively and take more than rules into account while making their decisions. Authority relations have power, but so do other types of relations. Elders derive power from kinship positions but other members of the lineage derive power from wealth, force of personality, generation, personal ability, and positions held in nonlineage domains—such as, for example, when a lineage member is a government chief. Such power relations impinge upon relations of authority as authorities use ritual means to blame deviants for family misfortunes. The divinatory process is a political process that provides an ordered forum for discussion, negotiation, conflict, and resolution of thorny issues. It can be seen as the Sisala solution to a universal problem: namely, how is society able to make binding decisions? Easton (1969:227) provides us with a heuristic format that we can use to understand ethnographic data on disputes when he says: "I suggest that there are at least five basically different kinds of activities in which members of a society must engage if binding decisions are to be made and put into effect: (1) the formulation of demands, (2) legislation, (3) administration, (4) adjudication, and (5) the marshaling of support and solidarity."

These five operations occur within the divinatory process, which comprises the perception of misfortune, the linking of that misfortune to deviance, the labeling of a deviant, and the resolution of the conflict. First, divination in Sisala-land makes it possible for parties to a conflict to formulate and press demands with regard to what they think should be done. This need arises from the very fact that a conflict in principles and/or opinions exists. Without this conflict there would be no need to make choices between alternative courses of action. Divination focuses the issues. It reduces possibilities to a limited set of alternatives and provides the elder with a method by which to choose one of them. At the oracle the client can synthesize conflicting points of view and sort out an acceptable solution.

Second, there exist processes that allow this alternative to be acted upon and converted into action. That is not to say that a formal binding decision is always reached. Decisions do not become legislation; rather, a situational solution emerges which is acceptable in light of general cultural values. It may become a precedent for a future situation of a similar nature, or it may be forgotten. In Sisala-land most disputes are not taken to the Ghanaian courts; they are handled at home by the elders. The result is a highly fluid set of unwritten principles, codes, and rules in use. When a specific case arises, the elders sift through the rules to arrive at a solution. Divination aids them in this sorting process.

Third, once a decision is reached there are administrative activities that allow its implementation. Sisala elders do this through the auspices of the ancestor cult. Specifically, an elder exercises his right to demand that a wrongdoer perform a public redressive rite. Once the oracle points out the deviant by defining his wrongdoing as the cause of family misfortune, the elder has the right to announce this publicly and demand that he make retribution for his wrongdoing. Should he refuse, the family remains in danger of being afflicted further. Thus, public opinion is firmly behind the elder in most cases.

Fourth, adjudication takes place through divination and the many palavers held before and after the divination. These palavers include the elders and any concerned parties. When this assembly points the finger at a person, he is called into the adjudicative process. He may try to sidestep the decision by requiring futher divination, since the ideal is multiple divination in serious cases. If they do this, he accompanies the elders to future sessions. In my experience, however, most persons accept the judgment and perform the postdivinatory sacrifice willingly. The performance of this redressive rite is so important that if the deviant cannot perform it, for whatever reason, it will be performed on his behalf by a close kinsman. This is done to avoid further misfortune, the threat of which always hangs over every dispute.

Lastly, the divinatory process results in the marshaling of support behind the decision. Since the family stands to receive further and continued affliction if the deviance is not redressed, public support is usually forthcoming. If factions with differing opinions exist, these opinions must be worked into a consensus through palavers in the course of the divinatory process. Sometimes

the elder consults the diviner and then meets with other househol
Sometimes they all consult together and palaver during the consultation.
Sometimes the consultation takes place and then they meet with all lineage
members. Whatever the makeup of the assemblage, the divinatory process is a
series of negotiations where general principles are applied to specific conditions. It is a common, though not the only, way of organizing political power
in Sisala-land.

The politics of divination are tied up with struggles between individuals
and those between kin groups. Political cleavages may exist between segments
of the lineage system. The divinatory process is a means of handling such
conflict. I see it as a symbolic arena in which people can work out their
problems. Under its symbolic cloak, people negotiate with and manipulate
each other. Whereas previous works have viewed kinship and religious
structures as directing or constraining behavior, which they do, I also see
people working out their rules in use. That is, they select certain rules to be
applied in certain cases and ignore others. They select the symbols they wish to
use to define a conflict situation. This power struggle over the use of symbols
within the divinatory process occurs not only between individuals and kin
segments but also between authorities and subordinates. I see flexibility built
into the process. People are not slaves to custom: rather, they work out ways in
which life can go on in spite of structural contradictions and conflicts of
interest.

Such concerns relate to another main theme of this book: namely, what
are the ways in which disputes are handled by ritual means? By understanding
how misfortune is linked to deviance and by understanding the consequences of
this linkage, we can better understand how the Sisala are able to reproduce their
social system over time. Briefly, in a segmentary lineage system, new settlements emerge near parental ones and come to have a structure similar to that of
the parent group. Through lineage fission, structure is reproduced. But how?
What are the actual means by which social form repeats itself? This book is an
effort to show how the process of labeling deviance through ritual means has
both political consequences and structural consequences, for disputants. Bailey
(1969:xiii) puts this point nicely when he says, "The edge of anarchy is fenced
off by rules"—that is to say, disputes are handled within the institutional
frames, and conformity and deviance are labels worked out through social
interaction according to system principles and rules. Conformers are people
whose activity others find valuable, and deviants are those whose behavior is
not valued. These evaluations, however, do not emerge out of a vacuum and are
not purely situational; rather, they are made by group members who share

common premises, symbols, and expectations. These may emerge out of prior social interaction but become, through time, social facts (Berger and Luckmann 1967).

II   Most Sisala are pagans, that is, they worship their ancestors through blood sacrifice. Islam has influenced the Voltaic region of West Africa for centuries, but few Sisala have adopted it. Those that have come in contact with it through emigration usually adopt it while abroad but revert to ancestor worship when they return home (Grindal 1973). Christianity came to Sisala-land with the coming of the British in 1906, but few Sisala have adopted this form of worship. In fact, there are nominal members of all three religions in the area. My experience has been that the Sisala are very eclectic in religious tastes. If they experience a misfortune, they are willing to approach Allah, Jesus, or the ancestors to receive relief. The traditional system of divination is used by members of all three religions. A member of a lineage may consider himself to be a Moslem or a Christian, but he still has kinship responsibilities to his fellow lineage members. These duties involve working a common farm and partici-pating in divination sessions, funerals, ancestral sacrifices, and other group rites. Thus, while persons may nominally adopt a world religion in certain non-Sisala contexts, world religions have had little impact on the religious authority of lineages over their members. Not to participate in such funda-mental kinship activities is tantamount to being non-Sisala.

One such vital rite is divination, which deals with life crises. It is a set of institutionalized procedures and roles for coping with calamities of all sorts. It is a system of symbolic beliefs and practices that can be used to diagnose, explain, and ameliorate misfortunes. These are its manifest functions. It can also be used by groups and individuals to influence the outcome of conflict situations. As a highly politicized process, it can be used by actors to further particular goals or those of society or, more importantly, to achieve particular-ism under the guise of universalism.

During a lifetime each member of society breaks social rules. Much of this deviance is ignored by others, but rule violation that is considered "trouble-causing" behavior is usually punished by those in authority positions. Divination ferrets out trouble and represents it to members of society according to acceptable standards. When the powerful hold such positions, the weak are at their mercy, but in Sisala-land office holders are seldom in total control of their subordinates. In other words, subordinates usually have strategies open to them because, while they may not have authority, they do have some degree of power. Rule enforcement is affected by the differential power of rule violators.

In Sisala-land the oldest male of each lineage is vested with the authority to punish his subordinates through ritual means. In the language of the Sisala they are -*tiina*. This translates as "custodian" or "officeholder." Such elders have the responsibility (*bene*) to enforce the dicta of the ancestors, and ideally they are free to do this with impunity. Yet there is a great paradox in Sisala social life: opportunities for individual economic advancement do not coincide with the cultural model, which forbids such individualism at the expense of the group. Authorities have the right and duty to uphold group mores. They have the authority to do so, but elders are economically dependent on their subordinates for support. Therein lies the power of subordinates over elders. Since subordinates have opportunities to withdraw their material support of elders— for example, they can move away—they do have some power to negotiate in cases of dispute. Elders must take into account the power of subordinates, just as subordinates must take into account the authority of elders.

The power of an elder lies in his authoritative control of the ancestor cult. It is vested in his office. While he may be weak, old, blind, or even bedridden, he has the authority to make vital decisions and to administer justice within the social unit that he heads. By virtue of the fact that he has exclusive access to the group's ancestors in matters of misfortune, subordinates are dependent upon him to solve such problems as serious sickness, injury, or anxiety over an unknown venture. Subordinates can withdraw their material support, but elders can accuse them of deviance. Such accusations are made through divination and draw the accused into institutionalized procedures designed to redress the wrongdoing and ameliorate misfortune. The trump card of subordinates is an economic one; that of the elders is a ritual one.

The elders find customary rules to their advantage in most cases. This is because such rules have evolved as previous elders faced similar situations, and it is not surprising to find that rules favor those who make them. Ideally all punishment comes from the ancestors, who watch over their descendants, but that power is exercised through the actions of the lineage elder and/or the elders' council. The authority is vested in the office, but it is important to remember that the officeholder is a human being with personal goals, prejudices, and enemies. Thus, the possibility arises that an elder could manipulate his role for personal reasons. In fact, this is one beauty of divination: an elder can impose his will and have it appear to be the wish of the ancestors.

The authority of an elder derives from his office as custodian of the lineage members, their shrines, the granary, and the farm. He is a father to them in that he holds economic, political, and religious rights and duties over them. The elder is the senior married male in the lineage. His age enhances his stature because it is thought to bring wisdom, and in general respect is given to the elderly. As an officeholder though, he rightfully receives more than generalized respect (*zile*): he receives fearful respect (*fa*), similar to that which a child feels for a stern father. When disputes arise within the group, he is entitled to invoke the ancestors to ensure conformity with the laws of the ancestors. He can approach them at their shrines and commune with them through divination. He is the leader of the ancestor cult and as such has the right and duty to divine on behalf of his subordinates and perform sacrifices for them. Divination and sacrifice, then, form the ritual foundation of the ancestor cult. They are key institutions in what I call the divinatory process (Mendonsa 1978*c*). When misfortune strikes, the elder must begin the ritual process to discover the cause and cure. If a dispute arises, he may use ritual to settle the matter. Such power derives from the belief that behind all he does, as custodian of the lineage, he has the backing of the dead.

The social interaction of members of a lineage involves both cooperation and conflict. When conflict arises, it is thought to cause misfortune within the group unless the conflict is dealt with in a straightforward manner and the dispute solved. It is thought wrong to hold bitter thoughts or feelings against other family members without trying to bring about a solution. Thus, when misfortune strikes the group, it is thought to be the result of secret envy, hatred, or a deviant act. It is the responsibility of the elder to find the deviant and redress the situation lest more misfortune befall the group.

The divinatory process includes diagnosis through divination and sacrificial efforts at redress and cure. This is a process wherein the elder accuses a member of the group of deviance, which is seen as the cause of group misfortune. The labeled deviant must then perform a piacular sacrifice to rid the group of the threat of continued affliction. It is important to keep in mind throughout this book that the symbolic forms and practices of divination are highly ambiguous and manipulable. In chapter 5 I provide details of this. Here let me just note that the diviner does little interpretation. The interpretative function lies with the consulting elder or client. The diviner is a functionary who performs a set ritual that is interpreted largely by the client, though the degree of explanation by the diviner varies with the expertise of the client. The experienced client may complete an hour-long consultation without even explaining why he has come to consult. The diviner is neither expected nor required to know, nor is the elder expected or required to verbalize his reason. Thus, in the interpretative function of the consulting elder lies the opportunity for divinatory manipulation. Competing individuals or factions often choose skilled persons to consult on their behalf. Elders are aware of and openly discuss this manipulation. It is thought that a divinatory pronouncement is a truthful statement by the ancestors *even if* the elder tries to pin the blame on a specific person whom he personally dislikes, for the ancestors will not let him make an error. In fact, in the ideology of divination, it is thought proper that the consulting elder should try to fool the ancestors by placing various names before the oracle. He should *test* the oracle in this way. Once the oracle has selected a given person as the deviant, the elder checks and rechecks this name with the oracle to test further the decision of the ancestors. It is thought that such testing ensures that the oracle, not the elder, makes the decision. When the elder emerges from the divining session, he is armed with an accusation backed by ancestral authority.

Most adult males consult diviners, but when lineage matters are at stake it is the responsibility (*bene*) of the elder to consult. This is normally when a misfortune has occurred. Once he begins the consultation, the ambiguity of divinatory symbolism and practice gives him great latitude to accuse others of deviance. It is paradoxical that this ambiguity allows the elder to particularize the situation. Through divination he is able to segregate from an infinite array of possibilities the exact cause and solution to a lineage problem. Divination provides him with categories of general scenarios from which he makes his choice. Then he and the diviner focus on that scenario, represented by a cluster of material symbols. It is the elder who determines who the deviant is by placing names before the oracle. He may do this silently, merely indicating by gesture that he wishes the diviner to make a binary choice. Obviously, this method offers great freedom to label deviants. He also determines which ancestor, kin group, and shrine have caused the misfortune to befall his group. The material symbols, or code objects, will also reveal the exact shrine where the piacular sacrifice must take place and the animals to be used.

Divination makes concrete and simple those issues that are complex and that involve thorny problems within the group. These may arise from interpersonal conflicts or interrelations of contradictory cultural principles. I shall present cases of each type of conflict later. Divination acts to organize human effort to solve these difficult issues. It makes life manageable in spite of them. The group may be rife with jealousy, interpersonal rivalries, factions, structural contradictions, role conflicts, and ambiguous rules, but family members are able to live their lives in spite of such imperfections because divination focuses a specific issue and segregates a cause and cure by which to define and manage the situation. In this process, social reality is constructed out of abstract principles and symbols and is applied to real-life situations. By using cultural symbols, elders manage the situation. I see power relations as being camouflaged by such ritual symbolism. In Sisala-land, both within families and in the relations between larger political units, such as maximal lineages and clans, most symbols, rules, and procedures are of a kinship and/or ritual nature and are used in divinatory attempts to control behavior. They are ambiguous and highly complicated. These qualities make them especially suited for use in political persuasion. I do not assume that all ritual symbols and rules are concerned with power relations or that power does not exist in other kinds of relations; I have merely chosen to analyze divination's power component.

Elders need to control the behavior of their subordinates because wives run away and there is always the danger that a group will lose its young men to emigration. Both young men and women have vital skills on which elders are dependent. Ever since the establishment of the colonial structure by Britain, the Sisala have migrated south in search of jobs in the urban areas and cacao fields. Young men also leave the lineage to work elsewhere in Sisala-land. Land is plentiful, so anyone who wishes to clear the bush can start farming in any clan area merely by asking permission of the clan elder, and a youth always has the formal right to seek residence in his mother's clan. A lineage can also lose personnel in this way. It is important, too, for a lineage to be able to attract and keep wives for its male members. If a wife is unhappy she may return to her natal clan or easily remarry into another clan. Thus, a lineage elder must be aware that he cannot make life too difficult for his subordinates for fear that they will leave the group.

Elders use symbolic formations to control subordinates because they derive power from outside opportunities. In spite of this control, fission of lineages does occur. Fission is the most serious breach of kinship amity, but, as I have pointed out elsewhere (Mendonsa 1979), it is not easy for a household to sever ritual ties with the parent lineage. One can make a new farm and build a new compound at a new site, but, for the first few years at least, the new group will have to sacrifice at the original ancestor shrines of the parent lineage. More importantly for our purposes here, they will remain subject to the authority of the lineage elder. He can still accuse them of causing misfortune within the parental lineage. Furthermore, they have no means of ameliorating their own misfortunes unless they submit to the authority of the elder. Complete ritual independence comes for the new group only after at least one generation has passed away and they have begun to venerate their own dead at shrines created in their own compound. This is how new lineages emerge in time, despite the fact that it is the responsibility of elders and ancestors to prevent fission through control of significant symbols of authority. Later in this work I will show how deviant persons and segments can reproduce the necessary symbolic formations that permit the new group to attain the status of a lineage. Viewed through time, structural relations undergo transformations as a result of biological, material, demographic, and social changes that affect a lineage population. When a lineage splits in half, the two halves at first stand in filial relation to each other; in other words, the new group is the "son" of the parent lineage. But after one or more generations the relation becomes fraternal: they are now "brother" lineages, with the former parental lineage becoming the "elder brother" (for the details, see Mendonsa 1979). The structure of the segmentary lineage system allows the new lineage to use another point of reference, a higher-order apical ancestor, by which to define its status once it has acquired the two most significant ritual symbols of a lineage, which are the lineage granary (*virebaliŋ*) and the lineage ancestor shrine *(lɛlɛɛ)*.

These transformations place a strain on the cultural ideal of the unity of the lineage. They do not, however, completely invalidate the ideal model, because the ritual system contains an elasticity that enables lineages to emerge in response to strains and conflict. If conflict splits the lineage, kinship relations between component households are not severed but merely transformed from one type of kin relation into another. Thus, if an elder and subordinate have a conflict that leads to a transformation of their kin relationship, this is reinterpreted according to another principle within the same cultural model that the transformation violates. The cultural model and the general form of society are not threatened because they contain principles that can be arbitrarily applied in different situations in order to make the circumstances appear to conform to the model.

Divination is seen as a means of maintaining the integrity and unity of the lineage community. The settlement of disputes within the divinatory process allows deviance, such as lineage fission, to occur without seriously altering the authority of the elders. I view this process, not as an institutionalized way of maintaining the social order, but as a set of institutionalized activities that enable lineage members to work out disputes. The political consequences of the divinatory process do not always result in harmony or maintenance of group unity. The elders do not always coerce subordinates as they wish, but their authority is not threatened by deviance because it can be explained by the cosmology of the ritual system. The exercise of power within this context is not revolutionary. When subordinates rebel and are labeled as deviants, their deviance, even their winning of a dispute, can be explained away by the premises and rules of the social system. Ideology is protected from divergent practices because those practices serve to highlight the rules and can be institutionally explained and dealt with within the authority structure of society.

III   There are many fine studies pertaining to the relation between political and mystical relations in Africa which show that authority is backed by ritual means (e.g., Goody 1962; Evans-Pritchard 1937; Fortes 1945; Middleton 1960; Turner 1957). Both Fortes and Goody, who worked in the Voltaic area of northern Ghana, have convincingly shown that the ancestor cult is instrumentally related to the structure of the lineage system, to territorial divisions, to political alignments, and to the organization of authority. Most of these studies have been done, however, within the structural-functional paradigm, and as such they have shown how the ancestor cult functions to maintain other institutions in society and allow elders to control subordinates. More recently, A. Cohen (1979) has presented the ancestor cult as a constraint on the abuse of power. In his view, its rules provide a frame for political struggle which has integrative functions for society at large.

These studies illustrate that there is conflict between the holders of authority and those who exert other kinds of power in opposition. The question of the source of this conflict comes up. In his classic study *Schism and Continuity in African Society*, Turner provides important data on the political processes involved in rituals of life crises among the Ndembu. He finds that conflict occurs over issues of succession, marriage, inheritance, and death payments. These disputes arise, he says, from structural contradictions such as the incompatibilities resulting from the coexistence of the principles of virilocal marriage and matrilineal descent. These structural contradictions create stresses and strains, but social cohesion is fostered partly by kinship ties, partly by economic and political cooperation, and partly by ritual reinforcement of communal ideology. His work shows how people work out solutions to thorny political problems through ritual means.

African witchcraft studies (e.g., Cohen 1969; Gluckman 1955; Marwick 1965; Nadel 1952; Parkin 1968) also cast ritual as having a political nature. Many studies have shown that accusations are not made randomly and that some members of society are able to label others as deviants through institutionalized procedures. In Sisala divination, as with African accusations of witchcraft, kinsmen blame kinsmen. Particular kin are chosen as deviants by those with the authority to accuse. Divination is an institution that highlights unwanted conflict in a group. Accusations and outcomes are influenced by the relative structural position and power of the parties to the conflict.

Previous studies have emphasized the influence of social structure on behavior. While recognizing this influence, this study points out that behavior is also influenced by other considerations and that actors use symbols creatively in an effort to influence others and to control the outcome of a dispute. The divinatory process provides a formal structure wherein people work out their disputes in such a way that the social structure retains its general form even though individuals deviate from its rules. This is not new. Gluckman and Turner have both shown that such political maneuvering occurs in an African tribal setting, but these early works seem to have assumed that the social systems they studied were in a state of equilibrium. I make no such assumption; instead, I wish to show how the exercise of power in institutional settings can resolve conflict produced by the system itself or introduce change or also function to preserve the overall institutional framework of society. Thus, conflict and change, though they may also come from external factors, may be generated within the social system by the processes of institutionalization and system maintenance.

The valuable theoretical contributions of consensus theorists and the important perspective of action theorists are, I feel, reconcilable. I shall attempt to show that these two extremes can be linked into a more unified theoretical model through the use of concepts from symbolic interactionism. Action theorists have reacted against the Durkheimian tradition by stressing the use of power by individuals and factions (Barth 1966*a*; Boissevain 1968; Mayer 1966; Nicholas 1965). Their theories are also useful, but one needs to avoid the extreme positions taken by some—for example, Boissevain (1968), who advocates a shift from the study of the group to that of the individual. Rather, the position I am advocating attempts to show how conscious and active individuals take structure into account and use symbols in the pursuit of their goals.

Some social anthropologists who have worked within the structuralist framework have also called into question structuralist assumptions about equilibrium (Barth 1966*a*; Firth 1951, 1964; Leach 1954, 1960; Murdock 1971). They complain that the concept of social structure is too abstract an explanatory device because it is a residual abstraction that results from events and thus cannot be used as a sole explanation of such events. Each has turned partly to individual choice and decision making to explain behavior and the emergence of sociocultural forms. Thus, there has been a reaction to macrostructural theories of society which has resulted in the opposite extreme, that is, a concentration on individual behavior, Before moving on, let us look briefly at the main tenets of consensus theory and the transactional model proposed by Barth.

The consensus model stresses that each culture has certain basic premises about the nature of relations, both between man and nature and among men in society. These premises constitute the moral order, or value system, of a society. From the general moral order flow more specific rules that define and instill "expectations of behavior between actors in concrete situations" (Van den Berghe 1973). Since, as this model hypothesizes, there is consensus among the members of society about such values, interaction is regulated and patterned by them. The communality of basic premises, values, and rules is the integrative force operative in society. Moreover, man codifies these assumptions into legitimate codes that are passed on from generation to generation, giving culture and society continuity. This harmony at the level of ideas and rules is translated, for the most part, to the actual behavior of people. Most of the time man conforms because he is sociable and socializable, although social control institutions are designed to regulate deviance. Basically, the social order is the natural outcome of social interaction, but it becomes a social fact in the Durkheimian tradition (1964) which, once established, governs man's thought and behavior. Not only is there harmony at the level of principles, but there is a strain toward the establishment of fit between rules and behavior. (See Gluckman 1968 on this point). Thus, institutions provide the means whereby authorities can implement rules to control deviance when other institutions fail to socialize persons adequately. The processes of socialization and institutionalization lead to a harmonious moral order and a social system that strains toward equilibrium. In this theoretical paradigm there is an overwhelming interest in the maintenance of the social order through the establishment of conformity. Radcliffe-Brown (1952:10) says that "any relationship is one in which the conduct of persons in their interactions with each other is controlled by norms, rules, or patterns."

Deviance is seen as dysfunctional, as a threat to equilibrium and the security of the system. Deviance is seen as a temporary aberration that must be put right if order and stability are to be maintained, although some theorists of this camp have tried to illustrate its positive contributions to the social order (see Cohen 1966; Dentler and Erikson 1959; Erikson 1966). These theorists view deviance as a means of redrawing group boundaries and clarifying rules, and they point out that the deviant may actually serve to solidify the group in reaction to deviance. In general, though, consensus theorists agree that there must be a close fit between rules and behavior if social order is to be maintained. Societal institutions serve to punish deviance, thereby controlling its incidence, and at the same time they highlight necessary rules.

In social anthropology the most ambitious attack on consensus theory was made by Barth (1966*b*), who initiated a new era in anthropology. He pioneered a shift from a structural-functional view of social order to an interactionist perspective (see also Bailey 1969; Kapferer 1976, 1979). Barth's beginning was important because he was concerned with how social order was generated, maintained, and changed. The concepts of emergent properties and social change have always been inadequately handled by social order theorists—in the work of Parsons (1951), for example, and in that of Radcliffe-Brown (1952). Barth seems to have been influenced by anthropologists who were leaning toward explaining social forms in terms of individual behavior (e.g., Firth 1954; Leach 1961), and exchange theorists from sociology (e.g., Homans 1958). He came to define social form as the regularity in individual behavior. Form, in this view, was the general feature of social process, the result of the repetitive nature of acts. This work was an attempt to bridge the gap between theories of action and theories of structure.

Since individual behavior played a significant role in Barth's theory, he had to come to grips with choice. What are the constraints and incentives that influence individual choice? In asking this question he rejected the mechanical view of social order and claimed that social form depends on the human capacity to evaluate rules and anticipate outcomes. But he does not believe in a totally random social universe. He claims nonrandom frequency distributions that can be discovered through ethnographic fieldwork do occur in human behavior. Barth complains that most ethnographies give only a description of patterns of regularity. But what are the processes that *make* the pattern? How do individual decisions get institutionalized?

According to Barth, individuals conform to rules because they receive rewards and punishments from others within the system. Interpersonal relations, rather than abstract moral rules, are brought to center stage. People are constrained or directed less by rules than by the actions of other people, especially those with whom they interact. Interpersonal relations are seen as transactional: they involve reciprocal exchanges. Individuals also *decide* what is appropriate for a given situation and *negotiate* to achieve an acceptable outcome. Barth sees sequences of interaction as governed by the principle of reciprocity, which I assume he takes to be a panhuman factor. He does not claim, however, that all relations are transactional but that transactional relations exist even in kinship-based societies. In such contexts, both authority roles and transactions determine outcomes.

Barth does not deny that values and structures exist or that they affect thought and action. Cultural values are seen as generalized incentives and constraints on choice. Structural rules also function in the same manner, but how does structure limit choice? Barth answers that values and rules influence action because people evaluate the profit and loss of any proposed activity, but in doing so, they take into account more than material profit or loss. They also take into account moral values and rules. Decision making occurs in a cultural and social context, and exact ledgers are not kept by real people involved in transactions. Since many social exchanges involve no transfer of *tangible* value and transactions sometimes consist only of *token* presentations, the meaning people place on them is based on their cultural values or their evaluation of whether the activity has occurred in the appropriate social context. Thus, social and cultural rules and principles affect decisions and interaction.

Barth seems unfamiliar with the American sociological theory called symbolic interactionism. It has a long tradition in America, going back to G. H. Mead, W. I. Thomas, and C. H. Cooley, founding fathers of American sociology. Its tenets have recently been synthesized by Herbert Blumer (1969). If we interpret what Barth is saying in symbolic interaction terms, we would say that social exchanges involve a transfer of *meanings*. Meaning is the key concept that, in my opinion, ties together the writings of action theorists, who emphasize individual choice, and social order theorists, who claim that cultural and social structures act as moral influences on thought and action because they see meaning as being worked out by actors in symbolic relations with others. Structure, or symbolic formations, influence people's thoughts and actions by their social reality. A man and woman who wish to have common children for example, will be influenced by their knowledge of marriage institutions in their society. In this case, meaning derives from their capacity to know of and evaluate this institution in the abstract. But action theorists stress that meaning also derives out of interaction with others; for example, how did the man and woman come to know about the society's marriage codes? As people interact, they use symbols to create meaning for themselves and others. For instance, the families of the man and the woman may influence their decision and action by symbolically interacting with them, using the premises, symbols, and constituted meaning embedded in the institution of marriage. Such institutions "come alive" in this kind of analysis.

In symbolic interactionist theory all *"things"* (Blumer's term) in the world have equal existential status in terms of their meaningful influence on human thought and behavior. A tree, the concept of liberty, or the status of herring-boat skipper are regarded as *things*. Any thing may be interpreted by any person, that is, human beings can apply an infinite variety of meanings to any thing. These meanings influence action toward the thing. For example, in Sisala-land a tree can be considered a sentient being capable of harming a human being, whereas a European missionary might consider it merely a thing of beauty. The meaning one applies influences how one behaves toward the thing.

According to this perspective, persons take into account meanings about things, be they trees, values, or social rules. The concept of subjective meaning can help us bridge the theoretical gap between social order and interactionist theories, but there is a significant difference to be remembered: social order theorists believe that meaning derives from a priori sociocultural structures. To them, people are socialized and therefore conform; or they are constrained in their actions by sanctions applied by legitimate authorities. Interactionists agree that socialization and social control processes are real and effective to a degree, but they also claim that one cannot assume they are always and equally effective because people are also influenced by situational factors. That is, actors take more than societal rules and meanings into account when making a decision. The meaning that ultimately influences their behavior may derive only partly from culture and social structure. Such meanings may be cultural in that they grow out of an inherited body of agreed-upon knowledge. Meaning may also emerge or become refined in the process of symbolic exchange among participants. A person may be influenced by a moral principle, a social position, another person, awareness of work opportunities beyond his tribal boundaries, or even a false belief that a spaceship is coming to save the group. Meanings are both social facts, in Durkheim's sense of the term, and emergent properties of action.

Action theory incorporates three concepts I have used so far, which need to be distinguished: exchange, transaction, and interaction. Exchange theories in anthropology have noted how natives exchange items such as shells, beads, and pigs. Barth's transactional theory added the point that some exchanges are tangible and others are not. According to Herbert Blumer, what is important, in any case, is that persons must *apply* meanings to exchange tangibles or intangibles, so we should be concerned with determining how meanings emerge and are used by people in interaction. Thus, action takes place within the context of a social relationship. When I speak of interactionist theory, I mean those theories that concentrate on an individual's meaning as it influences his transactions with others. I reject the reductionist position, which concentrates only on the individual and his behavior, but in order to link individual meaning with meaning embodied in larger symbolic formations, we must understand more about the mental processes that influence interaction and, ultimately, the formation of structures external to the individual. One important advance in interactionist theory has been the stress on *intention*. Humans are seen as goal-seeking, deciding, and negotiating beings. It is true that a person is born into a cultural system of rules and principles that are presented to him as a set of moral imperatives, but the universal presence of conflict and deviance seems to indicate that socialization of individuals is less than perfect (Edgerton 1976). Individuals have latitude to make choices, communicate them to others, revise their meanings, and engage in a variety of other intervening processes before an action is completed. Nonrandom patterns of behavior result from both an a priori system and the willful activity of goal-oriented beings who consciously, and with intent, use the symbols provided by their system to influence others. As they do so, their thoughts and actions are influenced and patterned by such structures.

The perspective of symbolic interactionism has much to offer anthropology, which has a long history of interest in exchange and meaning. Heretofore, however, anthropology has lacked an adequate theoretical construct to bring these two concepts together for the purpose of analyzing action. Symbolic interactionism provides three basic axioms that help us to understand the relation between forms of patterned social relationships and meaning: (1) Human beings' actions toward things are based on the meanings that the things have for them. (2) These meanings arise out of the social interaction humans have with their fellows. (3) Meanings are handled in and modified through a process of interpretation used by an individual as he deals with things (Blumer 1969). Central to this theory is the concept of interaction. Meaning arises out of interaction. It is an emergent property, but this does not negate the structuralist's emphasis on socialization. Children have both structured and unstructured interactions, and their formation is influenced by both. Meanings formulated by the child are also codes derived from previously held societal beliefs and those that arise from unique situations and personal interactions with specific others. Both culture and idiosyncratic meaning are acquired and passed on in the same way: through interaction, wherein meaning is exchanged with others. This theory also accounts for change because as children interact with societal members to learn their cultural codes, such codes are modified by the processes of interpretation and interaction. Cultural meaning is mixed with personal meaning and transmitted to others, who interpret it and pass it on to still others. By communicating and interpreting meaning, people imperceptibly alter codes in everyday life. The process may also be organized, as in the institutions of the divinatory process. According to this view, then, change processes are located in the processes of institutionalization. As socialization and social control processes are enacted, members of society change the symbolic formation through interpretation and interaction.

Meaning arises out of interaction with others *and* with other phenomena. Blumer purposefully calls these phenomena "things." A thing is an object plus the meaning applied to it. *Application* implies the conscious action of a sentient being. One advantage of this theory is that it takes into account the processes by which people think and act. An individual interacts with many kinds of things, including self. After all, an individual thinks or engages in "head talk." New meanings arise out of interaction both with others and with self. As individuals interact with and think about their environment, they formulate meanings. Through the process of symbolic interaction with others, they pass on these altered meanings. Others accept, reject, or alter these new meanings. Following the lead of Barth and others, anthropologists are becoming interested in interaction and even in the contributions of early sociological works on symbolic interaction (Evens 1977; Kapferer 1976, 1979). This promises to invigorate our established theoretical perspectives on culture and action and the relation between them.

IV To say that a priori symbolic formations influence thought and behavior is not necessarily to accept that symbols are in harmony or that there are no contradictions in the moral order or in institutional arrangements. I assume that the culture and social order of a society at any given moment are filled with internal contradictions between rules and principles (Murphy 1972). Furthermore, there are the contradictions between action and ideals which derive from economic, historical, and ecological constraints and forces working on culture. Barth began by criticizing the social order theorists' assumption that culture is an integrated whole (Kapferer 1976:2). He was concerned with how the various institutional elements of society become integrated. What are the processes by which people attempt to reduce uncertainty and produce shared meanings and understandings? I say "attempt" because I consider this always to be an incomplete process, except situationally.

Thus, divination and ancestral sacrifice in Sisala-land can produce a momentary feeling of unity and order. If, however, cases are followed over a period of time, this order and unity appear to be illusionary. At no time is an entire cultural system in perfect harmony, yet its overall form remains. Our theoretical concepts need to aid us in understanding how such form is maintained and reproduced in spite of deviations from the rules and contradictions among them. Recently Kelly (1977) has also questioned the assumption that society is a moral system. He sees the system as a collection of segregates, clumps of principles that hang together for a certain purpose. Within the segment itself, symbols may fit together well, but different segregates are not necessarily integrated one with another. In fact, he says, at a deep level they may stand in opposition to one another. Thus, the social system is the surface organization of these contradictions.

For example, in Sisala-land two segregates that stand in contradiction are polygynous marriage and the unified patrilineage. There exist an elaborate kinship ideology, body of rules, and rituals pertaining to the unity of the lineage based on the principle of agnatic descent. The general consensus is that this group should stay together, but within the moral order lie the seeds of fission. This is the segregate of polygynous marriage, which also has an ideology, rules, roles, and rites. As a lineage prospers, more and more men are able to fulfill the ideal of acquiring multiple wives. As each wife produces children, another segregate emerges at the level of analysis: the unity of the sibling group. Because of their common uterine descent, siblings of one mother should, and usually do, exhibit greater solidarity than siblings of one father by different mothers; thus, the lineage tends to fragment into its constituent matrifocal sibling groups as time passes.

Kelly (1977:28) has noted that structure, conceived as set of harmonious jural rules, cannot account for behavior that deviates from such rules. Equilibrium theorists have had to go beyond structural explanations in search of nonsocial explanations of deviance. The imperfect fit between ideology and behavior is generally attributed to the failure of the individual to conform. One attempt to cope with this apparent discrepancy is evidenced in the work of Sahlins (1965). In his view, there is little relation among ideology, structure, and events, but he rejects theories that engage in reductionism. Rather, he says that rule violations occur as a result of external demographic or ecological factors. Kelly rightly points out that Sahlin's theory can explain only the *discrepancy*, not the occurrence and patterning of such events in structural terms, because, in Sahlin's view, structure impinges on the events only by way of interpretation after the fact. Kelly (1977:3) also deals with the apparent incongruity between a view of the social order filled with contradictions and the fact that it endures over time as a recognizable system. He says

> The organization of contradictions is the essence of social structure, [and] cultural perception of the social order expresses an ideological denial of its dialectical basis. There is a conscious contextual segregation of rule systems at the surface level, while at a deeper level, the relationship between them is contradictory. These fundamental contradictions are empirically manifested in the totality of observed behavior—which includes both conformity and deviance. The patterning of deviance is thus a product of the structure itself, not of forces external to it.

A dialectical view of the social order (Etzioni 1968; Moore 1963; Murphy 1972) sees socialization as an always incomplete process; thus, there is always tension within individual personalities and between persons. Furthermore, society has conflicting rules and principles; hence, social order is difficult to achieve through either socialization or mechanisms of social control. Deviance derives from the inherently conflictual nature of the social order itself and the way this conflict is transmitted to society's members, and a societal reaction to such deviance does not necessarily restore balance, but may only lead to a new state of tension management (Edgerton 1976).

To say that the social order is dialectical and filled with conflict does not mean that it is unstable or unenduring. Conflict theorists have also had an interest in integration. Some have argued that social systems are integrated through crisscross lines of cleavage, which shift as alliances among individuals and factions shift. Since the lines of cleavage shift, differences of values and interests, which are seen by conflict theorists as inevitable in every society, do not create a rigid split that tears society apart. Conflict theorists have written mainly about modern societies (see Coser 1956 and Dahrendorf 1959), but Evans-Pritchard (1940), in his classic work on the Nuer, noted that their society was filled with cleavage and conflict yet remained a recognized and recognizable entity. He postulated that conflict is the binding force that unites the various factions of Nuer society into one system. The historical flow of Nuer society is one of fission and fusion of groups, with conflict dividing people at one level but uniting them at another. Since these lines of cleavage fluctuate over time, based, as they are, on a complex variety of social, historical, and environmental changes, the integrity of Nuer society is not threatened.

In this view, social order is maintained, not by consensus or by a harmonious moral order, but through conflict among competing social groups, none of which has enough power to dominate the others. The norms they use to support different goals are also in conflict because they have been established over time under varying conditions, and the accumulative process does not result in a harmonious ideology and social structure. Moreover, since the social order is filled with contradictory principles and a variety of rule sets or segregates, authorities may select different principles or sets to deal with particular cases and situations that arise in the everyday life. Competing factions may, however, use their power to select alternative principles and sets to explain the situation. Seen in this light, the process of labeling deviance through divination becomes a struggle among powerful persons and factions with opposing goals, each of whom tries to force a different set of principles on the situation so that they can control the outcome. Thus, like the interactionist model, this view emphasizes decision making by individuals and groups, who make choices about the best course of action in a given social situation. Actors are seen as attempting to manage the situation in order to effect a solution to problems.

Gluckman (1965, 1973) has also viewed the social order as a normative structure, but one with inherent contradictions that from time to time erupt in social conflict or in symbolic statements about such contradictions—for example, rituals of rebellion. Specifically, with regard to divination, he has pointed out that the diviner exaggerates the wickedness of individuals and holds them responsible for misfortunes that arise from struggles rooted in the social structure itself (Gluckman 1972:5). Throughout his writings, Gluckman demonstrated that he realizes norms are not entirely fixed or coercive. He rebelled against the overdeterministic view of the Durkheimians, who have taken norms to be largely determinative of action. He understood that norms are built up into a complex arrangement of overlapping sets, which sometimes are mutually contradictory. Different normative sets pertain to different domains of social life. Disputants refer to those normative sets that enhance their position in a dispute. This dialectical view of the relation between the ideal order and situational adjustments led him to conclude that the social order is worked out and altered in everyday interaction. Nevertheless, throughout his career he remained committed to the structural perspective, trying to salvage the concept of equilibrium (Gluckman 1968).

I maintain that a social theory of deviance correctly begins by locating the causes of deviance in the dialectical nature of the moral order and social structure, though we must also be aware of external factors. By moral order I mean the basic premises of a culture. By social structure I mean a set of rules about human behavior and the subsequent recognized relationships that link persons together. The rules list rights and duties that are inherent in roles, and they define relationships between persons who occupy given statuses. Structure is based on the premises of the moral order. These abstractions, moral order and structure, are made concrete in the lives of people as symbols and patterns of symbols, or symbolic formations. Real human beings are aware of and use such symbols in everyday life, and sometimes they also become aware of the larger patterns. This awareness is, of course, a variable, and some actors become very effective at influencing others as they become increasingly aware of society's complex patterns and dialectical nature. Symbols and patterns are not accepted passively. They are creatively used by actors who deviate and who also are influenced to conform by the actions of others. The dialectical view of the social order assumes that there is conflict among all the aspects of the system—premises conflict with premises, rules with rules, rules with premises—and also that behavior may be at odds with cultural symbols and patterns.

This last dialectic is created because a discrepancy always exists between symbols and their implementation, which may lead to a critical point at which behavior is very different from the ideal model of it. This dialectic becomes a force for change as persons discuss deviance and redress in situations of dispute, because actors can become aware of system imperfections and the discrepancy between ideology and events and use this awareness to their advantage.

In this work I am claiming that deviance is generated by culture itself, because culture is not a unified, harmonious set of principles and because it contains contradictory sets of principles and rules that are selectively applied. Yet this is the very kind of analysis that the Sisala must avoid, because they have a theory that postulates a perfect moral order and a personalistic concept of deviance. They use the divinatory process to mask the structural source of conflict and thereby to avoid reaching this conclusion. Social integration is enhanced when institutions serve as bridges between sets of principles which are inherently conflictual. These sets are not logically integrated or harmonious but are operationally and behaviorally separated in institutional settings so as to allow the principles to exist in spite of their contradictory natures and to make it appear that such principles serve as guides for moral behavior. Endemic conflicts among individuals and factions do not lead to a revolutionary change of the general structure of society because of the creative use of principles and rules to explain it *in terms of the axiomatic values of the system.* Depending on situational interests and the fact that actors intend to ignore some rules and use others to their advantage, alliances form and are dissolved. Factionalism and power struggles do not threaten the social whole because they can be explained by deviation from system principles, and the lines of cleavage change in covariation with the interests of actors and alliances among them. Such deviation and factionalism are generated by the system itself because different positions and levels of positions in the social order produce different interests and perspectives on the parts of individuals who occupy those positions. One of society's most significant conflicts arises because interests diverge between authorities and nonauthorities, and conflict and factionalism are generated. Dahrendorf (1959) has noted that the formation of conflict groups in society is ultimately caused by the dichotomous distribution of authority in society. Some men have it, others do not. Some men have access to legitimate institutions, others do not. Those who do not hold authority, however, may have nonauthoritative kinds of power which they may use to support or oppose established codes and authorities.

V   Individual members of society experience life as a dialectic between the ideal cultural representations and the situational realities of everyday life. Each tries to manipulate and arrange his life so as to maximize his pleasure as he defines it. He pursues life's prizes within a normative framework. When ideals and rules permit him to seek a goal, he can do so openly. When he must do so covertly, he must employ strategies to avoid being detected and sanctioned by society. Thus, social relations are power relations. As people interact with one another, they influence each other, consciously or unconsciously. In this view, the very act of using symbols to communicate and interact with others influences their meanings. The use of symbols is inherently powerful, whether the persons wish to influence or not, but, obviously, human beings can become aware of the power element in the use and control of symbols. If the control of symbols is power, then those who have access to societal institutions derive some degree of power by controlling such symbolic formations.

There are various ways to view power. Basically, it can be seen as a potential, as a force, or as a constraint on choice. Whatever the source of power, power inheres in relationships, sociologically speaking. There can be no powerful without the weak; there is no power holder without a power subject. Thus, power is not an essence of the powerful but exists in their relations with others (Van Doorn 1963). Viewed in this perspective, power stems from one's position in the social order and one's structural relations with others. It follows that all social relations have a power element. Emerson (1962) has shown that in a social relationship the power of A is equivalent to the dependence of B on A. This structural view of power states, then, that it is a structural property lying outside the individuals involved in the relations.

Power also has a subjective side, however. Power can be imputed to one by another. One can be attributed with power, rightly or wrongly, but the social attribution, or meaning, itself provides at least the potential to use that power. It is important to keep this subjective view of power in mind as we analyze the relations between elders and subordinates and their struggles with each other within the divinatory process. Not only do others attribute power to persons, but they also attribute it to social positions and institutions. When this is done, the institution or the position and its attached role are said to have legitimacy. A social position, such as that of lineage headman, may be thought to be legitimate because of cultural beliefs about the supernatural powers that back up the holder of such a position. These beliefs do not have to be real to produce real consequences in society. Throughout this book I shall show that it is legitimacy based on ritual beliefs which underpins the authority of office-holding elders. I shall also show that such authority is not completely coercive; that is to say, subordinates also have power, which they use to counter the authority of elders. In this work I shall show that the main power relations dealt with by divinatory means are those between seniors and juniors, elders and their charges, office holders and non-office holders. In the divinatory process the classic confrontation between authority and power takes place, and while the authorities do not always "win" the struggle, the symbolic formation is instituted so as to give the appearance of their infallibility. The structure of ritual cosmology and institutions leaves ample room for tautologous thought. As conflicts occur between authorities and their subordinates, power is exerted from both sides, but the system is organized so as to provide a symbolic "smoke screen" for personalistic manipulation of symbols by both sides of the conflict while leaving the symbolic formation intact following the dispute.

Power is the ability of a person or group to influence others. Power can be held by individuals in relation to others, factions in relations to others, or organized groups in relations to others. Abstract power is a meaningless concept sociologically. Power inheres in social relations and is carried out through social processes. As power is exercised in society, one social entity limits the activity of another. The exercise of power by one person, faction, or group thus restricts the action of another person, faction, or group. Sometimes the social processes by which power is exercised are institutionalized, and in other instances they are not; however, both legitimate and illegitimate procedures take place within a framework of social relations and instituted social processes. This study will focus on the exercise of power within the related institutions of divination and ancestor sacrifice, which constitute a sequence of procedures I call the divinatory process.

This view of power allows us to understand the nature of choice within the constraints provided by social institutions and social processes. Disputing actors have wills, make goals, calculate, make decisions, play games, conceive of factions, and act with the perceived backing of egocentric networks. They also take into account a priori symbolic formations, both ideological and social. The will to win a battle is not necessarily diminished by the power of others; only the range of action is restricted. Symbolic formations provide not only the arena of political struggle but also the weapons of battle. Symbols are powerful as they are used in human relations. They constrain human action in two major ways. On the one hand, in a mechanistic sense, their very presence influences human acts. The subjective component of the power of symbols consists in this: if people think symbols are real, they will have real effects. This is the structural influence pointed out by consensus theorists. Symbolic interactionism makes explicit the processes by which social formations, cosmologies, and institutions influence behavior. They are influential to the extent that meaning is created and sustained in the consciousness of the members of society. On the other hand, though, symbols are deliberately used by actors with the intent of influencing others. Any ritual act in the divinatory process may be viewed from these two perspectives, that is, the performance of a rite may influence others merely because it is carried out, or the person performing the act may intend a result of that action, and that intent may be the coercion of others or the constraint of their behavior.

Bailey (1969:5) has pointed out that political struggle has a public face and its private wisdom, that is, there are universalistic rules by which the game is played, but there are also covert pragmatic procedures. Universalistic rules provide a framework of constraints and guides that are used by actors in a creative way to construct their social reality through symbolic interaction with others; but not all actors are equal in their comprehension of universalistic rules, nor are they equally competent in their use. Generally, following Van den Berghe (1973), I see three types of actors in this regard. First, there are those who honestly believe in the rules and who attempt to use them as guides to their interaction with others. Second, there are those actors who do not believe in the rules. These cynics consciously manipulate the rules for their own particularistic ends. Third, in between these two polar types are those actors, probably in the majority, who believe that they or the members of their faction would follow the rules if they could, but since they assume that others will not, they are forced to engage in game playing. While they honestly believe that they attempt to behave impartially within the framework provided by universalistic rules and procedures, they do little more than mask their manipulative attempts to obtain their own goals at any cost. The feeling is this: Since others are going to cheat, I have to cheat, too, in order to win, although I would like it to be otherwise.

In any case of dispute, rules and procedures provide the universalistic criteria within which the struggle takes place. Those actors, of whatever ilk, with the best chance of winning are those who know the universalistic rules and procedures. Knowledge of them is necessary in order to engage in battle with opponents, because disputes overtly invoke universalistic criteria. Any overt deviation from the formal rules is a bad tactic because an opponent can use this as a power lever against one. Effective fighting requires a thorough familiarity with the rules, because the opponent's procedural mistakes are the most potent weapons to be used against him. Rules are tools that are used creatively by actors engaged in political struggle. In addition to being used to attack an opponent, rules also serve as a shield to one's own intentions and goals. One who knows the rules well can effectively use them to disguise one's own prejudices or the dishonorable aims of one's faction.

The basic assumption of most actors is that others will deviate from the universalistic criteria, if given the chance, in order to attain their goals. They are aware of the discrepancy between ideology and events, and they use this knowledge to their advantage. Thus, most disputes involve actors with zero-sum assumptions about conflict situations. Merely assuming that others will deviate, however, does not permit open deviation. In fact, there is general agreement to abide by the rules, but the real skill comes in using the rules to mask one's own prejudices and illicit goals while tripping up the opponent on procedural grounds. Direct attack is not possible, lest the universalistic criteria be defined as invalid; therefore, one must use the rules to catch an opponent in a weak position in order to further one's own particularistic interests.

No consensus theory assumption of internalization of rules is necessary to an understanding of the politics of divination. However much the actors have been socialized to the rules and have internalized them, they are *cognitively* aware of the rules and procedures that are the agreed-upon and taken-for-granted constraints to the conflict. Most actors at least partially abide by the rules in order to protect their own positions and to catch an opponent in a weak moment through the clever use of legalisms. Since the universalistic criteria do not form a unified body of premises and norms, a thorough knowledge of them provides the actor with ample scope for particularism in that he can maneuver among rule sets, selecting those that further his cause or those that damage his opponent when that opponent makes a procedural error or is insufficiently informed of all the rules.

I do not completely ignore the fact that societies develop ideals emphasizing unity and that these principles provide a moral framework for action. The Sisala come to any dispute with abstract cultural values that lead them to assume it will result in compromise and peace. The ambiguity of the normative system allows political interests to select and foster a certain mix of social rules to suit them on any given occasion. Opposing interests, if they lose the battle of the day, concede and compromise, leaving the abstract principles intact. Compromise is a culturally desirable end that is enhanced by the inconsistency of the rules. A formal set of consistently ordered rules would render one party right and another wrong, with less room for political manipulation. Yet a set of formal rules provides only an overt framework, behind which goal-oriented actors and factions can operate to achieve the best possible outcome in a given dispute. Conflict and struggle also occur through a set of unacknowledged, though known, covert procedures, under the guise of axiomatic, institution- alized principles and procedures such as divination and ancestral sacrifice. Thus, by using known covert procedures and the rules and means of goal attainment, actors protect the general value system, leaving ample room for manipulation of the rules and opponents.

I take power to be the ability to affect social situations. As such, there are four major categories of power criteria in Sisala society: authority, age, wealth, and sex. Of course, these criteria overlap each other in certain cases; for example, those who succeed to office are the eldest men in line to do so. On the basis of these criteria, we can identify five power categories of persons in Sisala-land: chiefs and government officials, pagan authorities, big men, the educated elite, and youth. Generally speaking, power stems from three sources: numbers of people, social organization, and resources (Bierstedt 1950). In Sisala-land, each estate derives its power from a different source. The chiefs get power from the state, which rests on the ultimate power, force. Pagan authorities derive their power from the symbolic formation we call the ancestor cult. Big men acquire power mainly through the acquisition of wealth and the maintenance of ties with other wealthy men who understand how to operate in the national-level economy. The educated elite derive their power from their schooling and their knowledge of the "modern world," principally the bureaucracy. Finally, youth derive their power from health, physical strength, and opportunities to work outside the control of their natal lineages.

These categories are defined according to the potential power of the persons in them. Actual power is exercised in social relationships. In daily social intercourse, persons from each of these categories interact with persons from others. Networks of persons from each category overlap and inter- penetrate. Officeholders of the authority structure interact with and are influ- enced by persons from each category, just as they try to influence others. I have chosen to concentrate on intralineage power struggles, but this is a heuristic necessity only. The politico-jural domain and the domestic domain impinge on each other in real-life situations, as do the power of individuals and that of groups beyond the limits of Sisala-land—the government, the churches, and non-Sisala ethnic groups, for example. Authorities who attempt to influence others through use of ritual symbolism are also themselves influenced by considerations of the power of nonauthorities.

In this introduction I have been concerned to show that, on the one hand, theories of power, or "action theory," and, on the other, theories of integration, or "consensus theory," are not competing theories of social organization. It has become a truism in political anthropology that all social relations have a power component and that when we talk of social organization, we are talking of the organization of power (Cohen 1976). In the following chapters I will focus on one process—the divinatory process—to show how interacting persons influence one another in an institutional framework. That such influence occurs in heterogenous societies has been documented and accepted (see Cohen 1976; Van den Berghe 1973). While Van den Berghe talks about the highly diffuse structure of academic politics in Nigeria and Cohen discusses the nature of interest groups in complex societies, I will try to show that political manipulation such as that which they describe also occurs in highly institutionalized settings—for example, divination and ancestral sacrifice in a segmentary lineage system where every individual is related to others by formal relations of kinship and affinity. The exercise of power in both heterogenous and homogeneous settings appears to involve conscious manipulation of symbols by those struggling for system rewards.

VI   After a brief introduction to the Sisala people in chapter 2, I will turn to a discussion of the kinship system and subsistence activity in chapter 3. It is necessary to understand the relations of authority within the domestic group and how they act as subsistence relations before we can understand how and why elders resort to divinatory means of social control. Chapter 4 is an analysis of the ideology behind illness, misfortune, and medical treatment. Some misfortunes never become linked with deviance, but others do when elders resort to divination as a means of explaining misfortune. This is a common occurrence in the daily lives of the Sisala. Almost everyone has had the experience of being divined for and/or accused of deviance. These actions are also influenced by symbolic formations and have consequences in the lives of the people and in their social organization. In chapter 5 I explain the symbolic formations of divination and ancestral sacrifice and the nature of the divinatory process, which includes the perception of misfortune, divination, and post-divinatory sacrifice. Elders resort to divinatory means when there is a sudden, dramatic onset of misfortune within the family or when medicine fails to alleviate an illness. When elders consult the oracle, it almost always links their problem with one or more deviant acts by members of the family and results in the performance of sacrifice to the ancestors by way of retribution. In chapter 6 I analyze the linkage of misfortune and deviance as viewed from the perspective of interactionism, especially that literature on the labeling of deviance. In this and the following chapter I present the bulk of my empirical cases. Chapter 7 is an attempt to understand the politics of divination in Sisala society in relation to a major controversy in the social sciences: What is the nature of the influence of social structure on behavior? How coercive are rules? Does action alter rules, and if so, how? What is the nature of power, manipulation of structure, and the process of applying principles and rules to specific cases of dispute? I will look at the two dominant structuralist theories, conflict and consensus, and at Weberian action theory, especially symbolic interactionism, in order to glean concepts to help us better understand the nature of political struggle. The resulting theoretical framework could be called a tension-management model. This view of the social order sees it as composed of highly abstract moral principles and contradictory social rules, which provide a general structural background to political struggle. Within this framework of principles and rules, actors use cognition, make choices, and negotiate and struggle with opponents to produce a dynamic social order, one filled with conflict and contradiction and one where ideology does not completely dominate man's consciousness. In this view, deviance is structurally produced and socially defined through institutional means, but in the process of labeling and punishing deviants, the social order is negotiated, reworked, and changed.

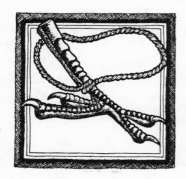

2
The People and
Their Country

I   Ever since the publication of *African Political Systems* (Fortes and Evans-
Pritchard 1940), social anthropologists have been interested in political
behavior in stateless societies. In such societies there is a lack of obvious central
organization of authority transcending the maximal level of lineage segmentation. In his preface to this work, Radcliffe-Brown observes that stateless
societies do not necessarily resort to the use of force to maintain social control.
Instead, they maintain social order through a variety of social institutions that
function to reinforce the communal ideology. Sanction lies in a set of authority
relations rather than in the use of force.

I am concerned in this work with how such relations of authority operate
within the lineage. Within this domestic domain, political control is vested in
institutions that are not considered overtly political in state societies, such as
kinship and ritual institutions.

But Sisala society is not a simple isolated stateless society today. The
Sisala live in the state of Ghana, the independent African state that came to
independence in 1957 after the British gave up their colony of the Gold Coast.
In Sisala-land there exists a chiefship that was established by the British
(Mendonsa 1975*b*). Chiefs, however, do not normally concern themselves with
intralineage matters. Much social control is still vested in the elders, who
govern with the chief in interlineage matters and alone in intralineage concerns. The segmentary lineage system and the formal administrative structure
of chiefship, courts, and police exist side by side, but they govern different
domains and have different concerns. Generally, the state is concerned with

defense against external threat, taxation, and secular delicts, while the elders deal with violations of kinship and ritual rules.

More recently, Smith (1956:47) presented a view of government rather different from the state-nonstate dichotomy put forth in *African Political Systems*. He says that government consists of aspects of all social institutions and actions "by which the public affairs of a people or any group are directed and managed." Thus, political functions may be embedded in seemingly nonpolitical social relations.

After a short introduction to the people and environment in Sisala-land, I will give a history of the contact between the Sisala and the British in terms of how that contact affected political organization in the domain of interlineage and interclan relations.

II The Sisala people reside primarily in the Tumu District of the Upper Region of northern Ghana, but a portion live in nearby Upper Volta (see maps 1 and 2). Sisala-land is bound on the east by the Sissili River and on the south by the Kulpawn River. The largest town in Sisala-land is Tumu, which became the most important center in the area with the arrival of the British in 1906 and the subsequent establishment of the paramount chief and administrative offices there. Furthermore, the main road built through Sisala-land runs through Tumu, which, because it lies halfway between Wa and Bolgatanga, became a main entrepôt.

The environment in Sisala-land is a harsh one. This is, fortunately, in direct contrast to the gentleness of the Sisala people. The harshness of the area deterred habitation until perhaps the seventeenth century. Even today the population density is low—less than twelve persons per square kilometer. The country is Guinea-savanna woodland that is heavily covered with a variety of fire-resistant trees interspersed among tall grasses. While the areas adjacent have been defoliated as a result of heavy population densities there, Sisala-land has not. It is generally considered a disease-ridden area.

The land is flat, mostly between 500 and 1,000 feet, but showing occasional granite outcrops and hills of between 1,000 and 2,000 feet. The soil is laterite. Since it can be easily compacted, it provides a good substance for house building, but it demands the utmost skill from those who wish to farm there because alternate leaching and evaporation cause the soil to form hardpan easily (Boateng 1959). In the past, the area was considered a prime hunting territory by nearby groups, but today it has become increasingly difficult to find any but the smaller animals, though there is certainly more game in Sisala-land than in nearby LoDagaa-land or Tale-land. Hunting looms large in Sisala lore. It is strongly associated with manhood. Even today many men hunt, some still using old flintlock rifles inherited from their forefathers.

The area's two seasons radically change the face of the land. From November to April the harmattan winds blow out of the north, drying out the land and causing severe shortages of water. In recent years this desiccation seems to have been on the rise. The extension of the dry season has caused several villages to abandon their sites. It also periodically causes crop failure throughout the land (Mendonsa 1980). During dry seasons there is little horticultural activity, since no irrigation exists. During this period men hunt, fish, repair their houses, and build new ones. People generally perform tasks that are postponed during the busy farming season, including funerals and other rites.

The rainy season lasts from May until September in a normal year. The majority of rain falls between the fourth week in July and the third week in September. The area has, typically, less than forty inches of rain per year. When the rains do come, though, they transform the land into a lush green state (Boateng 1959:33). During this time the rivers are full, cattle have plenty of feed and water, and the people are busy planting and cultivating their crops.

The temperature in Sisala-land can only be approximated from figures recorded at Navrongo, ninety kilometers to the east. Those figures range between 65 and 103 degrees Fahrenheit. Since the humidity is low, the heat is not too oppressive except during the hottest month of March. There are rapid shifts in temperature between seasons and even within one day. These sudden shifts in the weather frequently cause health problems, such as catarrh.

Illness and disease add to the harshness of life there. The surrounding tribes have long looked upon the area as being unhealthy, largely because of the incidence of endemic onchocerciasis, or "river blindness." Many people are afflicted with this disease. For example, in the village of Bujan, where I did most of my fieldwork, seven out of eight lineage headmen were blind from this disease. The disease forces many otherwise productive people into an early state of dependence on the labor of youthful, healthy members of the lineage. To date, the government's onchocerciasis eradication program has been unsuccessful.

The key to survival in Sisala-land is access to water for human and domestic animal consumption. No form of irrigation or water catchment is practiced, though the government maintains some wells and boreholes and is building earthen dams. The scarcity of water limits settlement. Villages are

91117

FERNALD LIBRARY
COLBY-SAWYER COLLEGE
NEW LONDON. N.H. 03257

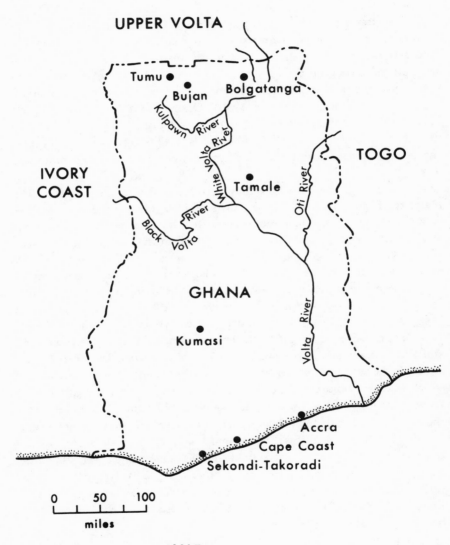

MAP 1

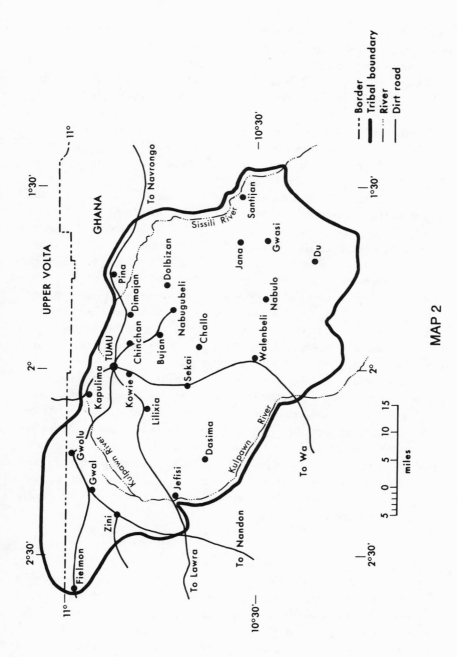

MAP 2

Border
Tribal boundary
River
Dirt road

UPPER VOLTA

GHANA

To Navrongo

Sissili River

Santijan

Jana

Gwasi

Du

Nabulo

Walenbeli

Pina

Dolbizan

Dimajan

Nabugubeli

Challo

TUMU

Chinchan

Bujan

Sekai

Kapulima

Kowie

Lilixia

Gwolu

Dasima

Gwal

Kulpawn River

Jefisi

Zini

Fielmon

To Nandon

To Lawra

To Wa

Kulpawn River

miles

5   0   5   10   15

11°

1°30'

2°

2°30'

10°30'

1°30'

2°

10°30'

11°

situated near water holes along the few rivers. Villagers are caught in a double bind: they must live near the water, but it also breeds many pests that afflict them, including the Simulium fly, which carries onchocerciasis.

Thus, the pattern in Sisala-land fits into the larger picture observable in the Middle Belt region of West Africa, which lies between seven or eight degrees and the eleventh degrees north meridians. It has sparser populations than its adjacent belts because of the limitations of a low-grade physical environment. In general, it has poor soil, lacks adequate water supplies, has widespread pest infestation affecting both humans and animals, is rife with diseases, and historically has been affected by heavy slave raiding (Trewartha 1972:187).

The people who inhabit this harsh land come of a conservative mold. They are a traditional people in the sense that they are preindustrial, preliterate, and prescientific. Their social organization is characterized by a low degree of role and institutional specialization. Tradition is cherished, and elders have the responsibility to protect the time-honored axioms and mores of the previous generations. Children are highly valued and warmly socialized into the culture. Few are ever cast off from society, deviants being given repeated chances to repent. The child is taught to respect "the Sisala way" (*woŋbiiŋ titi*). He is taught to order his life according to customary rights and duties inherent in his relations with others. These close and permanent reciprocal ties provide a seemingly secure social order for the individual.

Each newborn child begins a journey through a series of general age-grades (*wielee*; see table 2.1). Shortly after birth his kinsmen perform rites thought necessary to ensure his life and his place in society (Mendonsa 1975). From that point onward, his position in the kin group is assured. Males live their entire lives in their patrilineage, while females marry out but retain membership in their natal lineage forever. The lineage community is a major determinant of the child's attitudes, emotions, and behavior. In general, children long to be adults. Age is viewed positively, and elders are usually afforded high respect.

III   Archaeologists tell us that present-day northern Ghana has undergone immigration for centuries. A Saharan drought, which began about 1300 B.C., forced the southward migration of Neolithic peoples of the Sahel (Davies 1961). They mingled with a very late Paleolithic group of autochthons, and the result was that the people became hunters and makers of small

TABLE 2.1 Sisala Age-grades, or *Wielee* (ages are approximate)

	AGE (YEARS)	SISALA AGE-GRADE
Infant	0–1	*Bimulo/bimuluŋ* or *bifra/bifrasiŋ*
Child I	1–3	*Biwie/biwisiŋ*
Child II	3–5	*Heŋmie/heŋmisiŋ*
Child II	5–12	*Kuhiaŋbie/kuhiaŋbisiŋ*
Youth, male	12–20	*Bapuasuwie/bapuawisiŋ*
Youth, female	12–17	*Hatoluwie/hatolusisiŋ*
Adult, male	20–35	*Bapuasuŋ/bapuasaa*
Adult, female	18–35	*Hatolo/hatoluŋ*
Elder I	36–60	*Nihian/nihisiŋ**
Elder II, male	61 plus	*Banihiaŋ/banihiasiŋ*
Elder II, female	61 plus	*Hanihiaŋ/hanihiasiŋ*

**No sex differentiation.*

quartz microlithic tools: Their habitations have been uncovered along the main rivers of northern Ghana. This migration probably culminated about the end of the second millennium B.C. The drought ended about 900 B.C., when Neolithic arts became prominent throughout the area. They even began to penetrate the forest zone where a Neolithic culture, which arrived from the east, was already established. It was founded on the use of the stone hoe, with which the people cultivated yams.

Further north, near the lower valley of the Black Volta River, a very complex Neolithic culture, called Kintampo, diffused into northern Ghana from the bend in the Niger River. It had wattle-and-daub houses, villages built in sheltered places, very fine stone tools, and many beautiful artifacts. It appears that Kintampo culture, about A.D. 500–1000, suffered a military conquest by a less sophisticated people with a coarser material culture. Cattle and horses began to appear. So did copper and iron and beautiful arrowheads with long tapering barbs, which indicate an origin from the area north of Gao. These people were hunters and gatherers who ate mainly a diet of wild yams, game, and fish (Davies 1961).

Since we lack archaeological studies from Sisala-land, we can only infer that, given its remoteness from the major north-south trade routes and its unhealthy climate, it was probably settled toward the end of the great migrations that populated northern Ghana, about the seventeenth century A.D. It is also likely that the inhabitants of Sisala-land are descendants of those who migrated from nearby tribes of the north, such as the Mossi, the Mamprusi, and the Dagomba. These migrations are evidenced in their oral traditions. These migrations were probably caused by the spread of Islamized Mande-speakers about the early fifteenth century A.D. (Cardinal 1925:8—9). About this same time the Mossi and Dagomba states were formed, which gave protection to the established trade with the forest regions to the south (Bravmann 1974:51, 62—63). Sisala-land lies between these major trade routes, however, and was probably little affected by them, since traders would have avoided the unhealthy conditions there.

The Mande trade routes connected Jenne, Bobo-Dioulasso, Kong, and Bouna with the Akan regions in the fifteenth century. By the beginning of the eighteenth century, traders had established a continuous line of markets stretching from the modern-day border between Ghana and the Ivory Coast to the confluence of the White and Black Volta rivers (Bravmann 1974:65). During the second half of the seventeenth century, there was a decline in trade because the Akan began to trade with Hausa-land to the northeast and with the Europeans on the coast (Levitzion 1968:11—12).

Wilks (1975:319) reports that the area between the great states of Mossi and Asante was filled with stateless societies, similar to the Sisala. At the beginning of the nineteenth century, trade between these great powers was much reduced. It appears, however, that with the growth of the Salaga market, trade grew steadily throughout the century. It seems likely that Sisala-land felt the effects of this trade only slightly, if at all.

No east-west route bisected Sisala-land, but the north-south route between Jenne and Akan did pass through the southern Sisala village of Wallembelli, which was also linked in trade with Wa and Ouagadougou. Since there were no great towns in Sisala-land and no major trade routes passing through there, except in the peripheral town of Wallembelli mentioned above, Sisala-land probably was not greatly affected by trading activities, but it was greatly affected by slaving.

IV   Perhaps the greatest historical influences on the Sisala have been warfare and slave raiding. Because the Sisala lacked a state organization, they found it difficult to ward off attacks or retaliate against their more powerful neighbor states. Before the colonial era they were composed of scattered villages loosely held together by ties of clanship and exogamous marriage. The Sisala were continually raided by slavers and lived a defensive life

(Cardinal 1925:234−235). Today the Sisala have many stories of those times, which old men romantically relate. Manhood (*baalaŋ*) is linked with bravery (*twodolŋ*) and skill with weapons. Many such weapons still decorate the houses of men. The Sisala were no match for armed and mounted warriors, though, and more often than not they fled into the bush to hide until slaving armies passed. Their more sophisticated neighbors looked down on them and used them as a repository for slaves. They were called *grunshi* by the Dagomba and others. This was a pejorative term applied to stateless "bush" people. Slavers found such acephalous peoples easy prey for their highly organized slave raids. Genealogies collected in the field show that almost every household felt the effects of slaving. Slavers would sweep down on a village, taking as many captives as possible. They preferred youth but often caught the old and weak and ransomed them to villagers for strong young people who would survive the journey to the coast. In spite of the raids, the Sisala were never permanently conquered by any state until the arrival of the French and British at the turn of the century.

Tauxier (1912:354−355) writes of a specific example of such an external threat to Sisala-land. He relates how a Moslem named Mossa, around 1880, became wealthy through trading and founded a small state near Sati, a Nounouma (*sic*) village near Sisala-land. He began to expand south, raiding Sisala villages. He claimed to do this as a *jihad*, or holy war. He came into conflict with other slavers, who attacked Sati, killed Mossa, and incorporated his people and territory into their organization. They continued to raid the Sisala, but they also were bent on conquering territory. They had occupied several villages and extracted tribute from others. It appears that the arrival of the French in 1897 put an end to this state formation. The French drove them south, where they came into conflict with the British who were driving up from the south.

These raids and wars must have taken their toll on the Sisala. Lt. H. J. C. Leland, later to become the district commissioner at Tumu, wrote on first passing through Sisala-land in 1898:

> The inhabitants are as a whole very industrious and were very friendly to me, but owing to constant wars, first of all with Babatu [a slaver] and latterly with the French, they are at present in a very unsettled state; most of their towns and villages are in a very dilapidated and broken down condition, and they are showing no signs of building them up again. I did not pass through a single village that did not show signs of having been pillaged. There are hardly any cattle or sheep left in the country, and nearly all of the horses have been taken by Amahria [a slaver]. (COR 879/52, 358:335−336).

The Sisala did show organized resistance to slavers, but this was limited mainly to the level of the territorially based exogamous clan. The ritual guardian of the earth, the clan *tíŋteeŋ-tiina*, functioned as war leader, but he did not go into battle. The warriors were called *laliyuoroo, yuo* being the verb "to throw or fight." They used metal spears, bows and arrows, and clubs to fight the mounted slavers, who had guns and swords. There was no "Sisala army"; rather, each village or clan fought to defend its own people. Sometimes villages or clans banded together, but as clans were also hostile to each other, this happened only rarely.

Not only were the Sisala threatened by slavers, but historical evidence indicates that in precolonial times there was little interclan unity, and even cases of hostilities are recorded. Tauxier (1912:354) reports that the Sisala had difficulty keeping order and holding the peace within village settlements. Fights were known to break out frequently, even between lineages. Such intraclan attacks were carried out with clubs rather than bows and arrows in an effort to avoid bloodshed, which was considered polluting to the earth. He does, however, report the use of bows and arrows between clans. He says that raids were sporadic and intended for retaliation or for obtaining food and cattle.

Later, after the British-appointed chiefs were in control, this kind of strife was still a major problem in Sisala-land. Several years after the colonial takeover, Benpula, the chief of Bujan, tried to bring about peace among several feuding villages and even lineages that were at odds. During my fieldwork old men remembered times when it was unsafe for a woman to walk alone to the adjacent village of Tafiasi, six kilometers away, for fear of being abducted. The *Tumu District Record Book* records that in 1919 the Dolbizan villagers killed five crocodiles from the sacred pond of Bujan. Before the British came, such raids would have led to retaliation, but the British imposed an administrative structure on clans which united them under one judicial system. In this case the Bujan people sought redress through the district commissioner, who took the men in question before the chief's tribunal in Tumu, the seat of the British-appointed paramount chief (TDRB 62/5/1, 1919:13).

V Through the first years of the twentieth century, Sisala-land suffered warfare as well as disease and a harsh environment, conditions that curtailed population growth and inhibited immigration. The British arrived in Sisala-land in 1906, a time when Europe was against slavery, and therefore they tried to end slaving and warfare in the area. Both the French and British established overarching administrative structures to impose peace. To accomplish this they created a political system that took little heed of the acephalous nature of this kinship-based society.

Both European powers in the area had cultural assumptions about the nature of a polity that prevented them from seeing the existing political system in Sisala-land. The great works of European social anthropology were yet to reveal the political nature of acephalous societies and the segmentary lineage system. To Europeans of that day, a political structure meant hierarchy. They had to rely on their own cultural model of reality and their experience with West African states, such as the hierarchical Emirates of northern Nigeria. Thus, as they established an administration in the area, they altered the power base and created a system of dual governance. They appointed a chief (*kuoro*), who came to rule in spite of the existing traditional political structure composed of the ritual leader, the *tiŋteeŋ-tiina*, and the elders from each segment of the kinship system.

The French appeared first among the Sisala, anxious to make alliances with them. They thought that by securing written treaties with the "king" of the Sisala, they could secure legal right to rule. Because, however, they could find no such ruler, they settled on a stranger, a former slaver named Amirhea, and proclaimed him "king of the Grunshi." This fits the pattern followed by the French in other areas; for example, Alexandre (1970:3) describes their tactics this way: "The initial phase was that of the colonial or internal protectorate; annexations were consecrated by treaties in which French recognized X as the King of Y." French officers then forced various village leaders throughout Sisala-land to sign statements of allegiance to Amirhea. A typical case was that of Ninga, a notable at the Sisala village of Wallembelli, whose life the French threatened in order to make him sign this statement (COR 879/54, p. 101).

The French set up cantons over which they placed *chefs de canton*. Like their counterparts, the British, they had trouble recognizing appropriate leaders to fill these positions because they were ignorant of, or ignored, the indigenous leader, the *tiŋteeŋ-tiina*. They often settled on men of wealth. What brought these big men to the attention of the Europeans was that they exhibited symbols of wealth, which fit their stereotypes about the nature of chiefship. The kind of leader that the Europeans were looking for can be seen in the following reference by Dr. William Ryan, the district commissioner between 1913 and 1914. His reference is to the "chief" of the village of Sekai: "Sekai is an old man clad in a short shirt [i.e., not a long, Moslem-style gown] which is filthy dirty. He has absolutely no attributes of a chief: No appearance:

Dirty: No wives: No personal possessions: No authority" (ODTD, January 1, 1914).

The administrators wanted chiefs who looked the part. They should have been cleaner than average, better dressed, possessed of many wives: they should have exhibited such obvious signs of authority as palaces, fine Moslem-style robes, umbrellas, a court, an interpreter, a carved wooden staff, and talking drums.

After military conflicts with the French, and then with Babatu, the famous slave raider, the British finally secured the territory known as the Gold Coast south of the eleventh parallel. A military task force arrived in Tumu in December 1906. The leader immediately tried to determine who was "king" of the Sisala and who the "chiefs" were. This effort was entirely consistent with the policy of indirect rule as outlined by Lord Lugard, who had imposed a state model on the acephalous pagan peoples of the Middle Belt and the southern areas of Nigeria (Ballard 1972:3). Lugard (1970:34) had said of his policy: "The first step is to endeavour to find a man of influence as chief, and to group under him as many villagers and districts as possible, and to teach him to delegate powers, and to take an interest in his Native Policy, to support his authority, and to inculcate a sense of responsibility."

In 1899, Northcott, the first commandant and commissioner of the Northern Territories, said, "The essence of easy rule over the natives of West Africa is the existence of some convincing proof of paramountcy" (COR 879/58, p. 585).

Often the *tɩŋteeŋ-tiina* of an area was suspicious of this new powerful influence and did not come forth to claim legitimate leadership of his people. Sometimes he sent a messenger to deal with the British, who promptly made the messenger a chief. In some cases this messenger was merely a slave. In other instances, the new position was actively sought by men of intelligence and/or wealth who realized that the power base was about to shift. Thus, as the British established their political framework, positions of power were given out indiscriminately and to persons who had no legitimate claim to power. The *tɩŋteeŋ-tiina* remained in the background, unnoticed, either by choice or by chance. Some *tɩŋteeŋ-tiina* did become chiefs, as in the case of Wogery, the first chief of Tumu, but in some cases persons gained power who otherwise could not have done so. Rattray (1932) speaks of one Bata, the chief of Bulo, who was appointed chief of that village even though he belonged to an entirely different clan. More often than not the chief was a man of wealth and achievement, a big man (*kuoro*). In this way the word *kuoro* came to mean "chief." Today the Sisala use the term *kiaa-tiina* ("owner of things") to denote a big man.

It is clear from the records that the British found the political organization of the Sisala unintelligible. Upon arrival, Capt. G. A. E. Poole, the third administrator of the district, wrote:

> A matter which has been engaging my attention since I took over here, and which strikes me as peculiar in the Tumu District, consisting as it does of the country occupied by the Issala Race [*sic*], is the absence of any paramount Chief, and there being thirteen so-called Head-chiefs. This is, no doubt, due to the inter-tribal factions of the past times. . . . The day for this state of affairs has passed, and it is my hope gradually to create an inter-relationship between these various petty Chiefs, finally establishing one elected man from among them to lead the Race. (ODTD, June 2, 1914)

The "so-called Head-chiefs" that Captain Poole referred to were creations of the two district commissioners who preceded him between June 29, 1912, and November 14, 1913. They, along with other colonial officers, tried to bring some sort of order to the area. The important point is that Captain Poole was not satisfied with "this state of affairs" but wanted to "elect" a paramount chief to rule the area. In this way the British systematically created a political structure consistent with their own hierarchical ideas, one consistent with their previous experience with formal states such as the Dagomba, the Mamprusi, and, farther south, the Ashanti.

The British established districts, and the majority of Sisala fell into the Tumu District. This was divided into twelve divisions. Each village was assigned a chief, and one village chief was appointed as a division chief. At first all were under the authority of the district commissioner; later they came under the direct authority of the paramount chief (the *Tumukuoro*), who reported to the former.

In the beginning, chiefship was not accepted by the people. There was a transition period during which chiefs and their subjects struggled with each other while the British administrators supported the authority of their appointees. The people often considered the chief nothing more than an upstart without authority. Many complaints centered around the use of their offices by chiefs to enrich themselves and their own lineages at the expense of their larger constituency. With the backing of the colonial government, though, the power of chiefs increased, and chiefship became an accepted institution in the society. This process is illustrated in the following quote:

> Chief of Kwape with his subchiefs arrived and brought in fourteen Headmen of Compounds who the Chief reported had refused to obey his orders. A careful

inquiry was made and it would appear that the accused, mostly young men, had failed to carry out orders. Their excuse being that the work asked of them was excessive. . . . I carefully pointed out that the orders given by the Chief were by him received from the District Commissioner and as such were Government Orders. The District Commissioner further pointed out that in this Colony there were no taxes hence little money to pay out for labour. Their freedom from persecution and annihilation from such as Barbetu [*sic*; Babatu the slaver] and Samory [the slaver] was touched upon, and expense of walled towns and warlike stores saved to them. Any little work asked of them must be willingly supplied as a set off to the benefits they were duly receiving. All expressed regret at their behavior and said that their Chief would have no further cause to be vexed with them. (ODTD, April 30, 1914)

Once the British had appointed a number of chiefs, they sought to create a paramount chief. Initially they tried to establish the chief of Tumu, one Wogery, as the paramount. In 1910 a directive from the Northern Territories Headquarters at Tamale instructed all chiefs to deal with the district commissioner only through the chief of Tumu. The Tumu station was closed between February 1909 and June 1912, when a meeting of the chiefs was called wherein they were told to deal directly again with the district commissioner, bypassing the chief of Tumu (TDRB 1912:162). Later, however, the British reversed their policy and supported the *Tumukuoro* as the paramount. On July 1, 1914, Captain Poole called a council of chiefs to determine whether the Sisala would accept a paramount chief. The chiefs decided to follow the *Tumukuoro* (ODTD, July 1, 1914). This decision apparently was not adhered to, though, because the same meeting had to be held later during the rule of Kanton I as paramount. In this instance, Kanton I complained to the district commissioner that many chiefs were dealing directly with the latter. Again, as late as March 19, 1931, the district commissioner had to call a meeting of chiefs on this matter:

Col. P. F. Whittall D.S.O. held a meeting at Kwouchoggo of all the Issalla chiefs with a view to finding out whether there was any real hereditary chief of the Issallas. All chiefs gave the same statement: viz., that before the white man came there were no Issalla chiefs. They then voted to continue their support of the paramount chief, Kanton I. (TNA 1931:431)

Thus, it was only with the continual prodding of the colonial government that chiefship, especially the paramountcy, was established. The records show continual resistance by the people to the idea of chiefship, as well as intrigues by would-be chiefs vying for power. The paramountcy was established with the strong backing of the colonial administration, but its lasting nature also had much to do with the strong personality of Kanton I. He was an active and successful politician who played the people against the colonialist. He was considered by the people to be a powerful medicine man, and he clearly used his reputed supernatural powers to rule. Before his death he had managed to implant the office of paramount chief firmly in Sisala society. His powers were considered so great by the people that when his funeral was announced throughout the land, people did not come, thinking that he could not die. Today he remains a folk hero to the people of Tumu.

Although the Northern Territories Administrative Ordinance of 1902 informally sanctioned indirect rule, the concept was not formally applied until much later. From the beginning, however, administrators tried to rule indirectly because of the lack of money and personnel. By 1921 the policy had become more widely known in colonial circles. Governor Guggesberg tried to institute it formally in the Northern Territories at that time. In December 1929 Governor Slater finally established a formal system of indirect rule throughout the protectorate of the Gold Coast (Ferguson and Wilks 1970: 221—222).

In Sisala-land indirect rule was attempted from the beginning, but from time to time the district commissioner stepped in to rule. Colonial administrators were isolated in the hinterland and had a great deal of personal latitude in making decisions. In those days communications were bad, so, lacking a clear-cut directive from headquarters, they often applied ad hoc solutions that might or might not conform to the concept of indirect rule. It was not until March 1936, under the Native Authority Ordinance of 1932, that indirect rule was effectively applied among the Sisala. The ordinance gave chiefs the power to rule, but the watchful district commissioner was never far away (Packham 1950). Since chiefs wielded real power, in time their position in the community was established. The present-day structure of chiefship in Sisala-land is a historical result of the efforts of early colonialists and native opportunists to bypass the traditional political order and to supplant it with one consistent with hierarchical principles more familiar to Europeans.

Ballard (1972:7) notes the fundamental contradiction in this process when he says:

> The effective content of Lugard's policy was its insistence upon assimilating the administration of pagan areas [i.e., those with acephalous political systems] to the emirate model, based in so far as convenient on indigenous local institutions and using indigenous personnel. The inherent contradiction between applying the emirate model and developing indigenous institutions was given no official recognition.

The result of such contact with the colonial regime altered the power base in Sisala society. These changes, however, affected mainly relations between clans and those between villages. Intralineage and interlineage relations were, and still remain, largely unaffected by such changes in external political relations.

VI Today the Ghanaian government still supports the chiefship system established by the British, but the office of *tɪŋteeŋ-tiina* remains the central one in terms of kinship and ritual functions. Chiefs deal with such government matters as taxes and secular delicts, but they also consult with the *tɪŋteeŋ-tiina* and the village elders. Most deviance never comes before the chief because it is dealt with through divinatory means by the lineage elders and/or the *tɪŋteeŋ-tiina*.

Succession to the office of *tɪŋteeŋ-tiina* follows strict hierarchical rules based on position in the descent system and age. If the *tɪŋteeŋ-tiina* dies, his next younger married brother succeeds. If none exists, the office passes to his eldest son or to the senior male in the proximate descending generation. Today this office remains important in the everyday lives of the people. In every village I visited in Sisala-land there was a *tɪŋteeŋ-tiina*. This was not so with chiefs.

Chiefship seems to be dying out now, especially at the village level. During my fieldwork the government supported the paramount chief and divisional chiefs, who formed an important council that met periodically with the district officer, the government man in Tumu, but the government was not quick to replace dead village chiefs. Part of the reason is that there are usually squabbles over succession to chiefship because the rules of succession were never formalized; they changed with policy decisions of different colonial governors and, after Ghanaian independence, with the various policies of the multitude of political parties in power. Generally, succession to office is lateral and then vertical (Goody 1970), and this principle prevailed during my fieldwork when the paramount chief died and was succeeded by his younger brother, even though the dead chief had groomed his eldest son to succeed him and even though the younger brother had worked as a game reserve scout for a number of years outside of Sisala-land. Thus, it seems that chiefship is slowly being centralized as village chiefs are not replaced and their duties pass upward to divisional chiefs and the paramount. There is the feeling today that the *Tumukuoro* should appoint a new chief when there is a vacancy. He does work closely with the government district officer to make such appointments when the chief of an important village or town dies, but chiefs of lesser villages are not being rapidly replaced.

During the Nkrumah era in Ghanaian politics, the *Tumukuoro* was a staunch supporter of his party. After Kwame Nkrumah was deposed in a coup, the government stripped the Sisala chief of his paramountcy and generally weakened his role in administrative matters in Sisala-land. The district officer became more important during this time. The office is accepted by the people, however, and Luri, the *Tumukuoro*, retained the following of his people until his death in 1974, at which time the chiefship passed to his younger brother, Luribie.

During the post-Nkrumah years, it was the policy of President K. A. Busia not to replace village chiefs or at least to delay their replacement long enough to choose a "progressive" man for the position. He instituted a waiting period of one year, which was felt to give proper time for candidates to come forth and a fair election to be held. In some cases candidates did not emerge and offices were left vacant.

The roles of chief and *tiŋteeŋ-tiina* are thought to be different by the people. When it happens that the two offices fall to the same person, the chief delegates the powers of the other office to a senior member of his kinship group. The functions of the *tiŋteeŋ-tiina* are ritual in nature and concern primarily social control among kin groups that lie within larger units for which he is responsible. For example, every clan has a *tiŋteeŋ-tiina* who is responsible for relations between the constituent *jasing* (sing. *jaŋ*) which comprise the clan. Every *jaŋ* has a *tiŋteeŋ-tiina* who is responsible for the relations among the constituent *jachikei* (sing. *jachikiŋ*), the lineages. This realm of intergroup relations beyond the level of the *jachikiŋ* can be considered to be the political-jural domain and as such is presided over by the *tiŋteeŋ-tiina*.

The *tiŋteeŋ-tiina* also handles conflicts that arise between kin groups under his jurisdiction. He does this by palaver with the elder headmen of those groups and by recourse to divination. He performs all ancestral sacrifices for his constituency. The chief is never involved in such matters. No shrines are connected with chiefship. The office of *tiŋteeŋ-tiina*, though, is intimately tied up with the ancestor cult and social control at the supralineage level.

The ritual sanctions of the *tiŋteeŋ-tiina* are thought to be absolute. They stem directly from the ancestors, or *leleɛ* (sing. *leluŋ*). The *tiŋteeŋ-tiina* is the earthly executor of their power. When a matter arises which concerns a group of lineages, he is called upon to deal with the problem. For example, when an old man named Basijan in the village of Bujan was accused of witchcraft, he was called before the *tɪŋteeŋ-tiina* and the elders to answer the charge. The chief was not present or involved in the matter. The man was accused of wandering about the village at night. He claimed to have insomnia but said that he did not know if he was a witch or not because "any man may be a witch without knowing it." The *tɪŋteeŋ-tiina* required him to drink a calabash of water mixed with earth (*tɪŋteeŋ*). It was thought that if he was guilty, the ancestors would kill him. It so happened that shortly thereafter he did die, and it was explained to me that this was how the ancestors protect their descendants. Thus, in serious judicial ritual matters, the *tɪŋteeŋ-tiina*, rather than the chief, officiates.

The *tɪŋteeŋ-tiina* looks, lives, and works like any other elder in the village. He is visually and behaviorally indistinguishable from others of his age. The chief, however, does not farm. He is paid a salary by the government. He also possesses certain items that have come to be associated with chiefship: a large chair, fine robes, an elaborately carved staff, and a large umbrella that is brought out on ceremonial occasions. His house is usually a two-story affair, referred to by those who speak English as the "chief's palace." But whatever symbols of office the village chiefs have been able to acquire, the paramount chief has more. He has more and finer goods and many wives, and his family has become relatively wealthy because of his official influence through the decades since chiefship was instituted.

When one approaches the chief, it is customary to show respect by removing one's sandals and approaching at a crouch. Women and young men often avert their eyes. He is called only by title, "chief," and never by name. Such behavior contrasts sharply with both expected and observed behavior toward the *tɪŋteeŋ-tiina*. He is never shown obeisance greater than that due any elder.

The chief has also adopted certain court institutions—for example, the talking drums. Most informants claimed that the Sisala have always had them, but it appears that they have diffused from the Dagomba to the south. Today they are drummed on Friday mornings and evenings in the yard of the chief, though this is rarely done anymore except at Tumu. The drums announce the comings and goings of the *Tumukuoro* as well as funerals and special occasions, such as visits by government officials. Each individual has a drum name. If the people on distant farms hear drumming, they stop to listen for the name of a close relative. The chief's court contains a specialist who performs all ceremonial drumming.

In the beginning the chiefs wielded somewhat ruthless and unjust power. The British paid the chiefs for work done by their subjects, but at times the money did not go beyond the chief's hands. In this way chiefs built up the power and wealth of their own lineages. Chiefs were also known to tell their subjects that the district commissioner had fined them and then pocket the money (ODTD, December 30, 1913). Not all chiefs engaged in such deceitful practices, but enough did so that the district commissioner had to dismiss several chiefs and restrict the power of several more. Chiefs also demanded that their subjects work on their farms, a practice that remains to this day. In general, though, today the power of the chief is limited. He functions mainly as a figurehead and spokesman for the government. Judicial cases are brought before chiefs, but they have no sanctions except referral to the district court in Tumu. Wise chiefs, however, use persuasion and the prestige of office to settle cases before they reach this point. Villagers may bypass the chief and carry a case directly to the police and court in Tumu.

VII In summary, we can see that Sisala culture is relatively recent in origin. As a "tribe" it was a loose aggregate of semihostile clans prior to the coming of the colonialists, who established a new overall political organization of these clans. Clan-origin myths indicate diverse origins. In the seventeenth century these clans began to be established in the area by migration. Population density was low, and contact among clans was limited to combat and intermarriage. It seems that these clans were in the initial stages of adapting to this harsh environment when they came under the influence of slave raids in the nineteenth century and colonialism in the twentieth (Holden 1965).

With slave raiding at an end, Sisala clans became more unified under the colonial government. Chiefships were established in villages, giving them a measure of linkage with other settlements never before experienced. The British set up political relations and a system of communication that welded previously diverse units into a tribal unit.

Today there are three levels of social control in Sisala-land. The first is exercised by the government through chiefs, who are concerned with upholding national laws. Second, the *tiŋteeŋ-tiina* and the elders are concerned with upholding traditional codes governing relations among kinship units above the level of lineage (*jachikiŋ*). Third, codes governing intralineage behavior and relations among the composite units of the lineage are enforced by the lineage headman (*jachikiŋ-tiina*), who often uses the divinatory process to label deviants and enforce the rules. This third sphere of social control is the subject of this book.

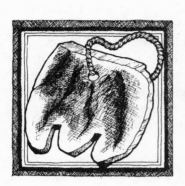

3
The
Patrilineage
and
Subsistence

I   This work is about power struggles among members of the lineage, especially those that end up in the divinatory process. The lineage headman (*jachikiŋ-tiina*) has the responsibility (*bene*) to enforce societal rules. His office is backed by the authority of the ancestor cult, but authority and power are frequently at odds in relations between elders and subordinates. While authority derives from the ideology of kinship, power comes to subordinates from the opportunities they have to escape that authority—such opportunities as the chance to remarry, for a married woman, or to get employment elsewhere, for a young man. Thus, within the lineage, the main dialectic exists between the authority of kinship and the power of youthful members.

    The lineage elder, or headman, has at his disposal the diagnostic powers of divination and the sanctions of the ancestor cult, which are applied primarily through ancestral sacrifice. He uses these in political interaction with his subordinates. When they break rules, he can consult the ancestors about such rule violation through the diviner. Ideally, this process labels a subordinate as deviant and prescribes a ritual remedy; the subordinate performs the rite; and the matter is set aside. But subordinates, either male or female, are neither powerless nor completely passive in such cases. They have options and employ strategies. An elder must also take into account more than the influence of his office. He also must gauge the relative power of persons and factions in the lineage as well as take into account personality differences. His use of the divinatory process for political action is limited by these factors and the more general cultural values of the community. Therefore, to bring about a solution to conflict through divination requires that the elder take such factors into account and develop strategies by which to overcome them.

The ideology of kinship forms the moral basis of West African societies like the Sisala (Fortes 1949, 1969). Ideally its codes and sanctions constrain behavior. Kinship relations are supposed to be inviolable and harmonious. Divination and the ancestor cult are known to be significant institutional mechanisms that are thought, by the natives themselves, to bring peace and order when deviance disrupts the harmony of the kin group (Fortes 1959, 1966). I approach kinship as an ideology, grounded in principles that are cultural in nature in that they exist only in the minds of kin group members and are passed from generation to generation by word of mouth. This ideology presents the kinship order as axiomatic, static, and inviolable. All goodness in life comes from adherence to its axioms. Deviance is thought to bring catastrophe and misfortune upon the heads of kin group members. Myths state that the dual institutions of divination and ancestral sacrifice were provided by God to guide human beings so that they might avoid such problems.

The works of Gluckman (1972, 1973) and, more recently, Kelly (1977), however, raise serious doubts as to whether the social system can be considered to have the degree of harmony claimed by the natives or those anthropologists who stress the harmonious nature of social systems. These works attempt to describe a different kind of social system. It emerges as one exhibiting structural contradictions that make the resolution of disputes difficult. Sisala social structure is based on an ideology of kinship. Society's significant rules are backed by institutions and sanctions that are kinshiplike in nature. I will show that although such structures are thought to be effective mechanisms to control behavior and to redress the social system when deviance disrupts life's harmony, in reality they do not always accomplish these goals.

Ideally, the descent group must retain its integrity through time. If a man farms alone without working on the lineage farm, he has committed a deviant act. It is also deviant to leave the lineage compound to build separately. Not to sacrifice on the ancestral shrines of the parent lineage is deviant as well. In short, independence from the parental lineage is seen as deviant, yet in his lifetime each adult male acquires some degree of independence. The degree is determined by situational factors such as birth order, the timing of his father's death, succession to headmanship within the lineage, and economic opportunities outside the lineage.

While the ideology of kinship postulates descent group unity, fission does occur. The static view denies such change, but change comes about slowly and is absorbed. This can happen because during any one lifetime little fission takes place, and what fission does take place is defined as being due to a deviant act rather than to any system fault. Economic and residential fission are denied for a long time before ritual fission is allowed to occur (Mendonsa 1979). This ideology, therefore, can be viewed as containing a certain flexibility that allows its continuation in spite of the dynamics of the developmental cycle of domestic groups (Fortes 1958; Goody 1958). It is also flexible enough to withstand the constant alterations in the social order brought about by power struggles among members of the descent group (Lewis 1961:298−299). Thus, the flexibility of the ideology permits the dynamic forces producing change to do so, and such change is incorporated within the overall form known as the segmentary lineage system (Smith 1956).

Authorities use kinship and ritual institutions in an attempt to regulate the behavior of their subordinates, but in many cases they fail to do so. In chapter 5 I present data to show that the outcome of fifty-three cases of divinatory efforts to settle disputes resulted in resolution in 32 percent of the cases, while 55 percent appeared to be unresolved after a reasonable amount of time. In 13 percent of the cases, I was unable to determine whether the outcome led to resolution or not.

In spite of such etic statistical evidence of inefficiency, authorities continue to believe in the efficacy of the divinatory process. Of course, they are unaware of these data and at any rate do not analyze their lives in this manner. To them, the divinatory process of settling disputes works. When it does not appear to work, the failure can be explained by a principle contained within the logic of the institution itself.

The ideology of kinship claims that the system works to regulate the behavior of those members of the kin unit who are subordinate to the authority of the headman and the ancestors. One thesis of my work is to suggest that this is not altogether true. It works some of the time, but those subordinates who are powerful successfully defy divinatory directives. Although they are labeled as deviants through divinatory means like everyone else, they have sufficient power to behave as before. Eventually, if they so desire, they are able to defy the principles supporting the group's unity by leaving (compare case 3 with cases 5, 7, and 8; see the list of cases on page 255).

The divinatory process not only hides the actual power of subordinates but also provides a ritual shield for the manipulation of the process by the elder when he perceives a deviant subordinate to be especially powerful (see cases 10 and 11). While the ideology of kinship claims that relations between kin should be harmonious, that is not always the case. Furthermore, kinship ideology states that breeches of kinship rules can be rectified by an exercise of authority on the part of the elder. My cases seem to indicate, however, that both the elder and subordinates must also take into account the relative power, especially economic power, of the parties to a dispute. They then attempt to influence the outcome of a dispute through the divinatory process. In order to understand how this manipulation occurs, let us now turn to an analysis of the ideology of kinship.

II   The descent system has many levels and units, but the lineage is the focal point of Sisala action. It is the main residential group. At night, when people are ready to sleep, the lineage gate (*boibalɨŋ*) is closed. No one but a witch will try to enter the lineage area after this door is closed. The lineage settlement is surrounded by a high mud wall, a structure designed to protect its members from contact with the dangers of the night. The lineage is also the main economic unit. The lineage members all farm a common farm, store their produce in a lineage granary (*virebalɨŋ*), and share food. In addition to being a corporate economic unit, the lineage is a political unit of major importance in the larger descent group. It is true that any unit of the segmentary lineage system can emerge as a political unit in relation to a like unit, but the lineage acts in this way more often than other segments. This work is concerned mainly with an explanation of the politics of divination within the lineage. I will therefore follow Fortes (1969) and refer to intralineage relations as the domestic domain and interlineage relations as the politico-jural domain. This work is an attempt to show that political struggles between individuals and households do occur within the domestic domain.

The ideology of kinship is the main paradigm of thought and expression in Sisala society. Descent (*lula*) is patrilineal, and postmarital residence is patrivirilocal. The senior male in line inherits property and succeeds to office. Males dominate all spheres of authority. Women perform tasks related primarily to food preparation and child-rearing. Unlike many African women, Sisala women do not farm.

The segmentary lineage system in Sisala-land is very similar to that described by Fortes for the nearby Tallensi (1949). The various segments are listed in table 3.1. Each segment is a corporate group that holds different kinds of rights over its members, but, conversely, an individual can demand different kinds of rights from different levels of the hierarchy. Members of each segment meet and act for different purposes. Aggregates that emerge as segments of the same level are in competition with each other, though this fact is played down.

TABLE 3.1 The Segmentary Lineage System

GROUP SIZE	CONSTITUENT UNITS	UNIFYING PRINCIPLE	COMMON ACTIVITIES	LAND TENURE	SHRINES HELD
		La Sisala (Tribe)			
59,000 (based on the 1960 census)	Unrelated clans of different origins	Chieftaincy established by the British and supported by the Ghanaian government	None; treated as a unit by government	None	None
		*Viara (Clan)**			
1,500	Agnatically related *jasiŋ* for villages in the southeastern part of Sisala-land	Agnatic descent from a common founding ancestor	Clan members do not meet, but elders do sacrifice on their behalf	Holds rights in usufruct over clan land	*Tinteeŋ, vene*
		Jaŋ (Village in Southeastern Sisala-land)			
400	Two agnatically related maximal lineages	Agnatic descent	Common rituals; elders form village government	Elders allocate clan-owned land	*Tinteeŋ, vene*
		Nyiŋniaa and Vaadoŋo (Maximal Lineage)			
One has 100, the other 300 persons	Patrilineages (*jachikiŋ, jachikisiŋ*)	Agnatic descent	They sacrifice together and bury the dead of the other maximal lineage in their village	None	Some hold shrines, others do not

Jachikiŋ (Lineage)

Average size is 42	Extended or joint fraternal families	Agnatic descent	Farm, live, and sacrifice together	While clan owns all land, lineages develop usufructory rights to plots, but land is freely given for the asking by the lineage head	*Lelee*, most commonly approached ancestral shrine, and *virebaliŋ*, the lineage granary.

Kaala (A Large Household)

10 to 20 persons	Normally composed of children of one father	Agnatic and/or uterine descent	Live together within the lineage settlement and cultivate a farm in addition to the lineage farm	None; they can use any clan land	Only personal shrines of members (*vuyaa*)

Diisiŋ or Dia (A Small Household)

4 to 10 persons	Normally composed of children of one mother	Uterine and/or agnatic descent	Normally farm with their lineage agnates, but they may decide to farm separately	None	Only personal shrines (*vuyaa*)

Dia (Room or Small Household)

1 to 3 people	Nuclear families	Marriage, agnatic, and/or uterine descent	Live together; may farm a separate plot	None	Only personal shrines (*Vuyaa*)

These data on the descent group are taken from the Crocodile clan of southeastern Sisala-land, near Bujan, for the year 1971.

Such competitive relations give way at a higher level to unity (Middleton and Tait 1958:6). Thus, while two "brother" lineages may compete with each other for access to women, land, water, grazing, and so forth, there exists a corpus of kinship codes that stress their noncompetitive nature because of their mutual inclusion in a larger descent group, the maximal lineage. As brothers should not compete, "brother" lineages should not compete. Coordinate groups are arranged in a state of continual segmentation and complementary opposition. Each smaller group nestles with its "brother" groups inside the larger one.

All segments of the segmentary kinship system in Sisala-land hold some kinds of rights in land and women, with the minor exception of the maximal lineage, which does not hold land in common, nor does its headman allocate rights to land. The clan holds rights over land and is an exogamous unit. Since land is plentiful, squabbles over land are rare. Subsegments of the clan, especially the lineage, occupy specific portions of clan land, which can be passed onto offspring, but this land is also freely given out to other clan members, or even to strangers, if there is enough land for family members. In Bujan, actual farms do not correspond with lineage land ownership; most lineage members farm on another lineage's land. This occurs because of shifting cultivation and the ease with which land is obtained for the asking. The *jang* also is thought to "own" the land around its settlement, but this too is freely given. Land that is no longer used by any subsegment of the clan reverts to general clan land. Land is not sold or exchanged between clans. In theory territory is an epiphenomenon of kinship, but in practice kin groups become associated with certain tracts of land. Jurally, all segments hold only right of use over the land.

Three principles underpin the kinship system: agnatic descent, sibling-ship, and age. Kin groups at every level of segmentation and hierarchy are organized according to the same organizational principles. Genealogical reckoning is the major way of determining relations and organizing groups and action in Sisala society. People descended from a common ancestor have more unity than nondescendants, and the corollary is also true: the more ancestors one has in common with another person, the greater the unity between the two. Siblings have more unity than nonsiblings, and the greatest unity exists among siblings of the same father by the same mother (*naaŋbiiriŋ*). Here is a major structural contradiction in the ideology of kinship, a contradiction that is at the root of its segmentary nature and allows fission to occur: the principles of the unity of the descent group and of the unity of *naaŋbiiriŋ* oppose each other. When the principles come into conflict in disputes, parties can justify action on the basis of either. Normally it is the responsibility (*bene*) of the lineage elder to maintain the unity of the lineage through time, while groups of children of different mothers by the same father may be rivals. This contradiction will be important in our discussion of how such disputes are handled by the lineage elder through divination.

Within all segments of the descent group, the principle of seniority based on age pervades. The Sisala believe that as a man becomes older he gains more wisdom (*wu-jimiŋ*) and, therefore, his governing capability increases. Consequently, an elder brother rules a younger one, a father has the right to control his son, and an ancestor is thought to be wiser than a living person. Authority relations are relations wherein the younger member should show great respect (*fa*) toward the senior member. All younger people should show respect (*zile*) to those older than they, but authority relations are tinged with *fa*, or fearful respect (Grindal 1972:33; Mendonsa 1976 *a*). *Zile* is general respect or politeness that is expected to be shown by all juniors toward seniors, whether male or female. One might say that *zile* recognizes the principle of age whereas *fa* recognizes authority. A woman or a junior male should exhibit *zile* toward all elders, but certain of them are officeholders (*tiina*), and as such represent authority (*biesaŋ*) and the political order. As an officeholder, a man has the responsibility for the protection (*poo*) of his subordinates. He is entitled to receive fearful respect, or *fa*, very much like that a father receives from a son. It is thought important for a father to instill *fa* in his child so that he will grow up respectful of authorities. Any authority position contains two counterposed rights and duties: *fa* and *poo*. Whenever there is an obligation on the part of the elder to provide protection (*poo*) for a subordinate, that subordinate owes him respect (*fa*). The father-son, especially the father—eldest son, relationship is the model for relations between subordinates and superiors and, ultimately, between the living and the dead. Gerontocratic principles pervade the kinship system and the ancestor cult.

The clan (*viaraa*) is the largest descent group. It is a named group of agnates who share a common genealogy and totemic taboo (see fig. 3.1). They occupy a known territory or parish. The parish is communally owned by clan members and administered by clan leaders. Each clan has common ancestral shrines. At times, though rarely, clan officials sacrifice at these shrines, but these sacrifices are not attended by the entire clan membership, nor do the members come together for any other purpose. The clan is corporate only in that all members share common ritual rights and duties and each member has the right to demand land within clan boundaries. The clan is concerned primarily with the fertility of the land and the fecundity of the women. The

| Bujan* | Nabugujang | Tafiasi | Nanchala | Dimajang |

*Autochthonal (*jaŋ*). The units are in descending order of seniority from left to right. I assume that this represents their order of emergence over time through fission.

FIGURE 3.1   The Structure of the Crocodile Clan

exogamous clan has a common concern in the produce of its land and in the offspring of its women. Ritual exists to enhance both, but sacrifice and social control at the clan level are rare. Most such activity occurs at lower levels of segmentation within the clan. When clan officials do meet to sacrifice, it involves a very serious breech of conduct which affects the ability of the earth to produce crops and the ability of women to bear children. The corporateness of the clan, then, involves rights and duties revolving around production and reproduction.

The clan is governed by a *tiŋteeŋ-tiina*, or custodian of the earth. He is the one who sacrifices on clan shrines on behalf of clan members. He is supported by an elders' council made up of the headmen of the clan's constituent units. He is the senior member of the clan's autochthonous lineage. He is a custodian (*tiina*) of the earth because his lineage occupied the area first. If a matter should arise which concerns all clan ancestors and members, he will consult a diviner and sacrifice on their behalf.

The clan is usually composed of one or more subunits called "*jaŋ*." This unit may or may not be territorially based. It may be a section of a village or an entire village, or it may encompass the entire clan, depending on the size of the clan and the complexity of its inner structure. In the southeastern area of Sisala-land, where I did the bulk of my fieldwork, the *jaŋ* and the village coincided. In northwestern Sisala-land, the clans are smaller and are subsections of villages. The important point to remember in either case is that the *jaŋ* is a social unit, not a territorial one. It is a group with certain rights and duties of a specific nature within the larger clan unit.

The *jaŋ* is a segment of the clan, but *jaŋ* is a generic term, usually used as a suffix, which denotes any visibly separate kin unit. Sometimes the term is used to refer to a village, sometimes to a section of that village. The *jaŋ*, as a subunit of the clan, is composed of a variety of agnatically related lineages, often divided into two maximal divisions, each composed of two or more lineages (see fig. 3.2). The *jaŋ* is headed by the senior male of the oldest lineage of the *jaŋ*. This *jaŋ-tiina* consults the diviner and sacrifices for the group when a matter arises concerning the whole group. He allocates land to strangers and generally acts like the *tiŋteeŋ-tiina* of the clan, but on a smaller scale. He is one

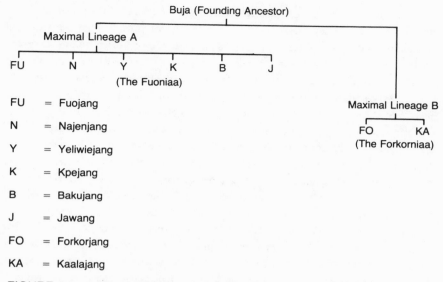

FU	= Fuojang
N	= Najenjang
Y	= Yeliwiejang
K	= Kpejang
B	= Bakujang
J	= Jawang
FO	= Forkorjang
KA	= Kaalajang

FIGURE 3.2   The Genealogical Structure of the Jang of Bujan

member of the clan elders council. Succession to this office occurs the same way as for the clan *tiŋteeŋ-tiina* office. The *jaŋ* is a ritual unit. It has common shrines at which the *jaŋ-tiina* officiates; in this capacity he is referred to as the *tiŋteeŋ-tiina* of the *jaŋ*. When a problem arises which affects all members of the *jaŋ* but not those members of the clan as a whole, the *jaŋ-tiina* consults a diviner and sacrifices on behalf of the membership of the *jaŋ*. In southeast Sisala-land the *jaŋ* is a separate village, and therefore this group does sacrifice frequently, though usually the sacrifice is attended only by the *jaŋ-tiina*, the village elders, and other interested males.

Each *jaŋ* is divided into two maximal lineages. These units are named after the autochtonous lineage in each—for example, the Fuoniaa and For-korniaa in figure 3.1. One maximal lineage is senior to the other. They are thought of as senior and junior "brothers." One's own maximal lineage is one's *vaadoŋo* group, while the other is one's *nyiŋniaa* group. Each maximal lineage has its own unique shrines, upon which its members alone sacrifice. These members share sacrificial meat, and therefore are said to be kin "who eat from the same bowl." Members of the opposite *nyiŋniaa* are never called on to partake of this meat.

These maximal lineages form reciprocal burial groups. The members of one unit have the responsibility to attend to the dead of the opposite maximal lineage. When a death occurs, the gravediggers (*kalibaa*) of the *nyiŋniaa* group are summoned. They clean and dress the body for burial. They sing funeral songs and carry the body to the grave. It is their responsibility to dig the grave and position the body therein. After the position of the body has been approved by a member of the dead person's *vaadoŋo*, the gravediggers close up the grave.

Sex with any female of one's own clan is considered incest, but one may have sex with wives of clan members beyond the level of one's own maximal lineage without causing ritual pollution of the earth. Incest pollutes the earth and requires sacrifices to unpollute it. Sex with the wife of a member of one's own maximal lineage also pollutes the earth in this way, unless permission has been given for the adultery through performance of the proper rites. This practice and the burial practices indicate that kin are considered closer within the *vaadoŋo* than are relatives who link the two groups.

The maximal lineage is primarily a ritual unit, however. Members share a common genealogy, sacrifice together, and "eat from the same bowl," but they do not occupy a common territory distinct from that of other *jaŋ* members, nor do they farm together or allocate land. The maximal lineage has no generic term other than *jaŋ*. Its ritual head is thus a *jaŋ-tiina*, but he is not usually called by this term, which is used to refer to the headman of the larger *jaŋ*. In the village of Bujan, he is referred to merely by name or as the elder of the maximal lineage in question (e.g., *nihiaŋ na fuoniaa*). Being resident within one settlement, members do sacrifice frequently together. The smaller size of this group allows all members to attend certain sacrifices—for example, those concerned with the naming of a child—hence the phrase, "we eat from one bowl." When any problems threaten this group which do not concern the other members of the larger *jaŋ*, the headman, the senior male in the autochthonous lineage of the maximal lineage, consults a diviner on behalf of his subordinates and performs the necessary postdivinatory rites.

The most important residential-subsistence unit is the lineage, or jachikiŋ (pl. *jachikisiŋ*). Each maximal lineage is composed of two or more lineages (see fig. 3.1). A lineage is named after its founding ancestor. The modal number of generations in Bujan lineages is three (see fig. 3.2). This extended family lives together, farms together, and sacrifices together at its ancestor shrines. The frequency of sacrifice is greater within the domestic domain (intralineage) than between units in the politico-jural domain. Usually each son knows only his father and grandfather. While genealogy is important in uniting persons into a descent group, this genealogy is usually six or seven generations in depth, and people who know each other personally form the functional domestic-residential-subsistence unit, the corporate lineage. This unit never exceeds four generations in depth (see fig. 3.2). Sisala lineage

TABLE 3.2 Demographic Characteristics of Bujan Lineages

CHARACTERISTICS	BUJAN LINEAGE INITIALS*									
	JA	YE	NE	BA	KP	FU	FO	KA	NUMBER	MEAN
Generation depth	2	3	4	4	3	4	3	3		3.3
Number of households	4	3	3	9	4	5	10	8	46	5.8
Number of married men	10	8	5	9	4	7	14	11	68	8.5
Number of unmarried adult men	1	3	2	2	0	0	2	0	10	1.3
Number of married women	14	9	5	20	8	14	22	19	111	13.9
Number of un-married adult women	0	2	3	1	0	1	3	2	12	1.5
Number of de-pendent boys	9	8	12	21	15	21	36	15	137	17.1
Number of de-pendent girls	9	8	6	13	12	13	9	14	84	10.5
Number of emi-grant males	3	3	4	6	1	2	8	2	29	3.6
Number of out-married girls	18	11	1	10	3	5	21	10	79	9.9
Total number of dependents	33	30	28	57	35	49	72	50	354	42.3
Number of wives per married males	1.4	1.3	1.0	2.2	2.0	2.0	1.6	1.7		1.6
Number of de-pendents per house-hold	8.3	10	9.3	6.3	8.8	9.8	7.2	6.3		7.7
Number of per-sons resident	40	35	29	60	38	54	79	59	394	50
Total lineage members	61	49	34	76	42	61	108	71	502	63

*Lineage initials: JA = Jawan, YE = Yeliwiejan, NA = Najenjan, BA = Bakujan (the chief's lineage), KP = Kpejan, FU = Fuojan, FO = Fokorjang (the tiŋteeŋ-tiina's lineage), KA = Kaalajan.

genealogies are characteristically unbranched at the upper levels. Branching into brother groups occurs nearer to the living members, because while the oldest living member may be able to remember collateral relatives, when he dies this information is lost. To say that there is a comprehensive, definitive genealogy is misleading. As each elder dies, some information is lost, and the pedigree becomes telescoped. Men who had large families are most commonly remembered. Women, children, and men who have died childless are most easily forgotten. In time, only the names of descent group principals and the apical ancestor are remembered. The name of the apical ancestor is often incorporated into the lineage name; for instance, Fuo was the founding ancestor of Fuojang. Everyone knows this name, but usually only very senior men know the names of other principals in their pedigree. Even then, elders argue about the names, numbers, and relations of such ancestors. Rules of descent are those that regulate membership by birthright in the lineage. These rules allow a continuous genealogical sequence through time. But since the lineage, as an empirical reality, is usually of a narrow span containing only brothers, fathers' brothers' sons, and fathers' fathers' brothers' sons, at a given point in time, forces must operate on the lineage to limit its size (see fig. 3.3). The main force is fission, which results from the fundamental conflict between the principles of agnatic and uterine unity. Some domestic groups within the lineage are united by agnatic descent, while others, *naaŋbiiriŋ*, are united by both agnatic and uterine descent. This structural contradiction is brought about by the practice of polygynous marriage, which produces different matrifocal groups of siblings

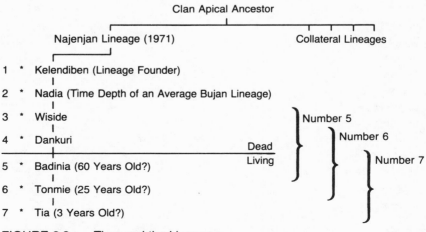

FIGURE 3.3   Time and the Lineage

by one father and different mothers (also see Fortes 1970). These contradictions lead to fission of the lineage along predictable lines of cleavage.

For example, the lineage in figure 3.4 underwent fission when the father of sibling group A (sib A) died. He had become the *jachikiŋ-tiina* (headman) at the death of his father. During his rule the lineage held together. While he was alive his next younger brother died, so when he died, the headmanship passed to his youngest brother. This caused a breakup of the descent group. Sibling A began to farm alone, as did siblings B and C. Sibling D was in charge of the lineage farm, and for a while members of A, B, and C siblings helped out and took their share. In time, however, sibling A established its own compound and farmed completely separately. At the time of fieldwork, siblings B and C were still farming and living together, but they had moved away from sibling D, which continued to be the trunk line of the original lineage and as such kept the ancestral shrines.

Kaala refers to the flat area outside of a group of houses used by household members within a lineage. It is the area of work for women and of play for children. It lends its name to a subdivision of the lineage. I call this a large household. It is usually composed of the children of one father, if the component matrifocal groups have not undergone fission. A *kaala*, however, may also be composed of a single group of *naaŋbiiriŋ* together with their wives and offspring. In either case, this group commonly has a farm in addition to the lineage farm, but they usually do not grow millet (*miaa*), which should be reserved for the lineage farm. If a *kaala* begins to grow millet on its own, this is thought to be a sign that fission is about to occur.

Most shrines owned by members of the *kaala* are personal shrines (*vuyaa*). If the household males have a common deceased father, however, they may have inherited from him one or more of his personal shrines. As they are inherited they are transformed into social shrines (*veŋsiŋ*), thought to protect his sons and their families. They will approach his ancestral spirit (*lɛluŋ*) at these shrines. Such shrines are kept by the senior male of the *kaala*. This link with their father gives them a degree of unity which sets them apart from their fellows within the lineage. It forms a nascent ancestor cult that, should fission

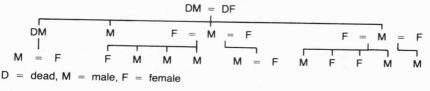

D = dead, M = male, F = female

FIGURE 3.4   Genealogy of Najenjang

occur, provides them with the structure to attain ritual independence of the parent lineage eventually.

The *dia* (pl. *diisiŋ*) is a small household. In fact, any unit of the lineage, including the lineage itself, may be referred to as *dia*, if the context is appropriate. I am using *diisiŋ* to refer specifically to the small household that is normally the offspring of one woman. As such, the unifying principle of the *diisiŋ* differs from that of all other segments. In addition to the fact that members are agnates, they also share the same uterine descent, which provides them with greater unity than other members of the lineage have. Behaviorally, members of this group often interact more frequently with each other than with others within the lineage. They are often visibly set apart as a distinct unit, even before they leave the group through fission. In practice a *diisiŋ* may be an agnatic household undivided by uterine cleavage, or a *kaala* may be composed of *naaŋbiiriŋ*; it all depends on the complexity of the internal divisions of the lineage.

The smallest social unit of the lineage is the *dia*, though this unit may grow into a *kaala*. It comprises the nuclear family, though it can be polygynous. Children are related to their father through agnation and to their mother through matrilineal ties. This group may farm alone, but its members usually farm with another segment of the lineage, normally a *naaŋbie* of the adult male.

III   The Sisala economy is based on farming (*periŋ*). It is performed through shifting cultivation with a long fallow of seven or more years. In 1960, 92.4 percent of employed males were engaged in agriculture (Hilton 1968:869). Economic activities are conducted by kinship units of the segmentary lineage system, especially those of the lineage and its constituent households. This system thus conforms to the model termed the domestic mode of production, or household production by Sahlins (1972). Farming is mainly a subsistence production system (but see Mendonsa 1980). That is, land, labor, capital, and entrepreneurial activities do not enter the market, although recently entrepreneurs have started a variety of enterprises, mostly concerned with trading. These, however, are restricted to a few wealthy men or non-Sisala who trade in the area. The majority of Sisala households produce and consume their own food. If a household member sells a cash crop or works for a wage, this is considered fortunate, as it brings the family extra cash, but the economic base of each household is farming, supplemented by gathering, fishing, hunting, and animal husbandry.

Hunting (*naŋbagiliŋ*) is a highly valued male activity. The Sisala fore-bears are called hunters in their myths. Many active older men still hunt using ancient muzzle-loading flintlock muskets (*laŋta*). Modern shotguns (*marifa*) are owned by some. The hunter (*naŋbagila*) usually hunts alone and at night, when the animals roam relatively freely. Most have miner's lamps, which they use to spot the animals. Nowadays game is scarce in the area, and gunpowder and shells are costly and hard to come by. Because of this, hunters must wait until they have a sure shot at a large animal. There are a few full-time hunters, but most men hunt as recreation or when they do not have farm work to do. Bush meat does provide some protein in the diet, but it is rare that a household gets much meat in this manner. If a hunter is lucky enough to kill a large animal, he gives some to his relatives and friends, smokes some to save, and sells the rest in the market. Some men also set traps. I never heard of or observed any communal hunts, though they are referred to in Sisala stories.

Men also fish using nets (*joŋ*) and traps (*sɔlɔ*). A fisherman (*chenfili-kpuura*) fishes in December and January, when the rains have finished and the streams have begun to dry up. There are few year-round waterways in Sisala-land, and many dry up and leave pools of trapped fish, which are easily caught once the pools begin to evaporate. Some men choose to fish, others do not. A fisherman provides fish for his family and friends, and his wife may sell some in the market. No communal fish drives or gathering is done.

Women gather wild fruits and nuts from the bush. This is a small but significant contribution to household economy. A wide variety of wild edible foods are known and collected, especially the shea nut (*chuunuŋ*), from which they make cooking oil by a laborious process of extraction. Women do this gathering when they collect firewood or water or when they are returning from a distant market. They also go to the bush in groups during seasons when certain fruits or nuts are known to be ripe. Men do not systematically gather, but they too know the flora. A man walking through the bush may pick fruit to eat on the spot or carry back to the village, but he will not normally go into the bush except, perhaps, to gather medicinal herbs and roots.

A domestic animal (*puna*) is distinguished from a wild one (*bagila*). Domestic animals are kept to eat and to sacrifice on shrines. Not all domestic animals are economically important: dogs, cats, and birds, for example, are kept as pets, though dogs are sacrificed on certain kinds of shrines and the meat is eaten. Men also have special hunting dogs (*golokpu*). I saw only two horses in Sisala-land, both kept as prestige items by wealthy men. Donkeys are not kept. Cattle (*neeŋ, nɛsiŋ*), sheep (*piese, piesee*), goats (*buuna, buunaa*), pigs (*tooŋ, toonuŋ*), chickens (*jimiŋ, jiŋŋee*), and guinea fowls (*suuŋ, suunuŋ*) are kept as sacrificial animals. The second bridewealth payment (*jaariŋ* or *ha-jaari-kiaa*) is paid from the cattle herds, which are not milked and which are normally guarded by small boys or Fulani who are employed for that purpose. Today, any of these animals can be sold in the market, and each has a price (*yaliŋ*), which changes with supply-and-demand factors. But households also guard a certain portion of their domestic animals which they keep as breeding stock and to sacrifice when the ancestors demand blood sacrifices. It is generally considered wrong to buy and sell cows involved in bridewealth transactions, though any surplus cattle can be sold; yet recent demand and high prices in large southern towns have caused truck-owning traders to transport cattle there to get large profits. These high cattle prices have caused some inflation in bridewealth payments as herds have been depleted through sales and lineages of outmarried wives demand cash payments equivalent to the going price of cows in the national economy. When stocks of domestic animals are depleted by sale or epidemic, the price rises in local markets. If, for a ritual, a man should require an animal that he does not own, he may have to sell part of his food stock to buy an animal in the market.

The Sisala divide the year into a rainy or farm season (*yibiiniŋ*) and dry season (*tafaaŋ*), but different times of the year are also connected with the various activities of farming—for instance, there are three sowing seasons, two weeding times, and a harvest (*miita*) (see table 3.3). At the beginning of the rainy season, farmers clear their fields and prepare mounds for planting. During May, the first tentative rains begin to fall, and there is much discussion about when to plant. With the uncertainty about rain and the tension produced by food shortages that occur as last year's stocks run short, this is a difficult time for the farmers. As the rains increase, though, and the first crops of beans and maize begin to ripen, life becomes better. The farming season is a period when men spend much time at the farm. Many maintain farm huts where they stay with their coworkers during the peak farming periods. Women and children and elders remain in the village settlement, but one woman may live at the farm to cook and care for the men. If not, food is prepared at the village and carried to the men at the farm, which usually lies one to four kilometers from the village. Men stay in the farms through harvest time. The month of September is especially crucial because the millet and maize have matured and must be protected from animals and birds. Men harvest the crops, and women carry them back to the village for storage.

Men learn farming as they grow up and work on their lineage farm with members of their family. They will, ideally, work on this farm all of their lives, first as unmarried boys, later as married men. When they become too old to work, others will feed them from the same farm. When a boy is about eight

TABLE 3.3 Work Calendar for Sisala Farming

April: First rains mark the coming of the rains. Mounds are made (*gbaa*) in preparation for the first sowing. Holes are dug for planting (*chɔsɔ*).

May: Sowing or planting (*duo*) is done. This is the time of the first sowing (*zagibele*) of early millet (*nɔrɔɔ*), maize (*kuorimiaa*), beans, and vegetables.

June: Rains increase in frequency and intensity. Second sowing (*zaginiiŋ*) of ordinary millet (*miipulima*), Guinea corn (*kadaagaa*), and yams (*piideree*). First weeding.

July: Heavy rains. Third sowing of rice (*miree*). Second weeding. Harvest of early maize, peanuts, and beans.

August: *Jepua*, the month of heavy rains. Crops are generally tended during this time of growth.

September: Rains abate in mid-month. Millet ripens and must be protected against animals and birds.

October: Maize is harvested (*kiila*).

November: Millet is harvested (*bori miaa*).

December: Yams are harvested (*bori piideree*).

January–February: Yams and rice harvested. New yam farms made.

March: Month of extreme heat.

---

years old, he is given a small hoe (*pire*). He is shown how to use it and encouraged to join in every time the men work. As he grows older, his responsibility in farm work increases. When he is a teenager, if he wishes, he may begin his own private plot in addition to working on his household farm and on the lineage farm. He can use the produce from this farm for his own purposes. It is not difficult to acquire the "capital" necessary to farm, since it consists essentially of "free" goods.

If we take *capital* to mean "accumulated wealth employed reproductively" (Bohannan and Bohannan 1968:118), then the Sisala do not have capital, except in the minimal sense of the word. The intent of their economic activities is to increase the size and well-being of the family by producing enough food. Like the Tiv, they "do not, as a goal, accumulate wealth to employ it reproductively." Their produced wealth is primarily for consumption. Even if a farmer has a good year, decay, mold, insects, and pests make it difficult to store the surplus. Land is a free good; it is neither bought nor sold. Farm implements, the hoe (*pire*), ax (*pire-saaŋ*), and the cutlass (*kariŋsia*), are inexpensive. By the time a boy is of marriageable age, he already has everything he needs to farm. Farmers do not produce a surplus to invest in other production factors. If there is investment, then it must be seen as social investment, that is, production designed to increase the size of the family and, therefore, the work force.

The clan holds rights in land for its members, but localized lineages normally come to have de facto rights over specific areas. Since there is no land shortage, however, in practice any stranger may ask for land and receive it. He is required merely to make a small sacrifice to the ancestors and provide a "first fruits" basket of millet to the headman who holds a claim to the land. Land not claimed by any subunit of the clan can be had if one asks the clan *tɨŋteeŋ-tiina*, following the same procedure. Such claims over land are very flexible. In the village of Bujan (map 3), each lineage has a farm area that it "owns." In fact, not all lineages farm on their own land. Some farm on the land of other lineages; others have started new farms on clan land. Members of a village use the land adjacent to it for farm purposes. Since they employ shifting cultivation techniques, they move their farms from time to time, and the "map" changes from generation to generation. Unused land reverts to clan ownership. The Sisala do not think of land as we do. It is not property in the way that a gun or a bowl is property. Kin groups only use the land. Land is an aspect of the group, not the basis of the group. The Sisala are interested in land as the spatial dimension of social relations. Land cannot be bought, sold, or rented. When a social group is a unified unit, it works a common parcel of land. If fission occurs, one group keeps the original farm, and the new group starts its own farm on clan land.

Access to land is not a limiting factor in production, but access to labor is. In household production, family members supply farm labor. A farmer can also call on the labor of certain nonkinsmen over whom he has certain kinds of institutionalized rights. He can ask for help from the in-laws of his married daughters, from his friends with whom he has institutionalized friendship relations (*naŋdɔsuŋ*), or even from a man who is the institutionalized lover (*hiila*) of his wife. A farmer who lacks hands from his immediate household to help him can acquire help through such relations. Labor is not for hire in the traditional system, though with the coming of all-purpose money and modern farming (Mendonsa 1980) labor did begin to enter the market in a very limited number of cases. To increase his access to labor, a farmer has two strategies open to him: he can increase his offspring, or he can increase his relations with nonkin on whom he can call for reciprocal farm work.

Labor is controlled by the headman of the kin group that forms a farm group. He directs farm activities and assigns tasks. If he is old and does not go to the farm regularly, he appoints a farm foreman (*tɨŋtinni-hiaŋ*) from among

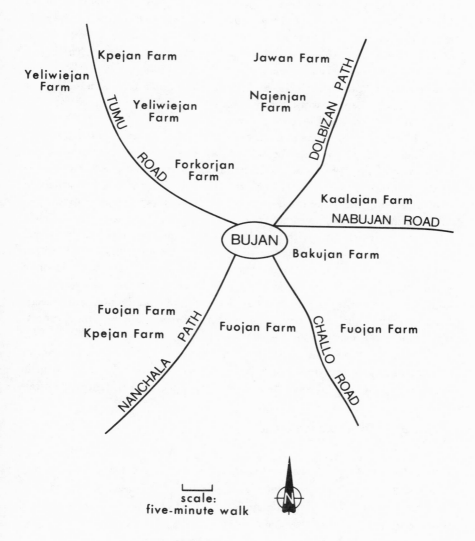

MAP 3

his subordinates. This is normally the most senior active farmer in the household. Agricultural products are also controlled and allocated by the headman.

The Sisala say that they perform work (*tɪ̀ɲtɪ̀ɲŋaa*) to avoid poverty (*sunʊ̀ŋ*). This is the state of not being able to feed yourself or provide the basic necessities of life. They are very clear on this point: security comes from membership in a kinship unit and through cooperation (*nii-maga*). To be poor is not so much a reflection on the individual as it is on his kinsmen. Sharing in production and profits is the basis of household production, but a member of the group who cannot work because of illness or infirmity is cared for until death through the work of his family.

The division of labor in household production is based on sex (see table 3.4), age, and position in the family structure. Senior males control the economic processes of production, distribution, and consumption. Men do the heavy clearing of trees and brush by the slash-and-burn method. They all do work involving the use of the hoe. Women are not allowed to take up the hoe. Women may be called on to help out in the farm if there is a shortage of male labor, but they help only with planting, weeding, and carrying crops back after the harvest. Since growing older is thought to bring wisdom, older people are always in charge of younger ones. There is no formal instruction in economic tasks. One learns by doing. Knowledgeable persons work alongside youngsters and teach them the proper methods. In household production, the lineage headman is the final authority, though he may delegate supervision to others. The senior wife in the house usually directs women's tasks.

Economic decisions are made by those who hold office in the authority structure of the lineage and its subdivisions. Such office holders are always male members of the patrilineage. As such, they have the right to control the labor

TABLE 3.4   Sexual Division of Labor

MEN	WOMEN	BOTH
Heavy farm work	Food preparation	Planting and harvesting
Cultivating	Housecleaning	Cultivating of gardens
Hunting and fishing	Child care	Basket making
Wood carving	Collecting of bush products	Sewing
Blacksmithing	Pottery production	Marketing
Musicianship		Divination
Gunpowder production		
Production of medicines		

of their subordinates. Thus, while young men and women can easily acquire the means of production, tools, and land, they are not free to allocate their own labor. They may have a separate garden or farm, but when the lineage elder requires them to work for the lineage, they must do so, and this work has priority over their own. Thus, control of economic processes is a function of position in the structure of the domestic group. The largest social unit that acts as a work group in Sisala-land is the lineage (*jachikiŋ*). Depending on its size and degree of internal differentiation, other households within may also form work units.

Economics can be seen as a concrete set of activities and institutions through which people organize the flow of goods and services (Nash 1966:3). In general, economics are embedded in kinship relations, and the segmentary structure of the lineage forms the basis of work. Production, distribution, and consumption do not go beyond the boundaries of the corporate lineage. Fraternally related lineages, which form a maximal lineage, have emerged from a single parental lineage through the process of fission, and therefore they say that they "eat from the same bowl," but this is true only in the ritual sense. That is, they share food and sacrificial meat only on ritual occasions.

The lineage head decides where to make the farm. He will have succeeded to control over specific fields, but he may decide to make new ones elsewhere. Normally, fields lie within a one-hour walk, or four kilometers, from the lineage settlement (Chisholm 1970; Prussin 1969:111). The Sisala do not farm the area directly adjacent to the village because they allow their domestic animals to roam throughout the village. Kitchen gardens must therefore be fenced. Lineage compounds are walled, though the village is not. On rare occasion, a cow will wander into a man's farm and destroy some of his crops. Generally, however, domestic animals stay near the village, and therefore the fields are not fenced or protected. It is thought best to herd cattle during farm season because, unlike the other domestic animals, they tend to range far into the bush, and sometimes they harm the crops in the farms.

Once a farm site has been selected, a lineage work party clears the brush, leaving only the large trees. This brush is burned in the field. Men then make mounds in preparation for planting. When many mounds must be made, as with a new field, the headman will try to get other men to help by providing beer. He normally calls on his married daughter's husband to bring a work party. He may also ask friends or neighbors to help, and he will reciprocate at a later time.

Another time when outside labor is needed is during the two weeding periods. Indeed, the men of one lineage can clear and plant much more land than they are able to control effectively during the growing season. The reason for this is the farmers' inability to keep down the growth of weeds, which choke off their crops. This environmental factor thus limits the size of farms (Hunter 1967:111). The rains produce weeds at the same rate everywhere, so all weeding is done more or less at the same time, which makes the demand for labor great during such periods. The shortage of labor limits farm size and production capacity.

Three kinds of fields exist in Sisala-land: the lineage field, fields of households or individuals within the lineage, and kitchen gardens. Thus, there are several farm groups within the lineage (see table 3.5). The average number of such farm groups was nearly four per lineage in the village of Bujan, at the time of my fieldwork. There were 6.4 residents for each farmer and 12.7 persons per farm group. Also, as table 3.6 shows, there was at least one kitchen garden per lineage. The average number of gardens per lineage was 1.9 for the village of Bujan. Such gardens are usually tended by women or aged men. Gardens are usually small, about a quarter of a hectare. The fields of the lineage and households which are cleared in the bush produce the bulk of the crops. Each may be composed of one or more of the following types of field: the *baga naaŋ*, the main cereal farm containing millet, maize, and Guinea corn; the *pii-yaŋ*, or the yam field; the *miiri-yaŋ*, the rice field, usually a low-lying spot that catches lots of rain water; and the *jisiŋ-yaŋ*, the peanut field.

Any social segment of the lineage may have a separate farm exclusively for their group, as long as they contribute labor to the lineage farm. It is also thought bad form to grow millet, which should be reserved for the lineage

TABLE 3.5   Bujan Farm Groups*

LINEAGE	NUMBER OF FARM GROUPS	NUMBER OF RESIDENTS	PERSONS PER FARM GROUP
Jawang	4	40	10.0
Yeliwiejang	2	35	17.5
Najenjang	1	29	29.0
Bakujang	8	60	7.5
Kpejang	2	38	19.0
Fuojang	4	54	13.5
Forkorjang	6	79	13.2
Kaalajang	4	59	14.8
Total	31	394	Average = 12.7

*Sixty-two men were farmers in Bujan, making 1 farmer for every 6.4 residents at the time of the study (1971).

TABLE 3.6   Lineage Kitchen Gardens of Bujan

LINEAGE	NUMBER OF KITCHEN GARDENS
Fuojang	2
Yeliwiejang	2
Bakujang	3
Fokorjang	3
Kaalajang	2
Najenjang	1
Jawang	1
Kpejang	1
Average number per lineage	1.9

farm. Control of millet is the right of the lineage headman. When the crop is harvested, he supervises the work and tells the women in which granaries to deposit the grain. First, he fills the *virebaliŋ*, the large storage facility of the entire lineage. Then he divides portions according to need to be stored in the different granaries (*viresiŋ*) of the households. If the harvest is good, the surplus is allocated by household heads to various granaries in women's kitchens. The produce from each household field is apportioned to wives by the household head.

Granaries are made from a mixture of mud, broken bits of anthills, cow dung, and straw. They are sealed tightly to prevent pests and rodents from harming the contents. The Sisala call this *tuɔlɛ*, which means both "to store" and "to preserve." They have also learned to treat the grain with certain herbs that may enhance preservation. Storage is a major problem because this produce must last the family from November until the following July, when new crops begin to become available. If any portion of the stored goods is lost, for any reason, it can prove disastrous for the family. Problems in storing produce for long periods of time also prevent a man from accumulating capital in this way. It is better to give a surplus to another group, as one may be in need at some time in the future.

Women cook (*chɔɔ*). When a wife needs food, she goes to her granary. When that runs low, she asks her husband to fill it from the household granary. If the household granary runs low, the household head appeals to the lineage head for more supplies. It is the responsibility (*bene*) of the lineage head to ensure that stocks are not depleted before the following year's crops are ready to eat. This duty is supported by the belief that any person who takes food from the *virebaliŋ* without his permission will be killed by the ancestors.

Social units form the basis of economic activities, including the transmission of property (*duaha*) from one man to another and from one generation to the next. The *tika* is the male heir who both succeeds to office and inherits the rights over property. Inheritance and succession rights are characteristics of kinship position. The Sisala call this process *dii*, which has the connotation of winning, earning, or receiving by right. Land as property is secondary to rights received over kinsmen. The legitimate right to control their labor and to allocate the products of that labor gives the headman control of the economic processes of production, distribution, and consumption.

A certain point is crucial for our present concern in this work: elders rule, not by virtue of their control of the means of production, but through exercise of the legitimate rights vested in their offices as defined by the ideology of kinship. The means of production sufficient to survive are available to all who choose to leave the lineage to pursue farming alone or with another group, such as one's mother's brother clan. An elder cannot control the behavior of a subordinate male by manipulating the means of production, for he cannot manipulate those means. His power derives directly from his authority as head and from the ritual sanctions of the ancestor cult at his disposal. He does not control subordinates because he controls economic processes; rather, he controls these processes and subordinates because he holds office in the kinship unit.

As the lineage subdivides internally in cell-like growth, it necessarily expands outward. As wives are added and children born, more housing is needed, farms are expanded, and households get a larger labor supply of their own. A man or a pair of brothers can have several strong young men under their control within fifteen years after marriage. At this time, if relations with the headman or others in the lineage are not good, fission may occur.

In this chapter I have described the structure of kinship and farming, which is the main economic activity in Sisala-land. Even when a man has other employment, as in the case of one employed by the government, he still maintains a farm. Other occupations have been introduced, however, since the advent of colonial rule. The roads built by the British, as well as modern transport, have strengthened market activity and allowed sellers to travel more widely and sell a greater variety of goods than previously. All-purpose money has facilitated trade and created a system of equivalency between goods and services that had no monetary value before—for example, the initial bride-wealth payments (*haala-kiaa*) or payments to a diviner. These socioeconomic changes have been described by Grindal (1972). I will not elaborate on them in this work, except where they affect the relationship between elders and subordinates. In general, I feel that new economic opportunities have weakened the power of elders over their charges. During my fieldwork in Sisala-land between 1971 and 1977, I witnessed a decline in the effect of the market and modern influences in the lives of the Sisala. Grindal's fieldwork was done in the sixties, when it looked as if the changes brought about through contact with the world economy would continue to make inroads into the traditional social and economic order in the area. In the seventies, however, modernization slowed up, and by 1980 it had come to a virtual halt (Mendonsa 1980). At this writing, because of the poor economic situation in the nation-state and the relative isolation of Sisala-land, most modern influences have been reduced. Today there are fewer schools, less market transport, fewer markets linked by transport, fewer industrial goods in the markets, no petrol, phenomenally high prices, and little employment in the modern sector. In this time of acute scarcity, the majority of Sisala continue to live their lives as they always have. Modern goods are a luxury that have not altered the basic structure of kinship or economic relations.

4
Cosmology, Illness and Medical Treatment

I It is not startling that people do not always obey all of the rules all of the time, or, put another way, that they do not always live up to the expectations of others. This work is an attempt to show what reactions are made by authorities when such deviance occurs and, specifically, how lineage elders attempt to use the institutions of divination and the ancestor cult to sanction deviants. Such political action and the labeling of deviants are set against a background of cosmological ideas about the nature of the world and causation. More precisely, deviance is thought to be inherently tied up with illness and misfortune. When either strikes, rule violation is thought to be at the heart of the matter, especially if medicine fails to cure a minor illness, or if misfortune occurs repeatedly, or if the onset of either illness or misfortune is sudden and severe. Either lingering, nagging misfortune or sudden and severe misfortune are reasons to consult a diviner, but in normal cases people usually try first to set their misfortunes right in pragmatic ways and to cure illness with medicine or magic rather than resorting to ritual means, which draw in the spirits. This chapter will deal with the cosmology of the Sisala and their treatment of illness through magical and medicinal means. The next chapter will concern ritual means.

Once an individual defines himself as ill, he has three main methods of diagnosis and treatment available. His first option is to consult an herbalist (*daalusɩŋ-tiina*) to obtain medicine (*daalusɩŋ*). An herbalist is a member of the community who knows medicinal recipes for one or more illnesses. It is common knowledge that he has these, and his reputation is spread by word of mouth. If a community lacks such a person, the patient inquires of his kinsmen and friends until he comes up with one. Second, he may consult a diviner (*vugira*), although such a visit usually follows a series of efforts to find medicine and an herbal cure. If the herbalist cannot solve the problem, it becomes the responsibility of the patient's jural guardian to consult a diviner about the malady. Finally, in cases that are of a seemingly intractable nature, the patient may consult a fairy caller (*Kaŋtɔŋŋɔɔ yira*). While the first and last options are largely a personal decision on the part of the patient or his guardian, consulting a diviner involves the patient in a diagnostic process that links his illness to rule violation.

The etiology of misfortune assumes that, ultimately, all misfortune is due to the withdrawal of protection by the ancestors, who become angry about a wrongdoing (*haache*). Normally, this is a *haache* that produces trouble (*wii-juuluŋ*) between at least two persons. Bad feelings, words, or actions between kinsmen is an offense (*jomuŋ*) against the moral order and an insult to the ancestors. Thus, the Sisala believe that misfortune stems from the eruption of ill will in their midst. The traditional method for divining the etiology of misfortune is *vuguŋ*, or divination. Neither herbalists nor fairy callers contact the ancestors. When it is thought that the ancestors (*lɛlɛɛ*) are involved, it becomes the responsibility of the lineage elder (*jachikiŋ-tiina*) to consult a diviner on behalf of the patient. This normally happens when medicine fails to effect a cure.

This etiology embraces a theory of morals. Evil thoughts or feelings (*tuɔ-biinaa*, literally, "inside things") or bad actions are thought to cause misfortune. Personal animosities are thought to cause people to wish others harm. The logic of the ideology of illness provides a mechanism, divination, whereby hostile and antisocial feelings can be divined as the cause of misfortune. Because persons everywhere who live in close quarters with their fellows tend to have such feelings from time to time, there is no shortage of guilt. The accused may consider himself guilty, even though no deviant act was performed intentionally on his part. Normal, everyday bad feelings are thought to be the cause of misfortune within the lineage family.

An elder can cause misfortune among his subordinates, for example, merely by thinking bad thoughts about them; hence, it is considered taboo for him to go to sleep at night with bad feelings toward his people, as this might cause them harm. This belief illustrates the ambivalence of the position of those in authority: they are both persons and officials.

The private thoughts and feelings of the man may interfere with the office. Middleton (1960:36−37) says of the Lugbara:

> For an elder to invoke is part of his expected role. He conceals his action until sickness seizes the offender, and when the oracles point out his part in the affair he will acknowledge it. Indeed, it is usually he who puts the case to the oracles and so actually suggests himself as responsible, although the Lugbara do not see the importance of this aspect of oracles.

In Sisala-land in addition to sins of commission, those of omission can cause misfortune; for example, the elder has the duty to provide ritual protection against ancestral punishment by sacrificing periodically upon group shrines (*veŋsiŋ*). If he does not do this, it is the right of the ancestors to punish the elder by causing misfortune to any member of the group or to the group as a whole.

Misfortune brought on by ancestral wrath is thought to fall on the deviant or on a person subordinate to him, never on anyone senior. This logically follows, since elders have the responsibility (*bene*) to provide protection for their subordinates, and an attack on a subordinate is an attack on the senior's ability to protect his charges. A deviant act on the part of his subordinates cannot make the elder ill. Harm descends to juniors or extends to collaterals. Thus, illness may occur through an elder's legitimate responsibility to protect and right to curse his subordinates. Hence, misfortune and deviance within the group, normally a lineage, are linked with the authority structure of the group.

The man who must act as elder is in an ambivalent position. On one hand, he must remain on good relations with his subordinates, but on the other he is responsible, directly or indirectly, for their misfortune. This ambivalence is most obvious in the case of cursing (*kalibε*). While a man who curses his son is formally thought to be within his rights in doing so, his action is also bad (*u bi zoŋ*) because an impaired relationship may bring trouble to the group. A man who curses his subordinates is thought dangerous, in spite of his official status.

By looking closely at Sisala cosmology we will see that the exercise of authority (*hiεsaŋ*) in defense of the moral order (*kisiniŋ*) is intricately tied up with intragroup deviance (*haachε*) and trouble (*wii-juuluŋ*) on the one hand and misfortune (*dɔgisa*) and illness (*yawiiliŋ*) on the other. Later in this chapter I will outline the model that emerges from these ideas and, furthermore, show how individuals in office manipulate the rules to attain their own ends. The ambivalence about those in authority is well founded because at times men in office use their authority to accomplish personal goals.

II   Sisala cosmology does not consist of a rigid set of beliefs about the nature of the cosmos or mankind. To an extent, to write about cosmology solidifies it. Their beliefs tend to be applied to situations. Their belief system is dynamic. It also contains inconsistencies and incongruities. Nonetheless, there is an overall logic to their cosmology. Though the situations may vary, a pattern emerges from the analysis of informants' statements and behavior in this regard.

The Sisala do not distinguish between a natural and a supernatural order. Rather, they believe in a single cosmic order that includes an occult, material, and social reality. Cutting across each of these realities is a distinction between living and nonliving things. Behind and pervading all things is *doluŋ*, the force that operates the cosmos. *Doluŋ* can appear in several manifestations or different willful sentient entities. These entities may cause good or evil among the living. Ritual specialists are persons who have been endowed with the power (*doluŋ*) to do good, to counter evil (*bɔŋ*). They do this by maintaining contact between living men and their departed ancestors. Men in authority positions in the kinship organization and diviners have this power.

Central to the etiology of misfortune is the concept of time (see fig. 4.1). The Sisala have a two-dimensional concept of time similar to that described by Mbiti (1969:16 ff.). It is important to understand this concept because it

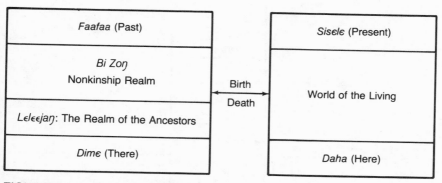

FIGURE 4.1   **Temporal-Spatial Concepts**

relates directly to the ritual process whereby the Sisala consult a diviner and carry out postdivinatory sacrifice. Additionally, it bears on their concept of causation, which is also two-dimensional in nature (see fig. 4.2). In Sisala cosmology both time and place are equated. *Faafaa* is both a time period and a realm where occult entities live. More correctly, *faafaa* is an occult or mythical condition. It is an eternal realm, a "timeless" reality that is believed in and that governs the behavior of the members of society.

God (*wia*) is seen as being "in the sky," the fairies are "in the bush," and the ancestors live in their village below the earth's surface; but all belong to *faafaa*. It is the realm of the mythological events concerning the beginning of the world, of the exploits of culture heroes and remembered ancestors. Occult causation is thought to originate in this state. The only way to determine such causation is by consulting a diviner, who has the power (*dolung*) to receive feedback from the ancestors, the underpinners of the cosmos. Indeed, the Sisala believe the ancestors to be the cause of much of their misfortune and illness.

Sisele is the sphere of *miisuŋ-tiŋa*, or "living things." All time within *sisele* is cyclical, recurring, and all eventually "returns" to *faafaa*. In contrast to Western linear concepts of time, it does not "progress" forward to a future state but "returns" to *faafaa*. This can be seen from the fact that the Sisala word *bua* is the word for time, a hole, or the rim of something like a jar—clearly a connotation of a circular concept of time. Human life is a natural cycle from birth to death. At birth the soul comes from God, and at death it returns to *faafaa*, specifically to *leleejaŋ*, the ancestor's village. *Sisele* time is event

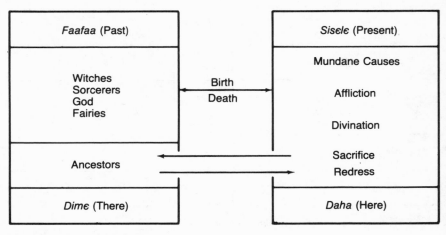

FIGURE 4.2   Sisala Etiology

oriented, that is, connected to concrete happenings. The concrete is more important than the abstract to the Sisala. They do not much concern themselves with the future, because no events have transpired yet in the future. There can be no significant future state, since it lacks events.

Faafaa, in contrast, has many events of significance—hence the orientation of the Sisala toward the past. The Sisala do, however, recognize cyclical *sisɛlɛ* time; for example, they will say, "Since it is now dry season, wet season will follow." This is calendrical time. It occurs within *Sisɛlɛ*, where the immediate future or naturally occurring events are known and spoken of; but a distant, abstract future state is not stressed in their culture. The word for future is *maachiɛ*, which literally means "also tomorrow."

Sisɛlɛ is a cyclical series of events beginning with birth and leading to death. Death returns the soul (*dima*) to *faafaa*, whence it came. Both *faafaa* and *sisɛlɛ* is concerned with life-history events of living persons. *Faafaa* is concerned with past events referred to in myths, and current etiological events from *faafaa* can be known only through divination. The living can relate to the mythical events because such events have spatial correlates in *sisɛlɛ*—shrines, rocks, rivers, and groves of trees, which figure prominently in mythical tales. Upon the instructions of a diviner, persons and groups experiencing misfortune perform sacrifices at such places, thus linking mythical events and places with current problems. These sacred places, or vesiŋ (sing. *vene*), are thought to be points of powerful connection between the realm of *faafaa* and the realm of *sisɛlɛ*.

All things are thought to come from and return to *faafaa*. Thus, ultimate causation and morality are located there. The ancestors, as underpinners of reality, control natural phenomena. Myth relates that God (*wia*) gave divination (*vugʉŋ*) to mankind (*nihuobiinee*) in order that people might be able to communicate with the ancestors, since the ancestors are charged with the responsibility (*bene*) of upholding the order. When the living deviate from this order, the ancestors rightfully have the duty to punish them by bringing illness and other forms of misfortune upon their heads. In order to remove this punishment, the living must consult an oracle to divine the cause of their affliction. In this regard, divination is a means of "looking backward," or tapping the moral wisdom of the ancestors. *Faafaa* is, therefore, seen as the moral foundation of *sisɛlɛ*, and the wisdom (*wu-jimĩ*) contained there is available to the living in the form of traditional codes or customs (*kisinĩ*) and through the institution of divination.

The moral rules are derived from precedents set by the forefathers of the living, who now constitute a group of occult ancestral spirits. The customs provide Sisala society with its social order, its direction. *Kisinɨŋ* provide the way. The customary way of the ancestors is called *wɔŋbiŋ-titi*, or the "true path." It is the proper way to act—indeed, the only way to act if society is to adhere. Their lore tells them that deviations from the laws bring misfortune. *Kisinɨŋ* and the *wɔŋbiŋ-titi* are unchanging and unchangeable.

The Sisala distinguish between sin (*haachɛ*) and a mistake (*perike*). *Perike* is a wrong turn taken, a violation of no great consequence. *Haachɛ* is a violation of custom (*kisinɨŋ*). Customs normally regulate relations between members and units of descent groups. They are thought to support peace and amity. The stress on amicable relations is especially evident among members of the lineage (*jachikɨŋ*), who live and work together in close proximity. In higher orders of the descent system, the frequency of sins is lower because disputes are more common among lineage members who interact daily, but any breech of the customs by individuals or groups within the clan is thought to be *haachɛ*. Such rule violation is backed by mystical sanctions. If a *perike* is committed, the deviant is thought to get his punishment directly and immediately. If for example, one walks bare-legged through tall grass, a snake is likely to bite him. No ancestral punishment is involved. If a person has committed a *haachɛ* and walks through the grass, though, the snakebite will result in illness or death. This is ancestral punishment.

When *Kisinɨŋ* are broken, the ancestors are thought to become piously angry, and consequently they cause a misfortune (*naabɔmuŋ*) to befall the deviant or one of his kinsmen. Thus, illness or misfortune within descent groups is interpreted as being due to the thoughts, feelings, or actions of other descent-group members. Ancestors are believed to do this to draw attention to the *haachɛ*, or sin. When misfortune strikes, then, the lineage headman must consult a diviner to determine the exact nature of the occult cause. Divination most frequently links it with a deviant act on the part of a close family member. It also provides details of the expiatory process whereby the deviant (*haachɛ-diire*) may remove the family misfortune at the same time he removes the stigma from himself. This is most frequently done through blood sacrifice (*kpaarɛ*). In this way deviance and misfortune are linked in a causal chain that leads the authorities to use the diagnostic ritual institution at their disposal, divination, which in turn leads to use of the curative institution, sacrifice. The series of events and actions performed by people as they use such institutions is what I call the divinatory process (Mendonsa 1973, 1978c).

Man's fate (*wiparɨŋ*) has its origin in *faafaa*. Whereas the living can appeal to the ancestors by way of the diviner, they sometimes fail to receive an adequate explanation of their problem, and the patient dies, or the misfortune lingers indefinitely. Such an affliction is defined as being due to fate. An inexplicable disease or an incurable illness is *kia la wia se taa*, "a thing that God has wrought." Whereas there is a possibility of controlling ancestral anger through expiatory sacrifice, it is difficult to control fate. One can pray (*chuɔlɛ*). Sometimes a diviner will instruct the client to apologize to God, which the client can do by leaving a few cowrie shells at a black-ant anthill or through a variety of other measures. If divination shows a misfortune to be due to fate, no violation of custom is involved. The only recourse is to appeal to God. But it is thought very difficult to alter events through prayer. The Sisala are fond of saying, *Wi la kala si che ne u ŋa, u ŋa ne*, or "Whatever will be, will be." One informant put it this way: "Diviners do and say things to bring life, but when your time comes to die, they can do nothing."

The Sisala theory of causation reflects their two-dimensional concept of time. Any event may have two causes: mundane and occult. For example, if a snake bites a man, he goes to the herbalist to get medicine. It is hoped that such treatment will be sufficient. It is thought that he has committed a *perike*, a mistake, by being where a snake was. If the medicine does not work and he becomes very ill or dies, *haachɛ* is thought to be involved. The only way to find out is to consult a diviner. If no *haachɛ* is involved, the misfortune can only be due to *wipariŋ* (fate). There are two questions to be answered with regard to misfortune: how it occurred and why (Gluckman 1973:84). The "how" is answered by commonsense empirical observation, while the "why" is obtained by divination. Thus, every misfortune can have three kinds of causes: empirical, ancestral, or those due to fate. Both the ancestors and God use empirical causes. It is obvious to the Sisala that a person burned in a cooking fire is burned by fire. The question is, Is there any cause behind the fire? Divination is a means of determining the exact cause of misfortune.

The soul (*dima*) is thought to begin a journey as it is created by God. Immediately after creation, God gives the soul its fate (*wipariŋ*) and sends it to be born of an earthly mother. A person's body (*yara*) is created in the mother's womb. The soul becomes attached to the body during the pregnancy. After the birth of the child, its relatives must perform several important rites to ensure that the soul and the body remain together (Mendonsa 1975*a*). Without the *dima* the body cannot have life (*miisiŋ*). The soul must not leave the body for more than three days for a man, four for a woman, or death will result. Upon the death of the body, the soul is thought to leave the body permanently and become a roaming ghost (*nidima*). This is a liminal phase and is ritually symbolized at a person's funeral when his soul bracelet (*nadima*) is hung upon a Y-shaped stick near the lineage ancestral shrine. Once the funeral is over and the sacrificial rites are completed, the *nadima* bracelet is removed from the stick and placed on the lineage ancestor shrine (*lɛlɛɛ*). This is symbolic of the fact that the *nidima* (ghost) is now thought to have become a *lɛlun* (ancestor) and, as such, has the right to enter *lɛlɛɛjan*, the village of the ancestors. The journey of the bracelet from its position in midair to its final resting place on the ground is symbolic of the journey of the soul through liminal ghost phase to its final resting place in *lɛlɛɛjan*, which is in the earth. The pile of *nadima* bracelets which constitutes a lineage's *lɛlɛɛ* shrine is symbolic of the ancestors who watch out for lineage members (Mendonsa 1975*a*, 1977*a*).

Ancestorhood is an ideal state and is thought to last forever if one vital condition is met: the living kinsmen of the dead ancestor must remember and revere (*ching*) the name of the ancestor, especially one from whom one has inherited. The name and personality of the ancestor must periodically be confirmed through sacrifice on lineage ancestral shrines. Ancestors are thought to be jealous and vindictive in their demand for this attention because without it a departed ancestor loses touch with his living descent group members. Mbiti (1969) contrasts ancestorhood, or what he calls the "living-dead," with those souls who are forgotten and who pass into "collective immortality," where their names and personalities are no longer remembered. Such souls are no longer members of their descent group. This is, to the Sisala, a fate worse than death.

The belief of the ancestors' fear of being forgotten is the key to understanding the emic model of the divinatory process. It explains their multiple theory of causation. Since ancestors must be remembered and revered (*ching*) in order to maintain their relations with a kinship group, they are thought to cause affliction in that group when they are forgotten. Since affliction leads to divination and postdivinatory sacrifice, the angered ancestor hears his name called out at the sacrifice, and he withdraws the punishment once the deviant has performed the necessary expiatory rite. Ancestors are thought to be justified in punishing both sins of commission and those of omission. They punish rule breakers and those who forget to perform confirmatory rites. Since most adult men have several shrines, divination may reveal that one of the many ancestors concerned with those shrines is the angry party. Ultimately, the ancestors are thought to be concerned with the maintenance of moral behavior and the punishment of deviance. Fortes (1949:329) notes that among the Tallensi all deaths are attributed to the ancestors because all other causes of death are controlled by them. Goody (1972:210) describes causation among the LoDagaa in this way:

> There are thus three levels of causation, the immediate, the efficient, and the final. The immediate is the technique used to kill the deceased; disease, snake bites, or other "natural" causes as well as forms of mystical aggression. The efficient is to be found among the members of the community itself, the person behind the act of killing. The final cause is the ancestor, the Earth shrine, or a medicine shrine.

Sisala etiology is similar to that described for their neighbors the LoDagaa and the Tallensi. As among them, divination is the mechanism used to discern the causes of misfortune. As this is done, a deviant is labeled as the specific descent group member responsible for the problem. It is thought that the deviant act committed by this individual is a trigger that angers a certain ancestor in the deviant's pedigree who is seen as the final cause.

It is important to understand the Sisala point of view on this matter. Health (*duorʋŋ*) is a function of having the supernatural protection of the ancestors. This protection is supplied through shrines of various types as well as through talismans (*sɛbɛ*). All are imbued with supernatural power (*dolʋŋ*), which provides protection for the living members of the descent group. When the ancestors are angered by rule violation, they withdraw this protection, and shrines and talismans lose efficacy. Natural and supernatural causes of misfortune are allowed to take their course. The ancestors do not directly attack their kinsman; rather, they remove their protection, much as a father does when he curses a son or as a lineage elder does when he curses a subordinate. The Sisala are very clear about this: a father, a headman, and an ancestor are all charged with the responsibility to protect (*poo*), and in return they have the right to demand obedience. If this is not forthcoming, they are within their rights to remove that protection to cause misfortune. Indeed, this is part of their responsibility, because if they overlook a single instance of misfortune, more will spring up within their descent group. It is the responsibility of those in authority to protect the entire membership of their group. It is therefore imperative that those in positions of responsibility act promptly when misfortune strikes. Divination is the diagnostic process and ancestral sacrifice the curative process in that sacrifice reinstates the mystical protection necessary to protect descent group members from illness, witches, sorcerers, and accident.

This raises the question of whether there is a true concept of "accident" in Sisala etiology. They have a word, *vuriki*, meaning to fall and break something "accidentally" (Blass 1975:151), but the sense of "accident" here derives from the sudden, unexpected onset of the event. Thus, the Sisala say, η *jaη vuriki tua bua*, or "You will unexpectedly fall into a hole." An accident occurs only at the level of immediate cause; the efficient and final causes must be divined.

From the perspective of Sisala logic, we see that illness and death are not merely caused—they are willed. There is no such thing as an unwilled accident. One may choose not to divine the willful intent of a misfortune, but further misfortune is possible because a sentient being, alive or dead, is thought to be behind the problem. Nevertheless, people do try to avoid delving too deeply into causation. The Sisala would certainly understand our proverb, "Let sleeping dogs lie." For example, one day in Bujan a neighbor's hut burned down. When I asked him if he was going to consult a diviner to determine the cause, he replied that he felt someone had willed his accident but he did not want to raise the matter with his guardian, his dead father's younger brother, whom he suspected of being involved in the matter.

With misfortunes of apparently minor consequences, the Sisala try to get by without taking recourse to divination. Minor illnesses are dealt with by the herbalist. It is only when medicine fails to cure or when the illness is sudden and/or severe that deeper causation is sought. It is known that illness can be caused by the ill will of one's kin. It is also thought that one can prevent such illness by having medicine shrines (*daaluno*) or protective talismen (*sebe*). These are protection against ill will and the machinations of witches. Diviners never reveal witches. Divination reveals the ill will of one's own kinsmen, which had led to misfortune. The average person is content to let minor problems pass if they will. When illness lingers or is severe, however, consultation of a diviner is in order.

Sisala etiology postulates that natural, social, mental, and emotional events are interrelated. This being true, bad thoughts, feelings, or actions may have like consequences in the natural world. This is why the Sisala agree that it is especially bad if the *tiηteeη-tiina*, or any headman, goes to sleep having bad feelings against a subordinate. The bad thoughts of a father toward his son, especially an elder son (the heir) or those of a headman toward his subordinate or those of an ancestor toward a living member of the descent group are thought to be dangerous to health. Bad thoughts upset the balance of nature and bring untoward events. Society and nature are morally interdependent, forming a single system of relations, and health is linked to the harmony of this system.

A strange event in the natural realm is a sign of a social problem. For example, one day a large, deerlike wild animal wandered into the village. The *tiηteeη-tiina* was immediately informed. He consulted a diviner about the event and determined that it was a sign the village was in for a bad harvest if certain rites were not performed. He assembled the village elders and they sacrificed several goats on the shrines of the *jaŋ*.

Hostility, whether hidden or expressed, can cause illness and misfortune. A father or an officeholder can openly curse (*kalihɛ*) a subordinate. Such a curse places the subordinate in a state of danger which can be removed only by his submission to the authority of the elder. Only the elder can perform the rites necessary to remove the curse. If, however, the father or elder thinks bad thoughts or has bad feelings against the subordinate, he will also fall into a state of danger. The message is clear: disharmony, whether felt or expressed, is bad and dangerous to the entire group. This is true for relations among all kinsmen but especially true in relations of authority.

Thus, violations of moral rules are linked to misfortune in Sisala etiology, particularly when the violation involves defiance of authority by a subordinate. When illness is recognized, the kin group reacts in one of two ways (see fig. 4.3). The first path is an attempt to treat the problem medically, with known herbs and medicines. If medicine fails, ritual methods are pursued. The institution of divination is the main link between etiology and therapy, and it also contains the key to understanding how deviance is behaviorally linked with misfortune. Through divination, a member of the group is labeled as a deviant. Divination acts to label deviants, but postdivinatory sacrifice serves to delabel them. Once divination reveals the deviant and spells out the necessary rite of retribution, the deviant is able to delabel himself by performing this rite, which is also thought to remove the misfortune from the family. All of this is done in a social context; that is, the group headman consults the diviner, often in the company of prominent elders of the group. As a group they inform the deviant of the accusation, and the expiatory rite is carried out under their authority.

Rule Violation → Recognition → Reaction → Outcome

Etiology: (Misfortune) → (Diagnosis) → (Therapy) → (Redress)

A rule violation occurs, causing → a minor misfortune, causing → visit to the herbalist, which may lead to health, or continued anger on the part of the ancestors and continued misfortune, causing → a consultation with the diviner.

A rule violation occurs, causing → a major misfortune, causing → an immediate visit to the diviner (possibly in conjunction with a visit to the herbalist), causing → piacular sacrifice to appease the ancestors' anger, causing → redress and reinstatement of ancestral protection.

FIGURE 4.3   Explanations of Deviance, Misfortune, and Therapy

Thus, the divinatory process—divination and postdivinatory rites—provides an institutionalized forum within which members can come together to discuss their social problems. Indeed, the term *vugiŋ*, meaning "divination," is etymologically linked with *vuure*, "to discuss." The institutional framework provides a context in which potentially disruptive deviance can be handled without any undue disruption in the daily routine of the group. This process of adjudication permits the accused to perform a redressive rite and remain a productive member of the group. In the Sisala view, the deviant has merely strayed momentarily from the proper path. The Sisala believe that an individual should follow the proper path, or *woŋbiŋ titi*, which is to say that he should obey the rules. This path is said to be straight, *tuula*. To deviate is to go crooked, *guɔra*. Straightness is equated with morality; for example, a child is reprimanded with the admonition: *N wi bi tuula*, "Your ways aren't straight." Moral behavior is seen a walking the path trod by the ancestors, but it is known, and expected, that from time to time people will step off that path. Divination serves as a guide, a gyroscope, as it were.

This function is expressed in the origin myth of divination. It recounts how God first gave shrines to man. Man did not know how to use them, and there was much sickness in the land. Later, God saw this and sent down the black ant (*chuŋchusumuŋ*), the first diviner, to act as a mediator between God and man. The Sisala hold an axiomatic belief that the presence of illness and misfortune is given in the world. Their creation myth indicates that God created both good and bad when he made the world.

The past (*faafaa*) is seen as the foundation of the present (*sisele*). Events and precedents of *faafaa* have established a moral order that is thought to serve as a guide to the living. Man must act in accordance with that order or else incur the wrath of the ancestors, to whom God has turned over the responsibility (*bene*) of maintaining that order. Therefore, the Sisala manifestly view the divinatory process as performing a political function. It is thought to keep people on the right path by reorienting them to the codes and mores of society.

Sisala cosmological beliefs determine how illness is regarded and dealt with in society. Medical and ritual practices overlap with misfortune and deviance. Their institutions are thought to clarify the relations between such variables and set them right. Bidney (1963:155–156) has put it this way: "Man's beliefs concerning his own nature and the nature of the world in which he lives have directly determined his interpretation of the etiology and methods of therapy to be employed in resolving these life crises."

I would suggest that the divinatory process is a method manifestly thought to make secret, occult forces known, and it is valuable because it clarifies emotions, interpersonal tensions, and social conflicts within the group. This function of divination is consistent with the general positive value placed on forthrightness and the negative value placed on "hidden things."

Furthermore, divination is thought to be a method of social control. I am in agreement with the native view in this respect, but, as I will show in some detail later, this process can be manipulated by the one consulting so as to achieve both public and private ends. This view is not altogether in conflict with the native model, for they see such an attempt at manipulation as legitimate. They rationalize it by saying that the ancestors will not allow a man to cheat unless his will and theirs coincide. Thus, in the hands of the headman, divination is an instrument whereby troublemakers are labeled, but he may also use it as a vindictive tool to label one against whom he has a private grudge.

III   The ethnomedical paradigm is well established in anthropological literature. Proponents of this approach view illness and illness behavior in cultural terms. Here I wish to illustrate the cultural nature of illness definitions, and in the next section I will proceed to a discussion of the cultural responses of the individual and his kin group to illness. I have already shown that the etiology of illness in Sisala-land is related to religious ideas. As we shall see, both diagnosis and treatment have religious as well as judicial components.

Ackerknecht (1971:15) has pointed out that non-Western medical systems are something more than embryonic miniatures of our Western scientific medical system. He says that "primitive medicine" is a separate category of phenomena. This uniqueness derives from the involvement of the "magical characteristics of primitive medicine." He says, quite rightly, that "primitive medicine appears quite clearly much more a function of culture than a function of biology."

In Sisala-land, it is sociocultural factors that organize and structure medically relevant behavior. Apart from the physical characteristics of illness, there are diagnostic and therapeutic alternatives that are framed within the field of social relations of the patient. Both diagnosis and treatment, then, are episodes that take place in the context of the patient's web of relations within his natal lineage or, in the case of married women, in their husband's lineage, though frequently they return home to receive treatment. This is due to the fact that a woman is never completely severed from her natal ties. In any case, an impairment of social relations is thought to cause illness, so treatment must address itself to such impairment.

As I have pointed out, Sisala-land has a harsh environment. Food and water are often in short supply. There are many endemic diseases and pest infestations in the area. I held a health clinic every morning in Bujan during my field period, and there I had the opportunity to examine and treat people firsthand. Most of them are afflicted by a variety of medical problems, and it is not uncommon for each person to be ill several days out of the month. Most people work with some degree of pain from such afflictions. Illness is not thought to be critical, however, until a person cannot work at all.

If a person falls seriously ill, that is, if he cannot perform his normal tasks, normally he seeks medical aid. The individual is not alone in this quest, however; he is buttressed by his kinsmen. Together they utilize their customs, medical lore, diagnostic and therapeutic techniques, and ritual processes and exhort their spiritual entities to cure illness. Nature is harsh, but the fight is not hopeless, because Sisala etiology posits a cause and cure for illness and misfortune. Illness is tied up with the violation of morals, especially those norms governing relations with kinsmen. When illness strikes, a search for cause and cure takes place within this social context, among the very kinsmen who may be directly or indirectly responsible for the patient's malady. Illness is thought to be controllable to the extent that behavior can be made to conform to the ideal model contained in the codes and customs of the ancestors.

The Sisala have what has been called by Lewis (1971:198) an "over-deterministic" theory of psychiatric causation. In similar fashion to Western psychiatry, they "assume that psychogenic and other mental disturbances have their roots in inter-personal and social conflict." Lewis points out that this in itself is not a bad view—indeed, it is not far from what today is popularly called "holistic medicine"; but the problem arises because "they also hold that the causes of purely organic disorders, as well as of misfortunes generally, can again be traced to the same nexus." Given this entanglement of illness with social relations, an analysis of the social structure of the patient and institutions of health care is crucial for our analysis.

Both health (*duoruη*) and illness (*yawiiliη*) are seen as deriving from a social context. The former is culturally equated with coolness (*fialiη*), the latter with hotness (*heyε*). The hot-cold syndrome in Sisala-land is a native model of the state of social relations. It constitutes a symbolic system thought to represent anxieties and conflicts. Health is believed to derive from proper behavior, which is defined as action that is cool, careful, and deliberate. In fact, the verb "to heal" (*fiεle*) is related to the noun *fialiη*, meaning "shade, coolness, or careful behavior." *Fiεle* means "to cool, heal, get well, or behave carefully."

A polite way of asking after a person's health is to say, *N yara fiɛla?* or "Is your body cool?"

In contrast, illness is thought to derive from improper behavior, which is defined as reckless, heated, or quickly done. *Hɛyɛ*, "heat," is the verbal noun of *hɛi*, "to be difficult, expensive, or hot." *Jima* means "to do something properly" and is linked with *jimm*, "careful attention, stillness, or slow action." If a member of the family is troublesome, the Sisala say of him, *U wiaa hɛyɛ*, or "His actions are heated/difficult." If one wants to say that someone is hard-hearted, one says, *U tuɔŋ hɛyɛ*, "His insides are hot." This is furthermore related with the noun *hɛɛŋ*, "suffering, sorrow." The equation of hotness with the internal state of the individual is evidenced in the phrase *U kala gaa hɛɛ nɛ*, "he was very worried." Another term for hot, the verb *haasɛ*, meaning "for the sun to get high," is related to the term for deviance, *haachɛ*. Both are linked to the adverb *haa*, which means "wide open" when used in a command, as in *Kɛŋ niiŋ haa*, "Open your mouth." Thus, an especially talkative person is thought to cause trouble as a result of his excess.

Another term, *Liiŋ* (pl. *lima*), means "to be or get hot." *Lima-lima* also means "to go quickly." Again, another way of saying that a person is worried is to say, *U kala lima nɛ*, literally, "He is completely hot." The term for illness itself, *yawiiliŋ*, is a combination of the term for "hurt," *wii*, and "hot," *liiŋ*. Generally, we can sketch these associations as shown in table 4.1.

Thus, action (*nagiŋ*), thoughts (*tuɔ-binaa*), and emotions (*tuɔŋ*, pl. *tuɔsaa*) are cognitively linked with both deviance and illness. Deviance is more than behavior. It includes thoughts and feelings. The body (*yara*) is thought to have social, psychological, and cultural significance. For example, the chest is thought to be the seat of bravery (*bɔy-duoŋ*). In the symbolism of divination rites, *hariŋ* (the back) signifies the maximal lineage of one's *jaŋ* other than one's own, while one's own maximal lineage is signified by the upper arm (*vaaŋ*). Regarding illness, a person can be made to be ill by improper emotions, either those located in his own body or those of a relative. The physical locus of

TABLE 4.1 Sisala Concepts of Health and Illness Symptoms

HEALTH (*DUORUŋ*)	ILLNESS (*YAWILIŋ*)
Coolness (*fialiŋ*)	Hotness (*hɛyɛ*)
Proper action (*jima*)	Deviance (*haache*)
Slow action (*fialiŋ*)	Quick action (*lima*)
Peaceful (*yarifiɛla*)	Worried (*tuɔŋ hɛyɛ*)

emotions and character (*tuɔŋ*) is the lower abdomen (*luobuŋ*). Hence, if you want to tell someone that you understand their feelings, you say, *Mi na ŋ bubuɔŋ ne*, literally, "I know your bottom."

In general, the body is a symbolic map to psychological and sociocultural life. Specific illnesses that affect various parts of the body are thought to have different causes and hence different diagnostic and therapeutic techniques. For example, an illness that causes a stomach pain is thought to be connected with worry or anxiety (*chila*) or suffering (*hɛɛŋ*) on the part of the patient. If the abdomen starts to swell, however, the illness is due to the anger (*baaniŋ*) of another or to witchcraft (*hilaŋ*). Various symptoms as they are interpreted in light of cultural beliefs alter the medical response to illness. Different institutions are involved in the cure of simple stomach problems and those considered to be caused by a witch. Thus, there are certain classes of illness that are thought, a priori, to be caused by certain kinds of agents that affect different parts of the body. In a divinatory session, the diviner's wand may point to various parts of the body which symbolize, for example, certain kinship groups, processes (e.g., childbirth—symbolized by thighs), or events (e.g., a journey—symbolized by the foot). The health of the body is thus symbolically linked to events.

We can see, then, that in general illness is related to notions about sin, friendship, rivalry, moral worth, envy, malevolence, and other social and psychological phenomena that are thought to have a physical locus in the body. The defining characteristics of illness involve a change in the internal and external state of being. Physiological changes in a person may indicate changes in feelings, thought, or self-concept.

Various criteria are taken to be symptomatic of illness: loss of appetite, thinness, and weakness are sure signs of illness. A sick person is called *ni-pugiŋ*, or "one who is weak" (*-pugiŋ* is etymologically linked with the verb *pugi*, "to impede or block"). Illness impedes one's normal strength (*doliŋ*). A patient is impeded from normal action, especially work. To be thin is another sign of illness. Thus a child suffering from kwashiorkor is called *bu-jagɛ*, a "lean child." Loss of sleep is another sign of illness. Insomnia is a common reason for consulting a diviner because it indicates a lingering problem. It is a sign that all is not well in a person's mind (*tuɔŋ*). Dreams (*duosiŋ*) are thought to be messages about one's state of health. In fact, the verb *duosi*, "to dream," serves as the root of the noun *duoso*, "news or an announcement." Other signs of illness include any noticeable change in natural bodily processes, such as micturation, defecation, expectoration, salivation, perspiration, a change in body temperature, or a change in temperament.

The Sisala are aware that certain diseases are contagious—for instance, tuberculosis (*kɛsibinɛ*). If a person is ill, it is thought that he should sleep alone lest he touch someone else in the night and make them ill as well. I suspect that this native concept of contagion has been enhanced by historical contact with colonials and, in the present, government health personnel. In the past the British, during times of epidemic, required the Sisala to build isolation huts in which to keep the sick. They also disapproved of the communal tombs in which the Sisala buried their dead for fear that gravediggers, who entered the tombs, would spread diseases. In any case, the Sisala today use two terms to refer to contagion. The first is *chol*, "to light a fire." Thus, *Nyanyalii-la cholu nɛ* means "He caught that disease." Secondly, *daagɛ* means "to spread," thus, *ŋ wuri-la daagɛmi nɛ*, "He caught that disease."

Pain or discomfort becomes an illness when the daily routine of the patient, especially his work (*tĩŋtimĩŋ*), is interrupted. This is a general rule of thumb, not a definitive criterion of illness. Indeed, many patients on the way to the farm stop to consult a diviner about a present ailment. Most minor maladies do not prevent a person from performing his daily duties. Minor discomfort sometimes develops to the point where the daily routine is impeded, however. If a person cannot work, members of his family become concerned, and the diagnostic process becomes the responsibility of the lineage authorities, beginning with the patient's immediate jural superior.

The severity of illness symptoms often determines what kind of help is sought. For example, if a man cuts his hand, he treats himself. If it becomes swollen, he consults an herbalist. If after the application of the medicine it continues to trouble the patient, he may consult a diviner. If he cannot work, his family becomes concerned, and his jural guardian may accompany him to consult the diviner. The Sisala also take severe and chronic cases to the government health center in Tumu, to either of the Christian missions there, or, in extreme cases, to the government hospital in Bolgatanga or the mission hospital in Jirapa. Access to these facilities is greater for those living in or adjacent to Tumu. Going to the hospital is seen as a last resort because that is where people go to die, in the Sisala view of things. Settlements located away from the main lines of transport present a greater problem of access to modern health facilities. An ill person either has to walk to Tumu or wait for the weekly market lorry, if there is one. In severe cases, villagers send for the ambulance from Tumu. Periodically, traveling government health clinics visit the outlying villagers, but this is rare. In general, the availability and quality of modern health facilities in Sisala-land are among the worst in Ghana. These problems are further exacerbated by corruption among health officials, some of whom sell medicine and services that are supposed to be free. Thus, most people try first to treat illness with local means.

Illnesses that are known to cause high death rates or ones that occur with sudden or severe onset cause an immediate family reaction. The patient's guardian immediately sets two medical episodes in motion: first, he contacts an herbalist (*daalusɪŋ-tiina*), and, second, he consults a diviner (*vugira*). If modern specialists are available, the Sisala consult them in addition to or instead of the herbalist; they are seen as merely another kind of *daalusɪŋ-tiina*.

These two treatment modalities are not viewed as mutually exclusive. Generally, the Sisala will try the easiest first. In severe cases, if the divination reveals no ancestral anger, the patient returns to the herbalist. If the illness persists, he consults a variety of herbalists, goes to a modern medical facility, or even consults other diviners to determine if the first divination may have missed something. If one diviner fails to discern a cause of the patient's illness, it does not mean that there is no cause beyond the apparent natural cause. Their etiological beliefs postulate the possibility of human and spiritual will as a cause of illness and misfortune. Because a given diviner may not be able to discern these hidden causes, one should always get a second opinion or even a third. There are a variety of institutionalized explanations for the failure of divination to reveal such causes in a specific instance of illness. The diviner may have been impure as a result of improper behavior on his part; sexual inter-course before a session, for example, can sap his divinatory power. Also, some diviners are thought to be imposters. No one knows which diviners are imposters, but they are thought to be ones who tell lies.

There is one other treatment modality that should be mentioned, though it is not a traditional technique among the Sisala. Other kinds of diviners exist in neighboring tribes. One such form has diffused to Sisala-land, called *kangtɔŋŋɔɔ-yiraŋ*, or fairy calling (see chap. 5). Normally, however, it is not the responsibility of the lineage authorities to pursue this avenue, and therefore fairy calling is not related to Sisala social structure, as is *vugɪŋ* divination. More commonly, individuals approach such diviners to determine solutions to personal problems, such as private concerns about love, wealth, or the attain-ment of employment in the modern sector. In general these diviners reveal solutions to achievement-oriented problems of individuals rather than to problems concerning violations of the moral order which have led to ancestral anger.

Thus, in general, it can be said that illness is a culturally patterned sociopsychological process or series of events involving the recognition of and reaction to illness. It responds to diagnostic and therapeutic procedures that are medicinal and ritual in nature. Ritual procedures follow from an etiology that postulates that illness abates when sociopsychological causes are revealed. Such causes are thought to involve strained or ruptured social relationships within the domestic domain, relations between descent groups, or a person's private relationship with a shrine, though this last is often a metaphor for one's relation to the ancestors. Illness that disrupts the normal life of the group is a family concern because it signals that the ancestors are concerned about the family's behavior. Illness and other types of misfortune are signs that deviance has occurred.

The verb *waaꜱɛ*, "to repair or put right," can be used to denote the performance of an expiatory rite; hence, *u waaꜱɛ wi-la*, "He performed the rite." Until the impaired relationship within the family group is diagnosed through divinatory means and rectified through expiatory sacrifice, it is thought the illness will continue. What is worse is that the continued presence of an illness signifies that the benevolent protection of the ancestors has been lifted. In such a state any member of the group is likely to be struck by further misfortune at any moment. This concept is cited as a reason why illness is a family concern, and it reflects actual poor health conditions in Sisala society in that there is a great deal of illness. Thus, this etiology postulates that both cause and cure of illness are connected with social relations, primarily those within the lineage. Sometimes, however, divination reveals that a patient has been made ill by impaired relations with agnates outside the lineage, with his matrilateral relatives, or with affines. As a rule, the closer and more frequent the interaction, the greater the likelihood of two persons becoming involved in divinatory and sacrificial solutions to illness.

Insanity (*nyiꜱnyiɛrɨꜱ*) is thought to be a form of illness. The Sisala have no special medicinal cure for this kind of malady, but insanity is often considered to be a calling to a person to become a specialist, including a diviner. If it is determined through divination that the patient is being called to be a diviner, he is subjected to a lengthy and complex initiation ceremony into the cult of the diviners (Mendonsa 1978*c*). I will give a detailed case (case 5) of this later. Suffice it to say here that this complex process of initiation constitutes a therapeutic process for those insane persons (*nyinnia-tiina*) who are not incurably psychotic.

A person is usually thought to go insane (*nyaaꜱɛ*) because of some personal trauma (*bugimi*). *Bugimi* is cognate with *bugirɨꜱ*, a "rocky place," and is associated with going rigid, as in *Aꜱwɔꜱ diu lɛ nɛ, u bugimi*, or "When the lion drew near, he went rigid." Any unsettling occurrence is thought to bring on a state of insanity. A *nyinnia-tiina* is thought to be very disturbed in his mind (*tuɔ-binaa*). Two major symptoms of mental anxiety are insomnia and talking in one's sleep (*giemi*).

The Sisala do not make a fine distinction among various kinds of insanity as they are defined by Western medicine (e.g., mental retardation, neurosis, and psychosis). They view all *nyinnia-tiina* as suffering from the same malady. This can be more or less intense, but it is still *nyaase*. While in Sisala-land, I encountered several persons thought to be insane, and I observed different strategies taken by the families to cope with this illness. Selection of the coping strategy is determined by the severity of the insanity. A woman named Haga, for example, was, by my estimation, mentally retarded. She exhibited all the outward signs of *nyaase*: she was unwashed, had matted dirty hair, and sat naked in the middle of the road, begging. She had had an illegitimate child for whom she could not care. She spoke a garbled mixture of languages. Haga was unable to carry on a normal life and had no kin to care for her. She had come from a village to the north and was cut off from normal kinship ties. Since the insane usually cannot fulfill their kinship obligations, they are troublesome and usually suffer a reduction of their moral and jural status, which involves a reduction in rights and duties (Edgerton 1976:63).

I also observed some persons who, upon suffering a shock, began to exhibit neurotic symptoms. One person, for instance, ran into the bush, only to return some days later, while another lost the ability to respond when questioned and remained sullen. Both were ignored because their behavior was only mildly disturbing and didn't cause trouble. I was told that when such a person causes trouble—by, for example, becoming dangerous to women and children—he is physically restrained by having his leg forced through a hole cut in a log.

Such people are watched for signs of normalcy. If they do not recover spontaneously, the family consults a diviner, since there is no medicine (*daaluno*) for insanity. Kiev (1964:5) claims that 35 percent of schizophrenics and 65 to 70 percent of neurotics recover spontaneously. During the divination, the guardian of the *nyinnia-tiina* searches for an explanation of the illness. There are two categories of etiological agent thought to cause insanity: shrines (*vuyaa*) and bush fairies (*kaŋtɔŋŋɔɔ*). If it is divined that the fairies are involved, then further divination is necessary to determine the deviant act that precipitated the removal of the benevolent protection of the ancestors and allowed the vindictiveness of the fairies to cause the insanity. Shrines are also thought to be sentient beings and therefore to be jealous and vindictive. A shrine can make a person ill if its owner fails to sacrifice to it or if it "wants" to be inherited by that person. Illness is removed when the patient sacrifices to the shrine or when he enters into a formal relationship with the shrine. The "placebo effect" noted by Kiev may account for the success of this form of therapy (Kennedy 1974:1178; Frank 1961).

Some persons told me that they did not want to own shrines for the simple reason that shrines demand sacrifices and afflict the owner if these are not forthcoming. Illness, however, may signal that a shrine "wishes" to be inherited, and the patient and his family have no choice but to accept a formal relationship with the shrine. Shrines owned by groups outside the domestic group—matrilateral and affinal shrines, for example—are often shown to be the cause of illness in this way. Of course, to enter into a relationship with a shrine can, sociologically, be seen as entering into a relationship with the group that owns the shrine, or, put more correctly, an existing relationship may be given an added dimension. Such a relationship may also be established with members of specialist cults, such as diviners, carvers, or musicians, all of whom have special shrines connected with their trade. In any case, the call by a shrine to inherit it may cause illness. Once a person has a relationship with the shrine, it must periodically be placated by blood sacrifice so as to prevent illness. Since any given individual and/or domestic group is entangled in a complex web of relations with shrines, both individually owned (*vuyaa*) and group-owned (*vesɲ*), their presence is used to explain the occurrence of misfortune. No one can actually provide every shrine with its due, so when illness occurs it is not hard to find a ritual explanation through divinatory means.

If illness is divined as being due to the "desire" of a shrine to be inherited by the patient, the family makes a promissory offering (*niɲ*) to the shrine. In so doing, the family promises to undertake full responsibility for transferring a portion of the shrine's power to an altar in the patient's residence, to sacrifice to the shrine periodically to renew that power, and to conform to the rules of the cult, if such a group is involved. Once this promise is made, the family waits for the patient to recover. If he does not, that is the will of the shrine. If he does, they must follow through on the promise. Commonly, people are slow to do this, which becomes another ritual explanation of future maladies that befall the individual or his family. Shrines are thought to demand sacrificial renewal. By establishing and renewing ties with shrines, individuals are linked to others and to groups, and groups are tied to each other in formal relations that inevitably involve reciprocal rights and duties. The failure to perform these rights and duties, whether they be of kinship, friendship, or artisanship roles, is considered a major cause of illness and misfortune in Sisala society.

In summary, then, the etiology of illness in Sisala-land can be termed a personalistic theory of causation (Foster 1976). According to this view, all misfortune is ultimately explained by the withdrawal of the ancestors' protection. They withdraw their benevolent protection because they become chagrined over immoral behavior on the part of their living kinsmen. Nevertheless, the behavioral response to illness and misfortune is not initially or exclusively concerned with appeasing ancestral anger. The living first try herbal and magical remedies, except when the onset of illness is severe or life threatening by definition. Only when medicine fails do they submit themselves to the offices of their jural guardian to pursue divination. In the Sisala view, the living are equated with children, and just as children try to avoid punishment, the living try to cure illness first by nonritual means. This tendency to postpone ritual means of diagnosis and cure is cited by informants as an explanation of the occurrence and continuation of illness. Thus, their ideology of illness is self-validating. Each new affliction can be explained by sins of omission and commission which may derive from past ritual attempts to diagnose and cure illness or from an attempt to acquire protective shrines and medicine.

IV   When misfortune strikes, the patient or his family have two main modes of solving the problem which do not require the use of a traditional diviner (*vugira*): they can consult either an herbalist or a fairy caller. A variety of typological factors affect the sequence of events regarding an illness (Fabrega 1972). One is the degree of behavioral constraint placed on the patient by the illness—in other words, whether the illness renders him incapable of seeking treatment. This does not affect the treatment process in Sisala-land to any great extent because it is the responsibility of the family to provide care, summon an herbalist, and collect herbs and roots thought to cure the patient's affliction. A bedridden patient is only at a slight disadvantage compared to an ambulatory one. If the patient is normally a healthy, productive member of the group, help is immediately sought. When the person is old, the family is sometimes less responsive to the illness. I have seen old people and those with incurable diseases ignored by family members, but this is not thought to be correct behavior.

Another factor is the degree to which the illness imposes role constraints on the patient. A cure is sought quickly for a patient who cannot work or play a vital role in the family—for example, when a strong young farmer falls ill or when a wife seems to be infertile. This is why the illness of the elderly is less threatening to the group: it is not trouble causing. Old people can continue to play their roles in the domestic group in spite of illness. More than once I have seen a lineage headman conduct a ritual from his sickbed. The illness of children and elders disrupts family life less than that which strikes middle-aged persons, who carry the productive and reproductive burden of the group.

A third factor is the duration of the illness, but this must always be viewed in light of the various forms of treatment attempted. A month-long illness that has not been treated is quite different from one of the same duration that has resisted several cures. In general, maladies that resist medical solutions lead to ritual ones.

There are also a number of relatively visible behavioral and biological symptoms that are used to classify the nature of an illness. These are well known by herbalists and are generally known by adults, since illness is one main topic of conversation in the context of daily life. To a great extent these symptoms determine how the illness is classified and treated. In a statistical cross-tabulation of symptoms with illness classification, I computed a lambda asymmetric of 0.85 with illness symptoms as a dependent variable. This is a proportional reduction of error statistic, so we can say that by knowing the symptoms of an illness we can expect an 85 percent reduction in error in guessing the name of the illness. I also determined that by knowing the symptoms we can reduce our error in guessing the type of cure sought. In other words, the types of symptoms of an illness are significant in determining how the Sisala think about and behave toward a given malady.

The mode of onset of these symptoms is also an important factor that influences the behavioral response to illness. If a person falls ill quickly, if the illness seems grave, or if death results, a diviner is called into the case. Divination is not incompatible with other treatment modalities, however. In severe cases, the family may pursue many avenues at once. The family may send for the government ambulance at the same time they call for the diviner.

All misfortune may occur in various levels of intensity, which determines the course of diagnosis and treatment. Many factors may affect the sequence of events, as pointed out by Alland (1970:114–115):

> In general, diseases which are ethnically defined as common and mild conditions of short duration are either self-diagnosed or, if a child's disease, diagnosed and treated by the parents or some near relative. Mild conditions which persist may provoke anxiety, but, if they are also common, may be classified outside the realm of disease and either ignored or self-treated in a rather haphazard manner. The severity of the symptoms which will be endured, however, depends upon such cultural factors as definitions of illness and such physiological factors as pain threshold as well as upon ecological conditions such as overall disease

incidence, frequency of illness in the community, and the types of disease prevalent. . . . When a disease is defined as serious an affected individual or his family may seek help from an outside specialist.

The behavior response to illness in Sisala-land involves a sequence of diagnostic and curative acts. Initially the symptoms of illness are experienced by the individual, who interprets them according to the conceptual categories of his culture. Illness is usually self-defined or defined by members of the patient's immediate family. Most domestic units have at least one person who is considered a *daalusɩŋ-tiina*, or herbalist. The herbalist examines the patient and confirms and/or disregards the self-diagnosis. He provides the patient with herbal medicine (*daalusɩŋ*) for a small fee. Sometimes the patient knows how to prepare the medicine himself, and he—or a member of his family, if he is not able—collects the necessary roots and herbs. Only men collect and make such medicines.

If the illness proves difficult to cure by medicinal means, ritual means are pursued, but this is not done immediately or lightly. The Sisala say, "We do not consult diviners by heart," meaning that careful consideration must be taken before becoming involved in the divinatory process. It is a serious matter, since it usually involves an accusation of deviance within the group, confession and submission by the accused, and the performance of an expiatory sacrifice on family ancestor shrines. The Sisala do not quickly seek mystical causes for their maladies; they certainly cannot be considered "superstitious" in this regard. But when medicine fails, mystical cause is suspected and ritual cures are sought.

The pharmacopoeia of those persons in Sisala-land who can be called herbalists (*daalusɩŋ-tiina*) is sparse. It consists mainly of medicines made from roots, leaves, and bark of a variety of trees indigenous to the savanna region of West Africa. These medicines are taken by one of several methods: inhalation, ingestion, and external application. In spite of this medical knowledge, some of which undoubtedly has validity based on trial and error, illness and death rates are high in Sisala-land, even when compared to those of other parts of Ghana. The Ghanaian government runs a health clinic in Tumu, but it serves primarily those persons living there. Most Sisala rely on herbalists for most medical problems. Infrequently, government health officials visit the outlying villages to hold temporary health clinics. In sum, adequate biomedical health care is lacking. People continue to frequent herbalists because they lack an alternative, although when alternative sources are available they may utilize the herbalists and the other curers too.

Alland (1970:134—135) has stated that, first, in nonliterate societies, herbalists thrive because such consultations are anxiety reducing. Second, pathological conditions are self-limiting, and there is usually spontaneous remission to illness. Third, a significant amount of illness is psychosomatic, and consultation is an active therapy. His fourth point is that medicine men surround their practice with a mystique obviously calculated to produce awe in the patient. In Sisala-land, however, the herbalists are not exotic medicine men or witch doctors decked out in Hollywood jungle garb. They are ordinary members of the community who have acquired knowledge about a limited range of treatments. Usually each herbalist knows only the treatment of a few related illnesses—for example, how to treat bites of insects and snakes. Herbalists become such if they inherit a medicine shrine, become ill and purchase a medicine shrine, or learn healing techniques by watching others. One herbalist described his experience in this way: "I became an herbalist because my child was sick and I needed medicine. Many of my children had died, and one remaining child was very sick. No one in Sisala-land could cure this child. A friend of mine from Upper Volta happened to pay a visit and saw the child. He told me that there was a medicine shrine in his area which could cure this illness. It is through him that I got my medicine shrine. I paid a great deal to get it, and every time I got money from the use of this shrine I sent some to my friend, but he is dead now.

"But you know that some people inherit their shrines from their fathers. In the case of inheritance, the heir must know how to prepare the medicine before the father dies; otherwise the fetish will be discarded. If the shrine is powerful it may also make its desire to go elsewhere known through the diviner."

Thus, most herbalists are small-time, part-time practitioners who practice because they possess a medicine shrine (*daaluno*) and therefore are considered specialists (*gɔgɔɔ*). They are paid little for their efforts, but they may make a considerable amount of money if someone wishes to split their shrine, therefore sharing its power. Some individuals use this role as a means of social achievement, like other specialist roles. I only knew one such individual, but he had worked himself into a de facto position of great political power in his village. In addition to being a successful farmer, he had acquired many wives, sired and educated many children, and built a two-story house, which is a prestige symbol in Sisala-land. He was a successful farmer and adept at political persuasion, but early in his life he also began to acquire medicine shrines from far and wide. He acquired a reputation throughout the immediate vicinity as a powerful *daalusuŋ-tiina*. At the time of my fieldwork, people still traveled for miles to consult him. He was the only person I knew who made considerable money from his doctoring.

While herbalists do not diagnose illness with reference to offenses against the moral order which involve the ancestors or the rites of the ancestor cult, they do possess more than mere biomedical or botanical knowledge. Their shrines give them access to universal power (*doluŋ*). The role of herbalist is a specialist role, as are those of musicians, carvers, diviners, hunters, and blacksmiths, all of whom have shrines that provide access to this power. No one can achieve anything in life without fate (*wipariŋ*), but given this, one can enhance one's position in life by gaining greater access to *doluŋ*. Once one becomes linked to *doluŋ* through specialist shrines (*daaluno* and *tɔmuŋ*), however, one is required to sacrifice to these sentient shrines—they must receive regular blood sacrifices to renew their power. Failure to sacrifice to a shrine may result in the occurrence of misfortune. The power of *daalusuŋ* derives not only from its herbal qualities but from the fact that it is imbued with *doluŋ*.

The herbalist's shrine is of a general class of shrines called *daaluno*. Their structure and appearance differ throughout Sisala-land and from specialization to specialization, but generally they are at least partially composed of a container that holds medicine, the actual herbs, roots, bark, and other materials that provide the power of the shrine and that permit the specialist to practice his trade. Lienhardt (1961:65) notes that in the preparation of medicines in Dinkaland, "roots of some kind are always included. The connection of the medicine with the earth is thus perhaps reinforced." This statement would certainly apply to Sisala-land, where the earth (*tɨŋteeŋ*) is equated with life-giving force (*doluŋ*).

Daalusuŋ is used for both treatment and magical protection. Medicinal herbs are often sewn into leather pouches that are worn on the body as amulets or charms (*sebε*). Such charms are thought to ward off illness or cure a person who is already ill. The concept of medicine in Sisala culture is not limited to protective or curative powers, however; it is also believed capable of maintaining or increasing wealth, or any other desirable quality. Further, it is more than a passive agent. It can be used aggressively against others. It can do harm. This is why one who owns many *daaluno* shrines is both respected and feared. Knowledge about the collection and preparation of medicinal herbs is another manner of tapping the universal power (*doluŋ*). This power can be used for good or evil by both living and supernatural entities.

The case that follows illustrates the medical and magical nature of the treatment process.

CASE 1.

Baho (all names throughout have been changed) was a small child who lived in a lineage near the one in which I resided in the village of Bujan. He was about four years old at the time of his illness. His symptoms included high fever, convulsions, and excessive crying at night. His parents brought him to my house to have me examine him. This was because I held a medical clinic every morning and was considered a doctor (*docta*) by the people. Baho seemed to be suffering from malnutrition, malaria, and catarrh. He had a high fever and no body perspiration. He was coughing up white sputum. I gave him a dose of chloroquine sulfate, aspirin, and a multiple vitamin.

After the visit to my house, Baho's mother took him to Kaluo, a local *daalusuŋ-tiina* who resided in her husband's lineage. Kaluo had emigrated as a young man in search of work. He had returned to the village with several medicines that he said he had acquired from different *daalusuŋ-tiina* in his travels. That he possessed these medicines was known mainly to his family, the villagers, and some close friends from beyond the village boundaries.

Kaluo examined Baho and declared that the illness was *diibie*, a commonly known illness. One informant said of this illness, "The illness came from Hausa-land. During the time of our forefathers the illness was unknown. But when the Hausa people came, they brought it. Only the Hausa people had the medicine for it. In Hausa-land they cut the child's body and put in the medicine." In any case, the Sisala consider *diibie* to be a common children's illness caused by the passage of the *diibie* bird over the child. Kaluo asked about this, and the mother told him that she and the child had been sleeping in the patio during the hot season. Kaluo said that the *diibie* bird had flown over them at midnight.

Kaluo accepted a payment by Baho's father of three kola nuts, threepence, and a small chicken (total worth equals about $0.75; one day's labor equals about $1.15). After accepting the payment, Kaluo placed the coins and kola nuts at the base of his *daaluno* shrine and "showed" the chicken to the shrine, after which it was placed in a small cage. He then took some medicine from inside the shrine and mixed it with water in a bowl. I was unable to determine the exact nature of the herbs, but Kaluo told me the mixture consisted of pounded roots and leaves of the *mummuluŋ* tree (*Ximenia americana*). He then went to the bush and gathered some grass and wove it into a wreath. He secured to part of it a piece of squirrel fur to form a squirrel's tail (*heldohoo*). To this he added two small red beads. He then picked up one of the two kola nuts and chewed a portion of it. He spat the red juice on the tail. At this point in the treatment, he briefly dipped the tail into the medicine solution and placed the wreath around Baho's neck, letting it hang under one arm. Kaluo then handed the bowl of medicine to the mother and told her to give him a sip of the medicine each night before he went to sleep.

Next, Kaluo turned to the father. He instructed him to go to his farm and dig up some *mummuluŋ* roots, dig two holes in the ground, divide a kola nut in half, and place one half in each hole, covering each. He was told then to dig up some roots of the pepper plant (*manjonaapoluŋ*) and place these together with the first roots in a pot, adding the leaves of the *karibasaŋ* (?) tree, together with a single toe cut from the foot of a chicken. These ingredients were to be mixed together in cold water and the boy's body washed with the solution. If the medicine were to spill on the earth while it was being made or applied, the child would not recover. If this were to happen the father was required to chew a kola nut and spit the juice on the wet spot three times.

The father did all these things and returned to Kaluo, as he had been instructed. Together they discarded the remaining medicine at a cross-roads (*woŋkpara*) along the path to the village from which Kaluo originally secured the knowledge of the medicine. Then Kaluo collected another chicken worth about $0.50, bringing the total cost of the treatment to about $1.25. When I returned to the village four years later, Baho had survived and was a relatively healthy child.

In contrast with the consultation of a diviner, a visit to a *daalusuŋ-tiina* is relatively costly. A man with many sick children is hard pressed to pay about a day's wages for each cure. If a family cannot afford such a cure, they may rely on their own home remedies, of which there are many in Sisala-land. Medicinal knowledge of various herbs and roots is widespread, but specialists are preferred. Also, the wait-and-see method is used: they leave any form of treatment until the illness becomes severe.

Another contrast with divination is that many of the medicinal recipes are acquired by those who have traveled outside of Sisala-land. These cures are thought to have the ability to tap into the universal power (*doluŋ*) but are not tied up with local social structure. Much cultural diffusion of medicinal recipes occurs in the Voltaic region of West Africa, and there is a general cultural agreement on the magical properties of herbs and roots, but divination (*vuguŋ*) is concerned with the revelation of rule violations against the laws of the ancestors. Divination also utilizes the generalized universal power, but it is more specifically concerned with uncovering deviance within the social order.

Divination involves many powerful symbols, nuances, and metaphors that express a causal correlation between deviance and illness. While the *daalusuŋ-tiina* is concerned to effect an immediate cure of the illness, the diviner is more interested in revealing the mystical and behavioral causes of the affliction.

In general, *daalusuŋ-tiina* are ordinary members of the community who possess specialized knowledge. The average herbalist does not become an entrepreneur through this activity; in fact, it is felt that he should not seek clients. Those who do are ridiculed behind their backs. People told me about one famous herbalist who "goes about like the traders, buying medicines in the market and trying to cure people." The implication is that while most herbalists provide their cures for a minimum fee upon request of the patient's family, some avaricious herbalists use their roles as a means of acquiring wealth and prestige.

Medicine shrines can be divided into parts and distributed among many persons. The material part of the shrine is merely an altar where the herbalist performs ritual action to concentrate universal power (*doluŋ*). The knowledge of these rites and the medicinal recipes are passed from herbalist to herbalist. Case 2 illustrates this process.

CASE 2.

Sibri is one of the senior men of the village of Bujan. He told me that while he was passing near Kumasi some bad trees (*tiabɔŋŋɔɔ*) attacked him and caused him to have severe pain in his joints. Later, after he returned home, some *tiabɔŋŋɔɔ* near his lineage caused him to have a chest cold. *Tiabɔŋŋɔɔ* are thought to be sentient forces. They look like other trees, but they harbor evil forces near their tops. These forces can swoop down on a passerby, causing him to become ill.

Some medicine shrines are thought to be especially good protection against *tiabɔŋŋɔɔ*. Sibri heard about such an anti-*tiabɔŋŋɔɔ* shrine named Korkulor, which was owned by someone in the distant village of Butuku. Shrines, being thought of as sentient beings, are named. A man from the nearby village of Tafiasi had told Sibri that this shrine had recently been purchased by someone in his village and that it had stopped many of the afflictions that had befallen several members of that community. Sibri had convinced himself that this shrine was his only hope. He had tried other medicine and divination, yet his cough persisted. He decided to make the journey to his friend's village to secure the medicine shrine for himself. Sibri mentioned this to the village elders, who decided that this would be a good shrine to have in Bujan. Therefore, they authorized Sibri to ask the Tafiasi elders to come and construct the shrine in Bujan.

Upon his arrival in Tafiasi, Sibri approached the owner of the medicine shrine, giving him a chicken. He told the owner of his illness and that
he had heard about the shrine through a friend from Tafiasi. The owner then
sacrificed the chicken on the shrine to ask (*kalibɛ*) if Sibri's illness was
being caused by *tiabɔŋŋɔɔ* and if the transfer of the shrine to Bujan would
be acceptable. The chicken died on its back, a sign of acceptance. Sibri
then presented a second chicken sent by the Bujan elders, and the
process was repeated, with the same outcome.

The owner told Sibri to rest the night and return the following day with
another chicken in order to get some medicine for his cough. The next day,
this was done, and the owner bathed Sibri's body with a solution. He then
put some medicine on Sibri's hat as protection against the *tiabɔŋŋɔɔ*. He
also put some herbs in a cow's horn and gave it to Sibri to use in the future,
carefully instructing him about the collection, preparation, and use of the
herbs.

Sibri returned to Bujan and informed the elders that the Tafiasi people
would come later to construct the altar. Sibri still had the cough but told me
that it was getting better. Later that year, near the end of rainy season, the
Tafiasi men brought the Korkulor shrine. They arrived in Bujan at dawn and
sent a message to the *tingteeŋ-tiina* (custodian of the earth) asking him to
dispatch a delegation to meet with them.

The shrine itself has two parts, and these are kept in a woven string
bag: a pot of medicine, which is considered the female part of the shrine,
and the hat, which is the male aspect. Only the owner of the shrine can
handle it. Anyone who accidentally touches it will die unless he provides a
goat to sacrifice on the shrine. The owner carries the shrine over his
shoulder. During the rites, the shrine's power forces him to the earth, and
speaks to him. He then rises and strikes the evil tree with his hand as a sign
that it is a *tiabɔŋŋɔɔ*. He then stands near the tree and recites what the
shrine has told him.

The Tafiasi men went around the village ritually ''killing'' the bad trees
in the village. No person can tell good trees from bad ones, but the shrine
can discern the difference. It destroys the evil nature of the bad trees while
allowing the trees to continue to live. After performing this rite, the men of
Tafiasi camped by the path to their village. They were given a goat and
several chickens by the Bujan elders. The following day the men marched
to an area of an abandoned lineage site which contained a tree named
Fuotia, an ancestral shrine of the lineage of Fuojang. It was thought that this
tree harbored evil forces that had killed several persons in that lineage.
These deaths had been the reason that the lineage site had been changed.
The tree was also accused of causing much illness in the lineage. Another
misdeed attributed to the evil of the tree, which reflects a felt relative
deprivation in Sisala-land, was the theft of cotton from farms. It was said
that the tree's evil forces stole the cotton, sold it in the southern markets,
and used the profits to buy trucks with which it made large profits in
transport.

In any event, the men arrived at the tree, and it was determined that the evil force was on a temporary journey to southern Ghana to buy its child some tinned fish. Therefore, the men waited another day in Bujan. That night there was a great storm with high winds. The men agreed that this was a sign of the return of the evil force. The next day they performed the rite to kill the tree's evil. They decided, however, to postpone the construction of the new altar. I did not get a chance to see that part of the rite.

This case illustrates how medicine shrines can spread from one area to another. This diffusion may take place within a tribal area or across tribal lines. Shrines normally follow already established relationships; a son may inherit one from his mother's brother, for example, or one friend may sell a portion of a shrine to another friend. Friendship (*naŋdɔsuŋ*) cuts across descent and ethnic boundaries. Persons who want to acquire a medicine shrine may cultivate a friendship with a shrine owner, but normally medicine shrines pass from one owner to another as part of the curative process. As friends try to help each other cure illness, they share herbal knowledge and ritual objects thought necessary to activate the herbs' power. There are many kinds of medicine that get shared in this way: those to cure illness, those for playing the xylophone, those for carvers, and some for a variety of other tasks. In general, medicine can be used as an avenue of achievement for individuals.

The Sisala pharmacopoeia is dynamic, and the people display an eclectic approach in both religion and medicine. New medicines are accepted from any quarter. If they appear to work, they are kept. The standard endemic diseases have standard cures, but occasionally a new cure is imported by someone who has traveled outside of Sisala-land or by stranger who comes to live in the area. There are also professional medicine men who sell their wares in the markets. They seem to travel from area to area selling their herbs and magical amulets at local markets. In these and other ways, the total range of cures is constantly changing. Also, new illnesses strike the area from time to time. This is the case with many diseases imported by Europeans. As new diseases strike the area, for example the measles epidemic of 1973 – 1974, new cures appear on the scene. Raymond Firth (1959:157) has commented on such flexibility: "Folk conceptions of health and disease are . . . by no means rigid. They have a flexibility which can absorb new ways and new ideas. But the result is on the whole to *enlarge* the scope of their therapy rather than radically to *overthrow* the framework of their health ideology" (emphasis his).

There is sufficient cultural uniformity among West African cultures to allow diffusion of concepts of health, disease, and curing from one area to another. The idea of *doluŋ* and the ability of shrines to be split and shared are concepts that aid in the expansion of the pharmacopoeia and curing strategies. Even apparently radical ideas, such as the germ theory of Western medicine, are easily incorporated into their conceptual framework. New ideas and methods do not alter the paradigm; they are merely added to it.

While, as Laughlin (1963:116) has pointed out, non-Western medicine contains a storehouse of empirical knowledge that aids in the restoration of health, many of the medical techniques of the Sisala are clearly of a magico-religious or nonbiomedical nature. They appear to work because "a knowledge of the etiology of a disease is not necessary for effective treatment" (Laughlin 1963:128), and most illnesses abate spontaneously (Alland 1970:127−128). Alland also points out that

> non-Western medical specialists generally practice within a social context which makes nonmedical demands upon them. They're social adjudicators as well as religious functionaries whose duty it is to restore relationships between men or between men and the supernatural. As such they treat social cause rather than disease. In addition, the limited range of treatment products available to them frequently coupled with diagnostic systems which tend to limit treatment to symptoms rather than the underlying pathological conditions puts severe restraints upon the development of scientific medicine.

Sisala *daalusuŋ-tiina* certainly are restricted in this manner, but as a rule they do not treat the social cause of illness. Their treatment, in contrast to that contained in the divinatory process, is an attempt to relieve the symptoms of illness with little concern for social etiology. This is left to the diviner, and it is when medicine fails that the Sisala turn to the diagnostic techniques of divination, which orient the patient and his family to the social causes and cures of illness. This is not to say that the curative process is completely linear. If divination and piacular sacrifice do not seem to cure an illness, the family will consult medicine men or other kinds of diviners.

In conclusion, the medical system is neither wholly ritual based nor entirely psychiatric nor completely biomedical. It is composed of a variety of etiological and treatment modalities. In general, the sequence includes, first, self- and medicinal treatment, and, next, treatment by divinatory means. Divination and piacular sacrifice lead the patient and his family into a discussion of the moral order and relations between persons and groups in the social order. It is to this divinatory process that I now wish to turn our attention.

5
The Divinatory
Process

I   *Vugʊŋ* divination is the method for connecting a deviant act with a
misfortune, and once a diviner is consulted, the clients are almost always
directed to perform an ancestral sacrifice. I will show how *vugʊŋ* divination is a
technique that allows elders to try to manipulate the behavior of their subordinates and also enables persons to justify the outcome of any social situation.
The viability of divination rests on the fact that a divinatory pronouncement
can never be proved wrong; it can only be seen as incomplete. First, though, I
will analyze the divinatory process as therapy, and later, in chapter 6, I will
address more fully the process whereby deviance is defined and deviants are
labeled through divinatory means.

One of my main theoretical points is that against a background of
cosmological ideas and cultural assumptions of reality, persons work out how
they are going to act toward one another in the process of interacting. This
sounds simplistic, but it has important implications for this study and for our
view of behavior in general. Rather than simply responding to norms and roles,
persons influence, create, and change the social order by their actions. They do
this by sending and interpreting meaningful messages. In the Sisala context,
vugʊŋ divination provides an institutionalized technique that enables persons
to do this when conflicts and disputes arise. Thus, divination is a major means
whereby authorities work out definitions of deviance and try to effect social
control.

The cases I present in this chapter illustrate that while a variety of
psychological and social functions can be hypothesized with regard to the

divinatory process, it can also be analyzed as a process that allows participants to negotiate solutions to problems. It is a way of working out answers to complicated situations. The otherwise vague systems of principles which we call the moral order is concretized by divination. *Vugɪŋ* provides participants with specific culturally prescribed choices, but they do more than merely accept these options. They redefine them and engage in accommodation and compromise with each other in relation to such principles. Their choices are based on the general principles of the moral order, not on a fixed set of rules. The outcome of any divination is as much a result of political struggle between involved parties as it is the result of rule enforcement. Participants take more than principles and rules into account when engaged in a divinatory confrontation with others. They also have personal goals, or ends that favor their particular faction within the group. They employ strategies to obtain these ends, and these particularistic interests are often cleverly couched in acceptable cultural terms to disguise personal and factional concerns.

Before looking at the microprocesses involved in *vugɪŋ* divination, I want to outline the two other forms of divination used by the Sisala and place *vugɪŋ* in relation to them and the mythical history of the area. *Vugɪŋ* is the key divinatory institution in the Sisala religion. The other forms seem to be used to discern probabilities about the future and life's problems which are not necessarily a concern of the ancestor cult.

II   In Sisala-land two peripheral forms of divination exist in addition to *vugɪŋ*: throwing cowries and calling fairies. The former is practiced mainly in the towns and larger villages in Sisala-land where there are several resident ethnic groups. It is a divinatory form that can be used by all such groups. It probably diffused from the Islamic peoples to the north and seems to be a method known widely throughout West Africa. Though some Sisala consult cowrie throwers, there are relatively few who practice this kind of divination. Mostly such diviners are strangers who pass through the area from time to time. Those few Sisala who practice this divinatory form are innovators who learned the technique while living outside of Sisala-land. It is my impression that they are also persons who have tried several other avenues to success, such as calling fairies, carving, or blacksmithing.

Pagan Sisala who consult *vugɪŋ* diviners tend to look down on cowrie throwing as a less reliable form of divination. Traditional diviners (*pl. vugiraa*) told me that if their verdict was too different from that of a cowrie thrower (*moribii-pula-tiina*), the latter would die because the ancestors would not allow him to continue telling lies. One diviner told me the following story: "The divining bag of *vugin* came from God. It was here prior to those who throw cowries and who only profess to see things. Anyone can become a cowrie thrower by going to another cowrie thrower and asking him to share his medicine. His face is washed with the medicine after he pays a fee, and he can start throwing cowries."

In reality there is little conflict between the practitioners of these two techniques because the cowrie throwers tend to be wandering entrepreneurs and are normally consulted about matters that do not have a bearing on structural matters—that is, matters of morality which are of interest to the ancestors and lineage authorities. For example, when a Wangara cowrie thrower came through Bujan village one day, many people consulted him in hopes of hearing "something good." It is my impression that such entrepreneurial diviners make a living at it precisely because this is what they provide. In general the treatment sequence begins with medicine. If it fails to cure, a diviner is consulted. If that fails, the family may try a variety of methods, including European medicine, Islamic healers, or distant healers whose reputations have spread throughout the Voltaic region of West Africa. One such type of healer is the fairy caller (*kangtɔŋ-yira*). He is usually consulted in cases of great difficulty which seem not to respond to easier and less expensive methods. Throughout the Voltaic region the fairies (*kangtɔŋ-yira*) are thought to be bush-dwelling spirits who act as intermediaries between God and mankind (Goody 1972). Some peoples have developed divinatory methods of capturing the fairies in an effort to communicate with God.

My reading of the early accounts about Sisala culture and my research in the area have led me to conclude that while the Sisala have a concept of the fairies, they did not have techniques of calling them until the colonial period. When the British and French governments established peace in the region, the Sisala were better able to travel and communicate with their neighbors. While there has always been some such intercourse, the slave raids of the nineteenth century had severely disrupted this communication. Increased communication allowed the diffusion of the technique of calling the fairies from the Kasena people in Upper Volta. While I was visiting a fairy caller in Kasena-land, informants confirmed this, and Sisala fairy callers agree that they have learned their trade from the Kasena, who have been practicing this art for a long time. I have attended seances in both areas and find them to be identical, except that the Kasena are more skillful and their seances more elaborate. The fame of some Kasena fairy callers is known as far as Ouagadougou and Kumasi. At one seance that I attended, there were clients from three different nations and from numerous tribes. The seance resembled a miniature United Nations conference, with the diviner's sons acting as simultaneous translators in several languages.

The fairies can been viewed as peripheral spirits (Lewis 1971); that is, they are not ancestral spirits and are in no way concerned with violations of moral rules. Their attacks are capricious and difficult to predict. Persons are made ill without moral cause, though ultimately, as I have said, all misfortune can be viewed as the result of the withdrawal of ancestral protection. Fairy callers form a peripheral cult that allows some individuals the chance to achieve prestige outside of the authority structure of society. These diviners usually become fairy callers because the fairies have caused their illness, especially mental illness. One fairy caller told me that the fairies "seized" him and made him insane for several months. Eventually, though, he learned to control their power, which he now uses to divine.

The Sisala do not normally consult fairy callers about illness or misfortune that can be dealt with by traditional means. Such diviners are scarce and costly. I did not gather much data on fairy callers, but my impression is that they are marginal individuals who act as cultural brokers for persons experiencing problems that do not neatly fall into a traditional treatment modality. They, and their clients, are frequently persons who operate in two worlds, the traditional and the modern. They are often persons who have jobs in the modern sector or who travel and experience problems beyond the scope of traditional *vuguŋ* divination. While *vuguŋ* divination solves problems by linking them to ancestral anger over violations against the moral order, fairy callers communicate with God through the fairies about general problems with which the ancestors are not concerned. These are such universal problems as a young man's concern over a love affair or a trader's fear of death in a truck accident. Fairy callers also deal with the future, more so than *vuguŋ* diviners; that is, they tell the client what he must do in order to achieve an end. *Vuguŋ* diviners tell a client what sin has disrupted the way things should be or the structure of social life. While Christians and Moslems generally boycott *vuguŋ* diviners, the universalistic character of fairy calling attracts persons with problems from all religions and ethnic groups. Of the 272 Sisala males I interviewed about their consulting habits, only 7.3 percent had ever been to a fairy caller, while 86 percent had consulted a *vuguŋ* diviner at least once in the month prior to the interview.

The *vuguŋ* diviner (*vugira*) is a person who occupies an accepted, traditional position in Sisala society. Neither the cowrie thrower nor the fairy caller hold such status. The office of *vugira* was instituted by God for the protection of the living. The first diviner is said to have been *chuŋchusumuŋ* (the black ant), who descended from God by way of the baobab tree. God had already given shrines to man, but man did not understnad their function. Affliction therefore was widespread on earth. Children were continually sick, wives died in childbirth, crops failed. God saw that man was confused and sent down the Black Ant to instruct man in the art of divination and the proper use of shrines. Today *chuŋchusumuŋ* remains the symbol of the divinatory link between God and man. For example, when a diviner tells a client that he should give twenty cowries to a "diviner" as a solution to a problem, he may give the cowries to a practicing diviner, or he may merely leave them on top of a black-ant anthill. When a diviner tells someone to "pray to God," he may take his offering (for example, three kola nuts and fifty cowries) to the anthill or to a diviner. Also, when people purchase medicine from a *daalusuŋtiina*, they must discard any remaining medicine on a black-ant anthill because "the medicine must be returned to God." The black ant is thought to be like God. Both are omnipresent and dangerous if certain precautions are not taken. The Sisala say that black ants never sleep. Anyone walking through the bush at night with a flashlight can see the ants busy at work at their hill. Black ants are also very strong and can destroy an entire millet harvest in one night if it is not properly protected.

Myth relates that God gave the divining shrine to man so that he could have a link with the occult world. It allowed him to communicate with the supernatural world and provided him with a feedback mechanism. Because of divination and ancestral shrines, man has a way of fighting affliction. Life is harsh and uncertain in Sisala-land. Divination is constantly used as a means to combat illness and misfortune, as can be seen from table 5.1, which shows that in the month previous to my interview, 86 percent of my informants had consulted a *vugira*, with a modal number of consultations of two.

Ancestors figure prominently in the etiological thinking of the Sisala. The specific reasons for consulting a diviner vary, but in most cases, the ancestors are thought to be behind the malady that drives the client to consult

TABLE 5.1   Number of Times Interviewees Consulted A Diviner in Previous Month

	0	1	2	3	4	5	6	7	8	9+	TOTAL
N	37	71	90	36	22	6	3	2	1	3	271
%	14	26	33	13	8	2	1	1	0	1	100

the diviner. Table 5.2 shows that the most common reason for consulting a diviner is illness. Thirty-eight percent of the sample said that illness was their motivation, while another 15 percent of the troubles mentioned were health related—for example, insomnia, childbirth, infertility, and death. Thus, over half of the explanations given by clients involved a health problem of some sort. Other reasons for consulting include the need to see if any rule violations have angered the ancestors prior to the performance of a vital rite, such as the naming of a child or a funeral, or prior to the performance of a critical act, such as a harvest or a long journey. The bottom line is always ancestral anger.

While the cults of the fairy callers and cowrie throwers are peripheral and intrusive to Sisala culture, *vuguŋ* forms the core means of contacting spirits within their religion. In the domestic domain of the lineage, the twin institutions of divination and ancestral sacrifice are key ways of knowing the state of interpersonal relations and of reordering impaired relations. As such, they clearly deal with social-structural concerns of the lineage authorities. These concerns involve kinship, economics, political relations, health, and such

TABLE 5.2   Reasons for Consulting a Diviner

REASONS	NUMBER OF CLIENTS	PERCENT
To find out about a journey	32	12
A matter of marriage	33	12
A child naming	4	1
An illness	102	38
Insomnia	12	4
Childbirth	18	8
Dreams bothering client	3	1
Wife's infertility	7	3
A death occurred	3	1
To learn about something in the future	3	1
Conflict occurring in the lineage	4	1
Some animals died	1	0
Wanted to know outcome of harvest	1	0
General trouble	10	4
No response to question	25	9
Totals	271	100

matters as impinge on the family member's lives. Neither *vugɩŋ* nor any other aspect of their religion can be analyzed in isolation from other parts of the total set of axiomatic values, institutions, and activities that occur in society. Each institution forms an integral part of the whole social fabric, and religious action is concerned with determining the proper way of maintaining the social order. Ruel (1968:649) says that one way to describe religion is as a "truth system," or an interconnected set of values to which are ascribed ultimate validity. Central to the Sisala "truth system" is the institution of divination. Much of their ritual behavior is concerned with finding the truth (*wutiti*) about the cause of trouble in the group, and it is designed to demostrate the proper way to ameliorate such trouble.

The writings of Victor Turner on divination have oriented me to view divination as a part of the total divinatory process. The following three statements have been especially instructive:

1. "The switchpoint between social crisis and performance of redressive ritual is the divinatory seance or consultation" (Turner 1968:25).

2. "All rituals of affliction are preceded by some recourse to divination, however perfunctory, and it is in the divinatory process that quarrels, competition and alignments among people are brought to light" (Turner 1968:27).

3. "The divinatory consultation is the central phase episode in the total process of coping with misfortune, and it looks both backwards to causation and forward to remedial measures" (Turner 1974:232).

I define the divinatory process as that sequence of events which begins with the perception of affliction, which leads to the consultation of a diviner, and which further leads to a retributive act thought to appease an offended spirit. This process is not unique to the Sisala; it has been identified in many African cultures (Fortes 1966; Bascom 1969; Turner 1961; Vaughn 1964; Willis 1968).

Divination forms a pivotal institution in Sisala socioreligious behavior. Without it the living are cut off from the occult world and have no way of ameliorating their frequent afflictions. Without divination, when affliction strikes, there is no way to guess or logically determine exactly which occult entity is causing the problem. Thus, divination is a key ritual institution in the total process of diagnosing and treating illness and other forms of affliction.

Sisala cosmology posits a link between deviance and misfortune. It is thought that the ancestors watch over their living descendants to ensure that they conform to the rules of the moral order. When they notice a rule violation, the ancestors are thought to become angry, and they remove the protection (*poo*) that prevents the living from having misfortune. Once the misfortune is felt among the living, the lineage elder (*jachikiŋ-tiina*) is charged with the responsibility (*bene*) to investigate the malady's cause through divinatory means. In so doing he is expected to provide a causal linkage between the deviant act, misfortune, and the ritual retribution to be carried out by the deviant.

I assume that ideas about ancestral action are a reflection of social life among the living. Furthermore, I feel that the key institution of divination is structured in such a way as to allow the living lineage authorities to manipulate its outcome. An additional hypothesis is that on the basis of this manipulability, elders attempt to control the behavior of their subordinates through the linked institutions of divination and piacular sacrifice, which make up the divinatory process. In this chapter I will provide empirical support of these hypotheses.

Case 3 illustrates the normal sequence of events following the perception of affliction.

CASE 3.

Siania had been suffering from chronic backache and insomnia. He tried several herbalists in the area, but met with no success. Finally he consulted a diviner and determined that his son, Nabie, had done something wrong, causing the lineage ancestors to be angry. He confronted Nabie with this accusation, and Nabie agreed to accompany his father to another diviner to ascertain the exact nature of Nabie's wrongdoing. The father asked his son to respond to various possibilities raised in the course of the consultation. One such was a category that dealt with "animals of the bush." When this was mentioned, Nabie became embarrassed and admitted that he had indeed done a bad thing regarding bush animals. He said he had trapped an antelope and sold it in the market for fourteen cedis. Instead of turning all the money over to his father, however, as an unmarried son should do, he had kept two cedies for himself. The father then said that the first diviner had mentioned that "some money has been spent in your house without your knowledge" (this is a common divinatory category). After the consultation Nabie was required to refund the two cedis and supplied his father with a chicken, which cost him three cedis in the market. The father sacrificed the chicken upon his hunting shrine. The meat was shared by all members of the family, including Nabie.

PLATES

A lineage unit with others in the background.

A diviner's shrine along with fertility dolls of "bush fairies." The shrine's name is "snake," the molded clay head of which can be seen protruding from the "spirit's door" in the shrine. The statues are placed next to the shrine in preparation for a sacrifice.

The lineage headman (shirtless) and a subordinate perform an ancestral sacrifice on the LɛLɛɛ (ancestor) shrine of their lineage.

A lineage headman (center) watches as the sacrificial goat's throat is cut and the blood is drained on the lineage shrine.

Gravediggers butcher their goat-of-payment as they dig the grave in the center of a lineage inner yard. The gravediggers are "strangers" in this lineage because, by custom, they must come from the village's other maximal lineage.

A divination proceeds with interested parties looking on as the client (seated on the ground) consults the diviner (holding his rattle aloft). Note that the diviner is a novice as symbolized by the fact that he has only a temporary reed basket instead of the customary goatskin bag. This divination is being held outside because it is a funeral divination.

The client (left) and the diviner follow the movement of the diviner's wand which they hold between them.

The diviner's wand points to a man in attendance who is thereby drawn into the verdict.

Those in attendance at the divination confer about the divination's meaning. They do so away from the diviner who awaits their return. At such a conference they may decide to pursue a particular line of questioning that has suggested itself in the previous part of the divination.

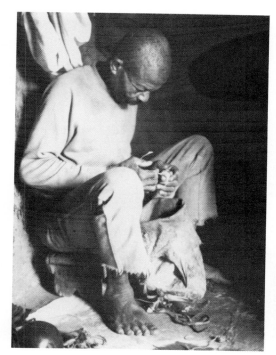

A diviner takes the code-objects out of his goatskin bag and examines each closely for signs of applicability to the case of the consulting client. After this, he explains the meaning of the object to the client.

The client (holding the wand) contemplates the diviner's explanation of the meaning of the code-objects before them.

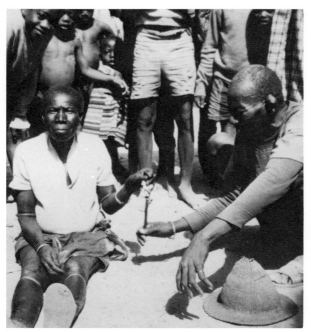

A female diviner is consulted in a busy marketplace by a man wishing to get a quick answer to a minor but pressing problem. She is a novice diviner as symbolized by the white cowry-shells on the top of her wand.

As this case shows, medicine is usually tried before divination, but when it fails to cure the patient or if the onset of illness is swift or severe, the patient seeks divinatory help. Divination is a set of standardized techniques and categories of possibilities which enable clients to pinpoint the cause of and solution to a problem. In a world of many questions, divination provides a person with answers. It also demonstrates a course of action by which he is supposed to be able to alleviate misfortune. Whereas medicine is thought to work directly to remove an illness, divination establishes a link with a behavioral cause of illness. The Sisala openly say that they avoid going to diviners when possible because divination is known to involve them in a discussion of deviance and the rites necessary to deal with it.

When an ancestor becomes angry over a deviant act within the family, he may afflict any family member, not necessarily the deviant. It is the responsibility of the headman to determine the cause of affliction. The patient rarely consults a diviner alone. Normally he asks the headman to go with him, or his father or another jural guardian. Subordinates, non-office-holding males, and females, must be accompanied by one office-holding authority. The practical side of such a rule is that most subordinates do not know the techniques of consulting very well. Elders have become familiar with them through years of watching and participation. Sometimes the patient goes along to the consultation; sometimes only elders go to consult on his or her behalf. The divinatory process there involves an interaction of persons who play institutionalized roles. During a consultation there are four main roles involved: diviner, client, observer(s), and patient.

The client is a person with knowledge of divination. Almost any elder acquires such knowledge through the years, especially after the death of his father, after which he normally consults on behalf of his own descendants. Until that time a subordinate male asks his father to consult for him. Learning the techniques of consulting a diviner comes along with the responsibilities of age and acquisition of office in the authority structure of the lineage. As one acquires more responsibility, through marriage and childbirth, one has more reason to consult a diviner. Thus, a mature man with a wife and children will have frequent occasion to consult a diviner. If his father is alive, he normally accompanies the father as an observer and, by watching, learns the techniques. Women never consult a diviner directly, although women may become diviners (Mendonsa 1978a).

The observer may be the patient himself or a representative of the patient. There may be several observers in important matters, such as, for example,

where death has occurred. The observer accompanies the client to the consultation to ensure that everything is conducted aboveboard. If the patient is a small
child or a woman, the father or husband normally accompanies the client. The
observer sits off to the side of the client, who faces the diviner over a cow skin
upon which the consultation takes place. The observer does not participate in
the actual consultation unless the client summons him to go outside, out of
earshot of the diviner, to discuss the consultation. At this point the client
discusses the revelations of the consultation—the nature of deviance revealed,
the ancestor who is angry, the deviant who has been accused, and/or the
sacrifices that need to be performed. As each of these points is brought out in
the consultation, the client may put down the divining wand and summon the
observer to step outside to discuss the matter, and together they will decide a
course of action. If, for example, the diviner has shown that a certain deviant
act has been committed, the client and the observer will decide which names to
place before the oracle as suspects. In important cases this group of discussants
may include all prominent men of the group.

Each consultation reveals a misdeed against the moral order and labels a
group member as the deviant. The group is usually that of the elder acting as
client, but the divination may reveal that another group is involved—for
instance, an agnatic descent group of wider scope, an affinal clan, or matrilateral relatives. Most frequently the deviant is found to be someone intimately
related to the patient, that is, someone within the limits of the corporate
lineage of the patient. I did not gather statistics on this, but it is my impression
that persons present at the consultation stand a high probability of becoming
labeled. Indeed, anyone present at the consultation can be drawn into the act.
Who gets labeled as the deviant depends on the questions placed before the
oracle by the client. Sometimes, however, he asks the general question, "Is the
culprit in this room?" At this point the diviner's wand, which is held at
opposite ends by the diviner and the client, moves and points to the accused or
makes a motion signifying a negative response.

The labeling of a deviant through divination is not, however, a straightforward process that occurs without discussion or conflict in most cases.
Especially when the accusation is grave or when many kinsmen are involved in
the decision, the labeling process involves negotiation, accommodation, and
compromise. Much depends on the relative power of the individuals and
factions involved. Observers at the consultation may disagree and vehemently
argue with each other. A consultation may end in indecision, requiring further
consultations. In serious matters, three or more consultations should be
performed. It is important to note that the nature of divinatory technique is

such that the elders can obtain almost any outcome they desire. The real decision is worked out by them through their interaction. As they discuss the matter before, during, or between consultations, they define and redefine the situation. Eventually conflicting points of view are accommodated, and their consensus becomes validated by divination.

III The technique of *vugʊŋ* divination is important to a complete understanding of how lineage elders attempt to use it as a means of social control. The Sisala have a "mechanical" form of divination that differs markedly from what Reynolds (1963:118) calls "mental" divination. In mental divination the diviner has a great deal of interpretive leeway. He usually goes into a trance and/or communicates with a spirit familiar. He then informs his client of the outcome. Mental divination is closer to fairy calling as it is practiced in Sisala-land, whereas *vugʊŋ* divinatory technique is more "mechanical" because the diviner is a technical expert, a keeper of the oracle, rather than one who is expected to have great personal insight or powers of perception. He merely performs his divinatory routine, and the outcome becomes clear to the client. It is unnecessary for the diviner to guess or know the problem involved. The entire consultation may pass without a single word being spoken. In this "mechanical" system of divination, the client silently supplies the options, and the oracle selects between binary choices. The primary effect of this process is that once a classification is made, the rest of the investigation becomes a search for evidence to confirm this classification. The standardized objects in the diviner's bag and technique provide cultural categories that stimulate the client to think along certain lines. Once the client has selected one such category, he pursues a course of questioning which leads him to find other categories that, when linked together, spell out an accusation of deviance thought to be responsible for the affliction in question.

In consultations where the client is accompanied by one observer and the matter is not too serious, they may openly discuss each category as it develops over the course of the consultation. If the matter is serious and many observers are involved, the group retires after each category to decide its significance and the line of questioning to follow. Thus, this method of divination leaves room for manipulation, negotiation, and interpretation by the clients, but not by the diviner. It is an encounter among actors who manipulate a variety of symbols—verbal, actional, and material—in order to reach a decision that is acceptable to them and to the membership of the group they represent. The cultural codes presented by the diviner provide the general limits to the investigation, but within these outer bounds, there is room for political maneuvering, persuasion, negotiation, and compromise.

The apparatus of divination includes the diviner's shrine (*vuya*) and a goatskin bag (*purʊŋ*) in which code objects (*vugira kpasɨŋ*), the divining wand (*vugira daaŋ*), two iron disks (*tayaŋba*), and the divining rattle (*chika*) are kept. In addition, each diviner has a cow skin (*nɛɛŋ purʊŋ*) on which he and the client sit during the consultation.

The consultation is an institutionalized ritual process having five sequential phases: (1) contact, (2) the opening of the skin bag, (3) the invocation of the ancestors, (4) the removal and interpretation of the code objects, and (5) interrogation. Just as the other aspects of the institution are largely uniform throughout Sisala society, the technique of divining everywhere comprises these five phases, which form a way of communicating with the occult world. Let us now look at the five phases of divination.

CONTACT

Diviners do not seek clients but, rather, are available to those who seek their services. Normally a client goes to the house of the diviner, although he may go to the diviner's farm if the diviner is working there. If he finds the diviner out but the diviner has left his divining bag behind, the client may take the bag home with him, and the diviner will have to go to the client's home upon hearing of this. If the diviner is in, the client enters his room without speaking and removes the skin bag from its hook on the wall. Not greeting the diviner is a sign that this is an official visit. If the client comes merely as a friend and wishes to chat, he will immediately greet the diviner from outside his door. If the diviner also has his cow skin hanging on the same wall hook, the client removes this too. In any case, the skin is spread on the floor between the diviner and client, who sit facing each other.

OPENING OF THE BAG

The diviner opens the bag and removes the wand rattle and the two metallic objects. He touches these metallic objects to his lips, the ground, his shrine, and the bag, then rubs them up and down on the wand. When this is done he places the instruments before him and picks up the rattle in his right hand.

Diviners explained that this procedure is designed to infuse the power of the earth (ancestors) into the divining objects.

INVOCATION OF THE ANCESTORS

At this point the diviner asks all present for permission to start the divination session. If someone enters the room later he will also stop the session and ask permission of them. The appropriate response is *Tɔ wia jaŋ pi*, meaning "OK, may God help you." Once the diviner begins to shake his rattle, often he yawns several times. Frequently the yawn develops into a "ho, ho, ho" sound. After the yawn he begins to call the ancestors. The diviner never goes into a trance or becomes disassociated. The rattle shaking and the ritual language and tone used by the diviner, however, lend the setting a ritual atmosphere: anyone entering the room recognizes that this is a ritual, not a conversational, situation. People who are watching the consultation are never reverent, as, for example, good Catholics should be in church, but they do quiet down during the invocation of the ancestors, more so than during the other phases of consultation, during which they may talk or go about their business, entering and leaving as they please. Here is one such invocation as an example: "God! What have I called? Savai [an ancestor] is the god. Which gods should I call? I should call Jevaha and Forkorbawie. They should call Gominabaah and Navrije. They should ask Salfuo and Jallo. Jallo should ask Janawia, the eldest river, and he should ask Dajare. Dajare is the eldest farm, and he should ask grandfather, who will ask God.

"God created the first ancestor, and he came down to earth. Then grandfather followed, and then grandmother. They went forward to the shrine Korsung [this is the diviner's *tomuŋ* shrine's name].

"A man's son went to sleep yesterday, but as for today, he hasn't slept, so he came to consult. Today a man's son has brought down the sitting skin to consult. My shrine is a big bush pig and doesn't even fit where the wind blows from. The shrine is a fish under water. It is a star in the sky. It is able to see everyone's door. It is a black ant that carries away every grain of millet. It is a razor that cuts out the pus without causing blood. Even if you go to a farm or to a river, this shrine follows. For a diviner to tell lies and collect things causes stomach pains. Even if the things are sweet or if they are hot, the shrine should tell the truth for each child of man. Korsung! If you have gone to the river or to the farm, come and we will see."

REMOVAL OF THE CODE OBJECTS

Once the invocation is finished, the diviner puts down the rattle, which he has been shaking slowly while speaking. He then places the skin bag between his legs and removes the code objects one by one. Attached to each object are two strings that are rubbed together in the palms of his hands so as to spin the object. Each object is said to have a pair of "eyes." These are the knots of the string. If they point toward the client, this indicates that the object has something to do with his problem. Code objects that face away from the client go into a reject pile. In this fashion the diviner goes through all his code objects to determine the parameters of the client's problem. The code objects pertaining to the client are placed in one or more piles by the diviner. Each pile can be viewed as a sentence or phrase that provides a definition of the problem and a solution to it. If there is more than one such pile, they are not necessarily mutually exclusive, though most clients try to narrow the subject down to one pile in the interrogation phase.

INTERROGATION

The diviner places the two metallic disks before the client. The diviner takes the wand by its top, and the client grasps it at the bottom. The client is now expected to question the ancestors about the cause and cure of his affliction. He tries to eliminate all but one pile of code objects by asking a series of binary questions about each grouping. Once he has determined which grouping or groupings pertain to him, he continues to ask binary questions about the configuration of symbols until he ascertains the ancestor responsible for his problem, the sin committed by one of the ancestor's descendants, the exact shrine upon which the sacrifice must take place, and the kind of animal or animals to be sacrificed on that shrine.

During these five phases the role of the diviner is a passive one. He acts much more as an oracle than as a psychiatrist. He performs his routine and gives culturally accepted interpretations to the code object configurations as they emerge from the skin bag. The client is expected to find the cause and cure of his affliction through the questioning process. This is not to say that the diviner does not direct the seance, for he does; but the symbols and categories used are general cultural symbols known to almost all adults which represent a variety of social categories and axiomatic principles. He organizes these symbols in accepted categories when he arranges the code objects into different piles, but once the client has selected a pile, he applies that interpretation to the specific problem facing him or his family. In other words, the client applies the general statement made by the diviner to a specific situation. He does this be asking silent binary questions about each code object in the relevant pile. Once he has formulated the question in his mind, he indicates to the diviner that he is ready to receive an answer, and the diviner guides the wand so as to strike one or the other of the metal objects, providing the "correct" answer to the binary question. They go through the configuration of code objects one by one in this way, until the client is satisfied that he has a proper explanation and solution to his problem. Since these binary questions are not voiced, the diviner never knows the exact nature of the client's problem, nor is he expected to guess it. The following excerpt from my field notes provides an example of a consultation beginning with phase 4:

> When the diviner finished with the invocation he spat on the metal disks and threw them down on the skin between himself and the client. [The client now has the option to take up the wand for any preliminary questions he may wish to ask the oracle before the code objects are brought out.] The client took up the two disks in his left hand and appeared to become momentarily lost in his own thoughts. The diviner sat, waiting silently. Then the client placed one disk carefully on his right. He appeared to be deep in thought while doing this. He lingered over his decision, holding his left thumb over the disk for a few moments. Then he placed the other disk down about six inches to the left of the first disk, following the same contemplative procedure. He then looked up at the diviner. When the diviner saw that the client had made his choice the dialogue went like this (C = client; D = diviner):

C: Whom do I call?

D: Call on Bosung (the name of the diviner's shrine).

C: What brought us here?

D: This brought you here (wand pointed to the left disk).

C: Is this what brought us here?

D: See, see, see (wand again struck the left disk very hard).

C: Why?

D: This is why? (wand hit the right disk)

C: Is this it? (client pointed to the left disk)

D: Yes (wand struck the left disk).

C: Who is it?

D: See, see, see (wand struck the left disk).

C: What did it ask me to do?

D: This (wand struck the right disk).

C: Why?

D: This is why (wand struck the right disk).

C: Who is it that wants me to do it?

D: This is who wants it (wand struck the right disk).

The client put down the wand; the diviner took a small portion of earth and threw it into his bag, saying: "All the gods come in. Baka, Fuong, Tomong. Whatever this man has brought, you are to tell me, for I know nothing." He shook the bag and continued saying: "Give me the grandmother. Whatever she tells me, I'll tell them." (He had inherited his divining shrine from his grandmother.) He then touched his right hand to his lips and placed his hand on the top of the bag and then quickly made a jerky movement of his hand over his right shoulder. He then began to remove the code objects one by one as follows:

Pile 1. Object 1. A piece of calabash with a notch and two protrusions, meaning, "You knew the truth but spoke in two different ways" (i.e., you lied).

Object 2. A piece of calabash with a hole in it, meaning, "This is life. If you stop telling lies you will have it."

Object 3. A small dried husk of a *nanpapamuŋ* tree fruit, meaning, "Your things will spoil if you go on telling lies."

Object 4. The dried black fruit of the *bubiŋa* tree, meaning, "It will be a black (bad) thing if you continue."

Object 5. A small bundle of twine, meaning, "You ran into this bird's nest by yourself. You buried your own head, and now people are coming to get you (your body at a funeral). You have tied yourself up in this mess."

Object 6. A Y-shaped stick, meaning, "This is a *liisiŋ*, and you are driving it into the ground upside down." [This is a reference to the support post of a Sisala house. Only a fool would try to drive this forked pole into the ground with the forked end down; in other words, someone has done something foolish.]

Object 7. A single cowrie shell, meaning, "You made a promise to a shrine and asked it for some things, but now you have forgotten your promise."

Here the client took up the wand, and the diviner grasped the top of it. The client again separated the metal disks as before.

D: You should do what your *tomoŋ* shrine tells you, or the shrine will give you a black heart.

C: Where did I say that?

D: Here is where you said it (wand hit the left disk).

C: Where did I say the thing?

D: You said it to this (wand again hit the left disk).

The client picked up both discs in his left hand and contemplated the situation for about fifteen seconds. He then placed them down as before.

C: I have put them down.

D: See, see, see (wand hit the right disk).

C: And what did I say?

D: This (wand hit the right disk).

C: Through what?

D: Through this (right disk).

The client put down the wand, and the diviner returned to the process of removing more code objects from his bag.

Some diviners remove all the code objects before doing any such questioning; others do it pile by pile. From this text we see that the diviner is not given specific information about the client's trouble, nor is he expected to discern it. Rather, the client provides possibilities that are randomly selected by the oracle. If the diviner understands the client's problem, he does so only in general terms. He may find, for example, that there is some sort of affliction the client wishes to remove from the family and he is therefore seeking the nature of the deviance and ancestral anger that triggered that affliction. Thus, the client, who is often the senior male within the lineage structure, has a great deal of control over the outcome of the inquiry as he places the names of family members before the oracle to determine whether they have violated a custom. Often, however, whether consciously or unconsciously, a person is selected as a deviant because of the way the client phrases the questions, the kinds of questions asked, and their sequence. I am saying that the client has a great deal of power to manipulate the oracle. Thus, an indivdual may be labeled as a deviant, not because he has violated a formal rule, but because of the violation of a series of informal rules which has piqued the elder doing the consulting. Therefore, decisions to sanction an individual may be based on a situational morality, rather than on rules stemming from the general moral order.

Once the divining session is over, the role of the diviner is finished. It is expected that the client and any observers he had with him will have reached a conclusion from the session. Any action based on that conclusion is their affair, and rarely is the diviner involved in the divinatory process beyond this point. Sometimes the divinatory instructions include a requirement to bring the diviner a small gift after the successful completion of the postdivinatory rites, but normally the client pursues the ritual remedy with only the help of his own lineage people, and the diviner is usually from another lineage or even another village.

If a client has not obtained a satisfactory solution to his problem with one diviner, he may seek another, or several. Usually these will be sought with different diviners, though one could go back to the same diviner since he cannot know the parameters of the problem. Also, if the client tries a ritual remedy that appears not to work, he may go to another diviner to see if the first divination revealed only part of the truth. Truth is seen as unending, and one never knows when one has enough of it to solve a problem. Ideally, a man should consult at least three diviners in order to get a solid verdict, but because of the time and effort involved, this is rarely done.

IV Once the divining session is completed and the client has received his sacrificial instructions, he must perform the sacrifice so that the patient will recover and/or further misfortune will be avoided. In the next chapter I will deal with the social control functions of sacrifice in some detail. Here I want to describe the nature of piacular sacrifice and its therapeutic value to both the individual and the social group.

Kpaare is the verb "to sacrifice to a shrine." It has the alternative meaning "to spill onto," reflecting the fact that in sacrificing upon a shrine, the Sisala pour a libation of water (*lin lon*) or millet porridge over the shrine. The person who pours the libation is called the *lii-looro*, the water offerer. Sacrifice is seen as an act of cooling (*fiele*), as in cooling a quarrel, or of cleansing something (*tiise*). An informant explained why water is used in sacrificial performances by saying, "The diviner tells us that the ancestors want a drink of water. That is why we pour a little bit of water each time we sacrifice. Water is life. It comes in the form of rain to make our crops grow. Without rain people cannot live."

Kpaare also contains the verb root *kpaa*, "to share, divide, or distribute," reflecting the fact that sacrifice usually takes place in a group context and the meat of the sacrificial animals is distributed to the various segments of the sacrificing group. One informant put it this way: "You can pray to God [*Wia*] alone, but when making a sacrifice to the ancestors you must assemble all your brothers and their people. It is taboo to go to the ancestors in secret."

I have elsewhere (Mendonsa 1975*a*), following Evans-Pritchard (1954), classified sacrifice in Sisala-land as being of two types: confirmatory and piacular. The former is made up of sacrifices that are prescribed by custom and that should be performed at certain times of the year to ensure the continued protection of the ancestors. The latter, piacular sacrifice, is of more concern to us here because it is the central feature of redressive rites (see also Turner 1957 and Wilson 1957; chap. 7).

Waasɛ wiaa is piacular sacrifice. It differs from confirmatory sacrifice in that it is performed in response to trouble within the group. *Waasɛ* is the verb "to repair something" or "to put something right." They say, *U waasɛ wii-la,* "He performed a rite." One informant said of piacular sacrifice, "This is done after something has gone wrong, for example, a quarrel or an act disrespectful of authority." *Waasɛ wiaa* is sacrifice that occurs as part of the divinatory process. In most cases it is performed to repair damaged social relations and to set right a deviant member of the group. Such a sacrifice may be performed by any segment of the lineage system that traces descent from a common ancestor and sacrifices upon a common shrine.

The actual shrine upon which the sacrifice will take place is determined in the course of divination. The shrine will be one at which the afflicted group can approach the ancestor held responsible for the affliction. Usually it is a shrine of any segment up to and including the patriclan of the deviant person. It may, however, be a shrine of a matrilateral or affinal group with which the deviant has some relationship.

Piacular sacrifice involves the killing of animals by throat cutting. The blood is always drained on the shrine and/or drunk by those in attendance. The meat is distributed according to custom to the heads of various segments of the ritual community, that is, those who share an interest in the ancestors being propitiated, in the shrine, and in the repair of social relations within the group. Thus, the ritual community corresponds to the troubled group. One informant explained it in this way: "The *vaadoŋo* [maximal lineage] are kin who share sacrificial meat [of the clan sacrifice]. They are those of the same share [*ma nɛ ɲila si pɛ kpaaliŋ*]. The animal is killed because our grandfathers and fathers are dead and we don't know where they are. Also, our fathers did the same thing. The animal goes to our fathers in their village [*lɛlɛɛjaŋ*]. A shrine requires blood. That is the food of the ancestors. It is their life. We do not know why, but we saw our fathers doing it."

Waasɛ wiaa are, then, redressive rites that are thought to bring about the return of a harmonic state of being to the ritual community. The shrines upon which the redressive rites are performed are visible, material focuses of the relationship between the ritual community and its ancestors (Middleton 1960:46 ff.). The activities associated with such shrines provide a ritual drama wherein the values of kinship unity are reinforced and restated. This is possible because the members of such ritual communities are dependent upon each other in a variety of ways. Trouble within the group has ramifications in many areas of the group members' lives. According to the native theory, redressive rites serve to reorder and repair broken or damaged social relations that threaten the unity of such a group.

Most social anthropologists, following the leads of Malinowski and Radcliffe-Brown, have assumed that these rites do indeed perform such redressive functions. In other words, the functionalists have taken the informants at their word. In my view, the rites are thought to be functional and may in fact be so in some cases and in some aspects; but such functionalism must always be taken as problematic. It remains an empirical hypothesis rather than an axiom. For me, piacular rites are a form of ritual drama that communicates rules and realities to the members of the group. It has a certain power over the individuals of the group, but this power is not absolute. There is room within the divinatory process for noncompliance. It is important that we do not blindly accept our informants' explanations of phenomena to the extent that we take ideals for actual behavior.

Before analyzing the ritual drama of piacular sacrifice as a form of psychotherapy, let me deal with the question of the so-called placebo effect (Frank 1961). Kiev (1964:5) claims that between 65 and 70 percent of neurotics and 35 percent of schizophrenics become well regardless of the type of treatment they receive. Alland (1970:132–133) says, of medical treatment in general, "Therapeutic procedures no matter how effective serve to reinforce social solidarity. In many cases it is not the efficacy of treatment that counts, but the fact that treatment takes place at all." This would appear to make all therapies successful to some degree (Kennedy 1974:1178). Coupled with the "placebo effect" is the closed nature of the thought system and the tendency to handle apparent discrepancies in the system by means of "secondary elaborations" (i.e., one part of the system explains the failure of another part of the system; see Horton 1967 and Gluckman 1973:105). Sacrifice appears to be an effective therapy, even when it is not; it is not axiomatic that it functions therapeutically for the individual and/or for the group that participates in the rite. The divinatory process is an interactive process of medical roles and relationships which is thought to be functional by the Sisala. It is also a labeling process, a characteristic of which the Sisala are also aware; but they do not see the labeling as the primary function of the process. The process labels and delabels two types of person: the patient and the deviant. The fate of the patient is dependent on the performance of a redressive rite by the deviant, just as the behavior of the deviant is responsible for the illness of the patient. From the symbolic standpoint, the divinatory process is a series of dramatic statements about the interdependence of members of the group.

Illness is believed to be a sign of a disturbance or rupture in a social relationship. Divination and expiatory sacrifice are ritual mechanisms that are thought to repair a "social" problem believed to be at the root of a "biomedical" problem. Divination is thought to be the diagnostic device, whereas piacular sacrifice is seen as the curing procedure necessary to effect a change in the health of the patient. Piacular ritual emphasizes the conflict that exists between at least two persons or groups participating in the rite. In theory, this conflict is seen as being due to personal deviation from the established rules and customs, and the rite supposedly reorders the social world by correcting such deviation: but in many cases the conflict is inherent in the structural order itself, and the deviant person is labeled as being at fault even though he acted in accordance with a social role, the behavior of which is in conflict with other aspects of the social system. In other words, while the Sisala's theory states that social problems are the cause of biomedical problems, they do not mean structural problems; they mean personal deviation from the structural rules. The system is seen as perfect; it is the inability of individuals and factions to obey the rules which leads to illness and misfortune. Redressive rites communicate the presence of conflict to the people, but they do not acknowledge structural imperfections, nor do they advocate structural transformation. Instead, it is assumed that retribution ameliorates the trouble.

There are two levels of communication in such rituals: manifest and latent. At the latent level, the ritual participants come to understand the imperfections of the social order as the disjunction between the ideal order and the real structure of power relations between living persons. Thus, when an elder accuses a young man of ignoring his work on the family farm in order to produce cotton for cash, the customs require that the young deviant perform a rite of propitiation of the ancestors. Individual entrepreneurship is not frowned on as long as it does not interfere with group economics, which come first. The rite supposedly realigns relations that had gotten out of order—in this case, the young man has pursued self-interests at the expense of group interests. But such rites also express power relations in society. The young man may be quite healthy and a capable farmer. As such, he is a great asset to the group. They cannot afford to lose him. While he may be amassing personal wealth that he does not share with the other group members, a direct confrontation on this point may cause him to leave the group to farm elsewhere. Ritual provides an authoritative cloak for political manipulation by the group's leaders. While the young man gets to keep most of his wealth, he is forced to share some of it through sacrifice of animals and is reminded at the same time of his obligations to the group.

Repeated ritual reenactment of system conflicts is a powerful means of communication with the public. Repeated ritual display of these conflicts is likely to provide a source of latent understanding. One must be cautious in making such assertions; but the ritual symbols contained in the divinatory process may be polysemous and metaphoric, and they may convey messages about a variety of phenomena at many levels. While the elders tolerate neither revolt nor rebellion in overt form, accusations of deviance provide ritual dramas in which structural problems may come to light under the guise of interpersonal problems or may be phrased as problems due to individual deviance. To this extent the divinatory process can be seen as a ritual of realignment, or at least accommodation, which labels deviants while at the same time acknowledging through ritual metaphor that the individual deviant, while guilty, is not inherently bad; and thus, the divinatory process is both a labeling and a delabeling process. The deviant is hooked and then is let off the hook in a ritual drama that highlights problems that arise in everyday life.

I am saying that ritual indirectly assaults their closed system of thought. Thus, the divinatory process, while appearing to maintain the value system, introduces change bit by bit through time and communicates this new information to the people in the ritual drama of the divinatory process. No one individual looks at the system as a whole at any given moment. Life is taken situationally. But ritual drama stops time and provides a liminal phase during which problems that are too threatening to deal with directly are dealt with indirectly. Ritual is said to have the capacity to bring about cohesion from conflict, but we must be careful not to assume that the native model is correct without empirical proof. The ritual enactment is merely a statement of the rightness of the moral order. As anthropologists we must go beyond this statement and follow cases to their conclusion in order to know whether ritual works in a direct manner to realign behavior with the moral order.

Ritual dramas do provide an opportunity to express that which cannot be expressed overtly and directly. It is a circumlocution, an indirect mode of communicating vital information to the members of the group. What cannot be said by any single member during the normal course of events can be stated through ritual drama and through the use of ritual symbols that have metaphoric qualities. Gluckman (1973:132) equates the degree to which hostility and conflict are openly expressed in ritual with the strength of the relationships involved and with the security of the social position being abused. Thus, rituals of rebellion are possible against Swazi kings because they are securely in charge; but where the social relations are more fragile, ritual is less directly expressive of hostility and conflict. The fragility of social relations within the Sisala lineage derives from the disparity between authority and power within the group. In short, while elders hold authority over women and younger men, both sexes have opportunities to leave the group and sever, strain, or otherwise alter their relations with the lineage. I will return to this point in detail later.

I now want to present an example of a redressive rite that ultimately leads to the public confession of the deviant. This example shows how redressive rites highlight trouble and conflict but do not immediately effect social change. In other words, while the rite may illustrate structural problems, the problems are not directly dealt with in that situation. Rather, ritual encourages the deviant to stop his deviant practices (which may be highly innovative) and to adhere to the ways of his forefathers.

CASE 4.

Gbenmie is a young man of about twenty-five. He became ill shortly after the death of his elder brother. After several attempts to cure the illness with medicine, he consulted a diviner, who informed him that his elder brother had been angry with him before his death and that the matter had not been cleared up. The elder brother had died angry and had remained so. The cause of the anger was Gbenmie's refusal to obey a command of his elder brother. The diviner stated that the brother had caused him to become ill and said that he must sacrifice to the elder brother on the lineage *lɛlɛɛ* shrine. Even though Gbenmie and his brother had been living in a farming community many miles from their natal home of Bujan, Gbenmie had to travel to Bujan to perform the sacrifice.

Gbenmie arrived with a goat for the sacrifice and approached the *jachikiŋ-tiina* (lineage headman), named Bayugo. Bayugo summoned the lineage elders to the *lɛlɛɛ* shrine, which was kept in his room. Then Bayugo removed his smock, as is the custom when addressing the ancestors. He said, "If you go against your elder brother you must beg his forgiveness. If you find this out by consulting a diviner it is because you have taken the wrong path. If you don't make him happy you will be sitting by fire and taking out your smock [this refers to a funeral, since during funerals people sit by fires during the cool hours of the night. The smock is a reference to the fact that a relative of the deceased must supply a smock for his burial dress]. When you go against your elder brother you must beg him to forgive you. That is why we are here today, to beg Gbenmie's elder brother to forgive him, as was done by the ancestors."

At this point, Nabong, the classificatory father of Gbenmie, instructed him to produce ten pesewas (eight cents) to beg the shrine to hear them and make them healthy "because everything we do," he said, "is to bring us health." Gbenmie did so, and then Jafal, another classificatory father of Gbenmie, said, "As we are sitting here, Bayugo is the senior. Gbenmie's elder brother was in Naverwie [the farming community], and he went there to help him. Many people deceived the elder brother into thinking that Gbenmie was keeping some things without giving them to his elder brother [it was common knowledge, even among those present at the ritual, that Gbenmie was indeed guilty of this act]. The elder brother became angry but died suddenly. According to the diviner he is still angry. Gbenmie didn't beg his brother to forgive him for taking the wrong path. We are now begging Gbenmie's brother to drop the quarrel."

Nabong then added, "Gbenmie, you should stop this thing so we can sit comfortably. When you listen to people outside your family you will do the wrong thing."

Gbenmie then gave two white chickens to Jafal, who handed them to Bayugo, who then said, "I have received the chickens, and our ancestor Nankene will take them to the other ancestors so that we will have peace. When they have accepted the chickens they will hear their son's begging."

Bayugo then squatted before the *lɛlɛɛ* shrine with one white chicken in one hand and a calabash of water in the other, saying: "*N ba wia*! [I call God!] You and your wife the earth should get up and get this water. If you do so, who should you give it to? You should give it to Fuotia, and also he should cry to Nanchala *woŋ* [a village shrine]. There is a small pond by this path by the same name which is a shrine. He should give it to Jallo, Salfuo, and Kasenmie. If you get this water you should cry to all the rivers. Budaba, you should get this water and cry to Vile Nakanaang. He should cry to Chakpasa, and if you get the water cry to Dajare. If you get this water, who should you give it to? Give it to Banawia. If you get it, give it to Gwoveng, and he wil give it to Tobwia. If you get it, give it to Gwonaba, and he will give it to Kaalaniapiling. They should cry to the Bujangtang, and he should give it to the Bujangvene, and then to the Bujangtinteeng, and to the Fokorbawietia, and he should cry to Najen. You should give it to Tiebuabene. He should give it to Kpe and Yeliwie, and they should bring it back and cry to Fuowii, and he should give it to Jawol, and he should give it to Tuobolnadima. If you get this water, give it to Bachene. Bachene is your Jebung [a skin smock formerly used by the lineage headmen] that is now with me and working. You should give it to Nankene. If you get it, cry to Nankentie, and he should cry to Bajongoli. Give it to Nakpang, and he will get this water, and take it to Bayboke. They should all get this water.

"Nankene!! Your teeth and your tongue always clash [i.e., you always hold your tongue]. We heard it from the diviners. They tell lies and people die, and they also tell lies and people live. Anytime we go to consult diviners they tell us that Gbenmie made Dima [his elder brother] angry. Dima then took the matter to the ancestors, and they are very sorry with this matter. We don't know the truth because diviners say things and people live, and again they say things and people die. You should get this chicken and give it to our ancestors Bayoke, Kajia, and Kuntosu. You all should receive the chicken."

Jafal began to cut the throat of the chicken. Bayugo continued: "Gbenmie has come to be his elder brother. If the ancestors don't get this chicken first, he cannot do so. So we give this up to you, the ancestors. We do this so Gbenmie can beg his elder brother to end the matter.

"The goat heard 'baa' from his mother [i.e., the living heard it from the ancestors]. Stop the quarrel and let us be healthy. When Gbenmie returns to Naverwie, you the ancestors should try to help him get things. When a person wrongs his elder brother, causing him to be angry, the younger one must beg the ancestors to ask the elder to drop the matter."

All present watched the chicken flop about the room until it came to rest on its back. This was a sign that the ancestors had accepted a sacrifice. All shouted *Janyo!!!*—the traditional shout made when the ancestors have shown that they agree with the living. Bayugo continued: "Grandfather, you have received your chicken. Nankene! We heard everything from your mouth, and you gave it to your son and went away, giving it to us, and we are struggling with it. See!! Gbenmie has done wrong against his elder brother, and the elder brother was not happy. So accept these twenty white cowries [represented by the ten pesewas] and these chickens and a goat. Father! Forefathers! Get up and hear this. Nankene! You get these things and beg Gbenmie's elder brother. If he were alive and his brother wronged him, he would accept these cowries and forgive his younger brother. But now he is dead, and he should do the same.

"Anywhere that Gbenmie goes he looks to avoid trouble, and he wants his name to last. This is why he brings the cowries. Let the Kaalaniaa [house people] be healthy. Let the younger brother have the name of his elder brother."

Jafal cut the throat of the second chicken, which he threw on the *lelee* shrine, and it eventually died on its back. Then the goat was led up to the shrine. Bayugo began anew: "Nankene! You are the person we all knew well. You take these things and beg Dima. This is the goat to beg him. All this unfortunate matter should end. If it is a hole, we are closing it."

Jafal cut the throat of the goat and drained a small portion of the blood on the shrine and caught the rest in a calabash to save to cook. A portion of the rope used to lead the goat was cut into small strips and placed on the shrine, as is the custom. Feathers from the chickens were used to mop up the excess blood, and they were stuck to the shrine as well. Gbenmie then produced a bottle of native gin (*apetishi*) and some kola nuts for his elders to enjoy, and the sacrifice was ended.

V   It is a truism in medical anthropology that the treatment of a sick person is a highly social matter (Firth 1959:135; Fortes 1975:142; Frank 1965; Kennedy 1974:1170; Ngubane 1976:277). Foster (1976) has shown how in personalistic medical systems, group treatment involves morality and the spiritual guardians of that morality. In such systems, curing becomes a ritual drama wherein the moral order is mapped out for the participants and the audience. Deviation from this axiomatic moral order is specifically indicated as the cause of misfortune, and a ritual remedy is enacted as the cure. This drama, it is assumed in the native model, realigns the social order—that is, it repairs impaired social relations.

During this process the patient is present, if possible, or informed if bedridden. The deviant, elders, and other members of the family are also present. From the very beginning, the entire divinatory process is a public matter. The divinatory process has roles that correspond to our understanding of "patient," "therapist," and "audience" (Kennedy 1974:1170). The consulting client is usually the jural guardian of the group, the headman. He rallies the group around the sick person. Of course, this attention and visible support by the family may, in itself, be therapeutic; but the divinatory process also reveals conflict within the group. The deviant is usually someone with whom the patient has intimate social relations, a family member. Thus, the divinatory process, including both divination and sacrifice, are involved in the revelation of wrongdoing. The ritual drama is a statement of opposition to the deviance, support of the patient, and acknowledgment that through the performance of the rite the patient is now permitted to get well.

I am saying that the divinatory process may have therapeutic value for the patient. He is not left alone to face illness, nor is he usually considered to be at blame (*dɔmɔ*). The blame is placed on another member of the group. However ineffective the Sisala medical system may be in the biomedical sense, it does seem to be structured so as to deal effectively with psychosomatic and psychological illnesses and ones that derive from interpersonal conflict. In this sense, the divinatory process is a form of psychotherapy. But Prince (1968:58*n*) warns us of the difference between Western psychotherapy and the kind just described. He says, "Insight and indeed the whole concept of the importance of childhood in the genesis of neurosis distinguishes our Western psychotherapies from all of the primitive systems." In Sisala therapy, the etiology of illness is thought to be located, not in childhood or in the distant past life history of the individual, but rather in the present interpersonal relations of family members. The patient is not encouraged to seek insight to achieve independence of others; instead, the divinatory process deeply involves the patient and labeled deviant in a series of ritual dramas designed to downgrade asocial impulses and behavior. Contrary to Western psychoanalytic attempts to disengage the individual from a tangled web of past relations that exist in his subconscious, Sisala therapy stresses the necessity of maintaining correct social relations with others; in other words, it emphasizes the need to acknowledge the dependence of the individual on the group. It is an effort to dramatize the interdependence of group members. Independence takes second place to conformity. Insight is not into past experiences but into the dynamics of everyday living and present social relations. Cure comes when the deviant is exposed and reintegrated into the "core of authority." This ritual act opens the way for the patient to get well. It is a dramatic signal to the patient that no social or supernatural reason stands in the way to recovery.

The divinatory process, by linking present difficulties with the moral imperatives of the group, immerses the afflicted person in meaning that stresses the need for the rejection of independence and for integration into the social group. It also communicates to the patient the fact that the group is behind him and his recovery. During times of chaos and misfortune, divination and subsequent rites imbue the illness situation with meaning. The diviner places the misfortune in its proper social context by virtue of his ability to receive direct feedback from the occult world. He ties the present to the past by linking the present situation with cultural precedents from the past—the myths and stories of the culture heroes, the moral imperatives of the fore-fathers. It is not the past history of the patient that is important—for example, a traumatic childhood—but rather the distant past and its moral rules. The divinatory rites orient the patient and his family toward expiatory sacrifice as a means of removing the illness. Furthermore, the postdivinatory sacrifice has an effect on the deviant, who also receives ritual messages of the need to reintegrate with group members.

The therapeutic message provided by the divinatory process to the patient, put simply, is that his malady is due to deviance on the part of a member of his social network and that the problem is soluble through ritual means. To the deviant it says, "You have done wrong. Now make amends and all will be well with your kinsman and our family." To both the patient and the deviant, as well as to the audience, the ritual drama signifies the importance of togetherness and group solidarity, and it plays down individualism.

In a way, both the patient and the deviant are the "odd man out." They are outsiders in that they have crossed a group limit or boundary. One is blameless but is nevertheless suffering because of another's deviance. Thus, the cure is a reintegration of both into the core of group values and relations. When the patient is suffering from mental illness (*nyinyieriŋ*), it is most likely that the divination will reveal that the patient is also the deviant and that his cure lies in formal initiation into one of the artisan cults, such as the diviners' cult, the blacksmiths' cult, or the praise singers' cult. In integration either with the family or with a cult, the patient and/or deviant is urged to adhere to a value system and obey legal authorities.

With regard to mental illness, the Sisala do not make fine distinctions among mental retardation, neurosis, and psychosis. They have the one term, *nyinyieriŋ*. This affliction is considered to be a special brand of the general category called illness (*yawiiliŋ*). It is especially thought to be caused by mystical power of shrines (*vuyaa*) of cult groups, although other illnesses may also be caused by these shrines. In Sisala etiology, *nyinyieriŋ* is especially associated with the calling to become a diviner; therefore, the family of the insane patient frequently consults a diviner to determine if the insanity is due to affliction by a shrine. In this way, an "odd" person is sometimes let alone when divination reveals no such causation; but more often he is formally labeled and brought within the framework of a cult group. Thus, the mentally ill person is not left to roam about, ignored. His relatives consult a diviner on his behalf to determine which of the various cult shrines or spirits has afflicted him. Once the patient is formally labeled in this manner, the group has a comprehensive tag for the individual—they can say, for example, "He's crazy"—and they have a means of controlling the aberrant behavior. In fact, the whole process of initiation into a cult group can be seen as a series of ritual events designed to reorient the deviant into a formal structure. As a member of a formal organization, the individual is placed in a formal relation to others. This is also the case with a patient who experiences a biomedical illness. He is reoriented to the core values of the lineage family. In both instances, ritual provides a meaningful place for the deviant and/or the patient.

Initiation into a cult, then, can be viewed as a form of therapy for persons suffering from personality disorders. As can be seen from the following case, the structure of this initiation process is such that those mentally disturbed persons who show signs of spontaneous recovery are initiated, while hopeless psychotics never are.

CASE 5.

Bidol was a young man of about twenty-five years. He was especially handsome and was constantly getting into trouble over women. He had a reputation for sleeping with other men's wives.

One day he was caught sleeping with the wife of a *vaadoŋo* brother, and the brother beat him severely with a club. (One's *vaadoŋo* are the members of one's maximal lineage. Since they "eat from the same bowl," sex with each other's wives is forbidden.) After Bidol recovered from the wounds inflicted in the beating, he began to show signs of madness. He would abuse people verbally and physically. Whenever small children were within reach, he would catch them and beat them. While on the way to the farm one day, he caught hold of a nine-year-old boy and beat him severely. Violence of this sort is almost unknown among the Sisala and is considered to be evidence of mental illness. Bidol also began waiting for women beside the farm paths. He would surprise them, beat them, and try to rape them. Furthermore, when given any small assignment by his father, he would not carry it out properly. One day, for example, he was instructed to weed the millet crops, which were yet small. He pulled up not only the weeds but the millet seedlings as well.

The elders decided to deal with Bidol in the traditional manner. They had a log cut and made a hole in it. Bidol's foot was then forced through the hole, and it became swollen, thus preventing escape. The log was such a burden to him that he could not catch hold of the small children or women. Bidol became a raving lunatic. He seemed to lose contact with people altogether and began to babble in a cacophonous mixture of dialects and languages.

At this point, the family decided to act. They consulted a diviner to determine the cause of Bidol's insanity. Divination revealed that he was being plagued by his dead grandfather's divining shrine, which had not been inherited by anyone after the old man's death some two years prior. In the words of a family member, "It was found that the shrine wanted to come to Bidol." Thus, Bidol's father, named Vene, informed the head diviner (*vugira-hiaŋ*) of the village divining cult. Together they approached the dilapidated shrine and informed the dead grandfather of their decision to initiate Bidol into the cult if he was allowed to get well. They sacrificed several chickens to the ancestor and "showed" him a hen, which they promised to him if he would allow Bidol to recover from his insanity. When the sacrifice was over, the *vugira-hiaŋ* took the meat and the live chicken. The meat was distributed to all the diviners of the village cult, and the *vugira-hiaŋ* kept the hen in his coop. Once the sacrifice was completed, the family waited and watched Bidol for signs of recovery. Slowly, he began to recover. Those who do not recover are left shackled to the log until they die. As Bidol regained his sanity, he was gradually reintegrated into a normal life within the community. First, he was released from his imprisonment; then he was given normal chores to perform. Finally the elders of the lineage, together with the village diviners, informed him of the reason for his recovery. They told him of the need to initiate him as a diviner, lest the insanity return.

The *vugira-hiaŋ* presented Bidol with the hen he had been guarding. He instructed Bidol to wait until the hen had laid eggs. The first cock of the brood to crow was to be separated from the rest, and this cock was to be used in the performance of the *u lani* rite, the rite of initiation to a diviners' cult. The head diviner then presented Bidol with a diviner's wand (*vugira daaŋ*) with white cowrie shells tied around the top. This type of wand is symbolic of divination initiates. While such initiates cannot yet perform a full divination, they can be consulted by persons who wish to "check" the verdict of another diviner. The initiates gain experience and save the money they earn to provide funds for the performance of the initiation ceremony.

When the hen's brood was grown and a cock's crow was heard, that cock was separated, and some of the remaining chickens were sold to raise money to buy a female goat. The goat was bred in hopes that she would give birth to a he-goat. At the time of the cock crow the head diviner was informed, and he called together the cult members for the performance of the *u lani* rite.

They gathered one evening at Bidol's compound. Only Bidol's lineage family and village diviners were present. The *vugira-hiaŋ* placed the cock in a cage. The diviners stayed in the compound all night, waiting for the cock's crow at dawn. The initiate was required to fast, but others enjoyed food and drink prepared by the women of Bidol's compound. They drank beer, told stories, and sang songs around the fire throughout the night. Bidol sat nearby in silence, listening to the diviners' lore.

At dawn the cock crowed, and the rite began with a chant by the diviners: *Ji-bele koŋ do dole do lana, buŋbaga nyuŋ tɔmuŋ be la do tu tɔgan na puna wia ko.* (This means: "The cock crowing is the time when we will see. The he-goat's beard wants to go south and see an animal with much hair." This stanza is repeated many times.

The women had prepared large quantities of millet porridge. The diviners and family all ate, but the initiate had to sit quietly and hungrily on the periphery of the group's circle. At this point in the rite, his "outsiderness" is symbolized by the fact that he does not eat or speak, nor does he sit and socialize with the others. He acts out the role of a deviant, the role of an insane person.

Once they had finished eating, the diviners replastered the divining shrine and sacrificed the cock upon it. The cock's head was completely severed, and the *vugira-hiaŋ* hid it somewhere in the compound. They then sacrificed one chicken to each of the major shrines of the lineage, the village, and the clan. They sacrificed another to all medicines and another to the ancestors in general. Another went to all living trees, and another went to all living rocks. The last chicken was sacrificed to "all shrines not yet mentioned."

If the he-goat is born and grown, the diviners sacrifice it and make the new divining skin bag (*puruŋ*) from it. In this case, however, the female goat had not yet given birth, so the initiate was temporarily given a woven reed basket in which to keep his divining implements until such time as the skin bag could be made. The Sisala frequently alter the sequence of rites according to exigencies in the work cycle. Rites of this nature are usually performed during the dry season, when men have less work to do than usual.

Next, the body of the headless cock was given to Bidol's mother to cook separately from the others. She was instructed to take care in its preparation so as not to break a single bone. She also prepared a special mixture of millet flour and honey. To this was added the meat of the headless cock and a bit of the meat of each of the other chickens. This was placed next to the divining shrine in a large calabash. No one but the initiate is allowed to partake of this mixture. The diviners took the feet, feathers, and some bones of the other chickens to make the first code objects (*tayaŋba*) for the initiate's use. These were placed in the divining basket, along with the initiate's wand, a new rattle (*chika*), and other apparatus of divination. This was also placed alongside of the shrine.

Then all of the diviners picked up their own rattles and went outside the walls of the lineage compound. The initiate stayed put. The *vugira-hiaŋ* then led the initiate to the shrine and removed all Bidol's clothing except his loincloth. He was made to sit with his back touching the shrine. When he touched the shrine with his back, the diviners began to shake their rattles and sing diviners' songs while entering the compound in single file. They surrounded the shrine and the initiate.

The *vugira-hiaŋ* handed the calabash of honeyed porridge (a very large quantity—I would estimate about four normal meals) to the initiate and instructed him to drink it all. The diviners were shaking their rattles and chanting, "Drink all, drink all, drink all. If you drink all, you will see all. If you leave part, you will see only parts" (see = divine). The amount and consistency of the porridge is such that no one can drink it all, and Bidol was no exception. The remainder of the porridge was smeared over his body, the divining shrine, and the divining basket. Several of the diviners came forward at this point and stuck the sacrificial chicken feathers on Bidol, the shrine, and the basket.

Next, the *vugira-hiaŋ* approached the initiate as if he were a client wishing to consult. The diviners of the circle instructed the initiate about his new role. They told him to pick up the wand. The *vugira-hiaŋ* took hold of the bottom of the wand, as a client does. Bidol was instructed as to how to hold the wand at the top. Together they roamed around the compound in search of the hidden cock's head. In this last part of the initiation, the initiate must find the cock's head to prove that he has acquired the power to discern hidden things.

Once they had found the cock's head, the entire company of diviners, including the initiate, marched from the compound to all the other village compounds singing songs and shaking their rattles to announce the initiation of the new diviner. At each compound the headman gave a gift to each diviner, and they replied, "Ah, now you have given us a gift, and we have deceived you." The rest of the day was taken up with drinking and merriment. That ended the *u lani* rite.

The *u lani* rite exhibits the themes of separation, marginality, and aggregation familiar in *rites de passage* (Gluckman 1962; Van Gennep 1960). In addition, this rite can be viewed as a therapeutic rite, one that sets the mental patient apart from his family and society and then dramatically reintegrates him into society in a new and prestigious position and role in the diviners' cult (Mendonsa 1973). The chaos of insanity is supplanted by the order of a formal role in this cult and a valued relationship to the community at large. The theme of "repair" (*waas e*) also runs through this ritual drama. The shrine is repaired, an act symbolic of the repair of the relationship of Bidol with his family and the former owner of the shrine and also symbolic of the restored health of Bidol.

Frank (1961:61–64) has emphasized the therapeutic value of such rites. The reintegration of a confused person into a formal role structure can, he says, arouse faith and hope, which stimulate the patient's self-worth and his esteem in the eyes of the community. Such a rite sets the world right again by restructuring both the patient's and the community's view of the mental illness. No longer something strange and frightening, it is made knowable and socially useful by the initiation of the patient into the cult. In the words of Kennedy (1974:1169–1171), it has an "organizing effect of a plan of action on the bewildered patient; it is cure by 'symbolic bombardment.' "

This rite, like piacular sacrifice, is a dramatic restatement of the social good and of the need for unity. The honeyed porridge rubbed over the patient, his grandfather's shrine, and the divining basket constitute a powerful symbolic message to the patient: he is back from chaos, he now has a valued place in the social life of the village. This bears out Kennedy's (1974:1176) statement that "in most nonwestern psychotherapies, action, including the manipulation of nonverbal symbols, is the main treatment modality, not talk." Unlike a Western psychiatrist's patient, the initiate does not talk, nor does he explore motives or trauma in his personal history. Only when the rite is complete does he take up his rattle and begin to sing diviners' songs with the others. Therapy, if it is effected by this rite, lies in the ritual symbols of a return from liminality.

In general, it is thought that invisible forces are responsible for illness. Thus, therapy is the process of making manifest those forces by symbolic means and then manipulating the symbols to cause change in the occult realm, which is thought to cause a change in the condition of the patient. If one substitutes "mind" for occult realm, the process is not unlike psychoanalysis in Western therapy. These ritual symbols appear to be based on sympathetic, contagious, and homeopathic magical principles (Frazer 1922; Turner 1963). Like psychoanalysis, association and analogy form the basis of the symbolic cure.

In Sisala cosmology, the cosmos is divided into things seen and things unseen. Spiritual entities are occult and have the capacity to cause misfortune in the everyday world. The process of therapy is partly a process of making occult forces known to the afflicted. By doing so, the afflicted parties are capable of redressive action. I am suggesting that the divinatory process is manifestly designed to make secret occult forces known but latently acts to reveal and clarify interpersonal tensions, social conflict, and, perhaps at a deeper level, an understanding of structural imperfections. Like psychoanalysis, the rites uncover hidden phenomena that are thought to cause illness. The therapy process is, therefore, one that makes unclear things clear, implicit things explicit, and hidden apparent. Rather than a psychoanalytic paradigm, however, this is a social-psychological one, because individual problems are not treated as isolable; in other words, the cause and cure are always located in social relationships, especially those relations that have a jural component. Thus, the cause and cure of illness are to be found in the context of social structure. Personal illness, whether biomedical or mental by Western standards, is viewed by the Sisala to have a social cause. The curative process involves revealing the cause, making retribution for the misdeed, and making a promise to shun such deviant behavior in the future.

The symbols of the divinatory process are repositories of information about the major structural values of Sisala culture. These symbols provide meaning, and their periodic reiteration in redressive rites serves as a powerful therapeutic tool for the cure of individuals, irrespective of social functions. Curing is an integral aspect of ritual in non-Western society because ritual language is therapeutic language, that is, that which communicates with the patient at many levels, thereby bringing insight into the social causes of his illness. Furthermore, the repetition of axiomatic values associated with the deeply meaningful ancestral code (*kisiniŋ*) links the affliction with a betrayal of that code. Therapy is couched in terms of a return to the proper order of things. In Sisala etiology, health is equated with order in the social realm, and illness is equated with conflict. Once the patient is convinced that the conflict has been removed, the way is open to recovery.

The act of sacrifice signifies that the deviant is shunning his aberrant ways, which permits the patient to shun illness. Piacular sacrifice symbolizes a return to a state of health and a renewal of life-giving conformity to the ancestral code. Lienhardt (1961: 153) poetically puts it this way with regard to the Dinka:

> The theme of separation of an image, the active counterpart of the passive element in human experience, from the self is carried further in the symbolic action taken by the Dinka to deal with suffering once its grounds are recognized. . . . the power is said to be "cut off" or "separated" from the man, and his suffering and guilt placed "upon the back" of the sacrificial victim, to

which the man's *passio* is thus transferred, to be carried away with its death. The recognition of a formal separation, within the person of the sufferer, between the self and the Power, is thus followed by the positive *enactment*, in dedication and sacrifice, of a material division also. The "inner" division of experience is sacramentally and externally confirmed.

Fortes (1975: 138— 139) describes the prayer accompanying each piacular sacrifice among the Tallensi as having a cathartic effect upon the patient. In the following passage he describes a therapeutic model equally applicable to the Tallensi or the Sisala:

> Prayer serves, then, as the main cathartic element of the ritual by making public and thus bringing into the open of social acceptability the state of affairs that is believed to lie behind the crisis. Now, in general all of this is known to the responsible participants, that is to say the lineage and family elders and the close relatives of the principals by whom or on whose behalf the offering is made. In many cases the relevant circumstances will also be known to a wider public. But revealing them in public in what amounts to a kind of confession, giving them explicit utterance in the ritually legitimizing situation of the sacrifice, gives the prayer its cathartic value. It enables the crisis to be grasped and interpreted and finally mastered. The fears and compunctions evoked by the crisis are openly expressed, the faults in question are admitted; and promises of the appropriate ritual services for restoring amity with the ancestors and other mystical powers are announced. . . . The catharsis may be personal for the individual making the offering on his own behalf. The prayer, however, is always a public and open utterance, directed as much at the company present as at the mystical powers addressed.

Life crises are anxiety-producing situations. The anxiety is not limited to the patient but runs throughout his immediate family. The divinatory process creates an opportunity for a catharsis of anxiety not only in the patient but also among family members who attend the postdivinatory rites. It provides a diagnosis that labels an offender, identifies the offended mystical entity, and prescribes a piacular rite as a cure. This curative rite supplies an avenue for the release of tension through confession, which can provide the individual and group with a cathartic release of affect. By publicly purging the family of conflict, guilt, and tension, the piacular rite is beneficial at both the individual and the social levels. While internalization of norms is very difficult to speak of with any precision, I will say that the average individual in Sisala-land still has a strong belief in the efficacy of the moral order. Guilt (*cheye*) is a crucial concept in the discussion of the divinatory process as therapy and is central to that moral order. One who breaks the rules is supposed to suffer guilt. A guilty person is said to suffer a "fall" (*tel*). *Cheye* actually means "to be spoiled, broken, dirty, or guilty." Guilt is strongly linked with the destruction of the "house" (*dia*), a metaphor for family relations or kinship unity. When there is conflict in the lineage, for example, the Sisala say, *Dia-la cheye nɛ*, "The house has broken down." Informants clearly understand this to mean that the house or family is in for more trouble if the *cheye* is not removed. Implicit in this assumption is the need for discussion (*vuuruŋ*) and openness (*wuolo*).

The handling of the patient and deviant will be discussed later at some length. Let me just say here that Sisala theory and practice allow a deviant to be labeled for his wrongdoing, but they also allow delabeling to occur. By this I mean that once the deviant, whether he is the patient or a relative of the patient, accepts responsibility for having caused the affliction, the group permits a return to a state of normalcy after his confession. There is no thought of expelling the deviant. I feel that the reasons for such leniency can be found in the need for economic labor on the lineage farm, a fact that is reflected in the ideological stress on kinship amity and unity. This, however, is a tentative hypothesis that would need to be validated by cross-cultural comparison of groups with and without such labor needs.

This lenient handling of the deviant is not unlike "integrity therapy" (Drakeford 1967:305), whereby a neurotic patient suffering from guilt is made to accept responsibility for his deviant acts, confess them to significant others, and make retribution for them. Then, it is thought, a state of health returns. In the Sisala case, this process takes place, not under the guidance of a professional therapist, but rather under the authority of the lineage elders, the ancestor cult. It is an effort to treat more than one patient; indeed, it is group therapy, because the patient's illness and deviance by a group member or faction within the group are linked. The process is thought to work not only when the patient is the deviant but whenever the group carries out the piacular rites, because, in a meaningful sense, the group is the real patient and the real deviant. Therapy is directed not only at the person as patient but at the group as patient.

While having a therapeutic value, the divinatory process may appear to serve a social control function. Because of the seemingly authoritatively objective nature of divinatory diagnosis, coming as it does from the ancestors themselves, lineage authorities are able to make accusations of deviance against subordinates with impunity. Sisala cosmology, like that of many other African societies, presents an ideal model of society wherein kinship amity prevails and selfish desire is wrong. As Lambo (1969:207) points out, "The African is the possessor of a type of knowledge that teaches that reality consists in the relation not of men with things, but of men with other men, and of all men with spirits." Along such lines, Sisala cosmology postulates that improper behavior leads to ancestral anger rather than to anger among the living or among the authorities. The postulated relationship of human beings with spirits enables the elders to label and punish those involved in misdeeds within the context of the core of authority vested in the ancestor cult. Felt animosity should be expressed, not kept within to fester and produce conflict (see also Harris 1978). Cult rites provide elders with an opportunity to accuse their subordinates of deviant acts within a sacred context that necessarily limits retaliation and danger to the cohesiveness of the group. Thus, we may view redressive rites as having cathartic and social functions, but we must be cautious not to believe that such rites always accomplish their stated goals, as the following case points out.

CASE 6.

Wengkuoro's wife, Hakuu, was accused of stealing food from the lineage granary. This was revealed after she had become ill. Wengkuoro and his elder brother, the lineage headman, consulted a diviner about the cause of her illness. It was found that Hakuu's theft of food had angered the ancestors, who allowed her to fall ill. Wengkuoro, however, who was not on good terms with his elder brother, disregarded the divinatory verdict. Instead, he traveled to a distant village and consulted another diviner, who told him that a shrine was responsible for the illness. Wengkuoro returned and sacrificed to that shrine, but his wife died shortly after the sacrifice. At the funerary divination it was determined that Hakuu had been a thief and that the ancestors were also angry with Wengkuoro for going against the first divinatory verdict determined by his elder brother. It was revealed that Wengkuoro must sacrifice a cow to the lineage ancestors in order to avoid further death in the family. This divinatory decision made Wengkuoro angry, but he reluctantly complied with it. At the sacrifice of the cow he admitted that his wife had been taking grain from the granary and that he had been insubordinate to his elder brother. Shortly after the sacrifice, though, Wengkuoro started to build a new house outside of the lineage compound. He built it near his private farm, which he had been tending in his spare time but to which he now devoted all his efforts. In the two years following this incident, nothing untoward happened to Wengkuoro or his family.

Here we have a case wherein the redressive rite was performed but was unable to heal the growing rift between Wengkuoro and his elder brother, who had inherited the patrimony at their father's death. The structural conflict between the two men had errupted in a series of petty quarrels ever since their father's death. The divinatory directive and the redressive rite, rather than ameloriating this tension, may have added to it. It is difficult to pinpoint causation in these matters. Certainly fission was initiated after the rite and was well under way at the time of my study. A word of caution here, however. One needs to follow these cases over an extended period in order to understand them fully, and I was unable to do that with this case. It would be interesting to know if Wengkuoro will deal with future illness through the ancestral shrines under the control of his elder brother or if instead he will establish his own medicine shrines in the new compound and "go it alone."

I would posit that structural conflicts produce fission. Role conflicts centering around inclusion in or exclusion from patrimonial inheritance and succession to the headmanship of the lineage are particularly important determinants of group fission. Where such conflicts occur, I would hypothesize that redressive rites only temporarily forestall, if at all, the inevitable fission of the group into two separate lineages. Elsewhere (Mendonsa 1980) I have shown that segments of the lineage undergo three phases of fission: economic, residential, and ritual. When a junior member of the lineage is able to establish independence in these three ways, this process appears to be sequential and spread out over time. If the junior person is no longer economically dependent on the lineage, it is more likely that residential and ritual fission will occur. Normally, ritual fission does not occur until a family establishes economic independence from the parent lineage and lives apart. I would say that the occurrence of the process of fission is influenced more by structural conflicts within the parent lineage and by work opportunities outside the lineage than by rituals that are thought to hold the group together.

The following case illustrates how a subordinate may be defined as dependent on his jural guardian in more than the economic sense. It shows that a situational mix of relevant factors determines whether a dependent member of the lineage behaves in such a way as to give the appearance of redress.

CASE 7.

Kazaar's eldest son, Benie, was thought to be an especially troublesome son. At times he acted as a disrespectful child (bi-yaya). He began to spend his extra spending money on amphetamines, which were easily obtained in the local market. He also began to drink apetishi, the local gin made from distilled sugar. Benie has been raised as a farm boy without formal education, but at the age of twenty-two he refused to farm any longer for his father. In fact, he became quite lazy, usually lying about drunk and useless. When it came time for Kazaar to pay the head tax on his family members, he refused to pay the tax for Benie. "No work, no tax," he told his son. Eventually the police were sent by the district officer to investigate the affair. Kazaar explained the situation to them, and they arrested Benie for failure to pay the government head tax. He stayed in jail for six months, and there he fell ill. Because of the illness he was removed to a government hospital, and his parents were informed that he was seriously ill. In due time, he was released from the hospital and allowed to return home, but he was still very ill. Unable to walk properly, he lay in the house, too ill to move.

Kazaar went with the lineage headman to consult a diviner about Benie's illness. It was determined that the ancestors were angry with Benie for being disrespectful to his father. Benie was instructed to apologize by sacrifice (*a chuala*) to the lineage ancestor shrine (*lɛlɛɛ*) and to his father's personal hunting shrine (*tomuŋ*). He was to give a white fowl to the *lɛlɛɛ* shrine and a colored chicken to the *tomuŋ* shrine. The whiteness of the fowl for the ancestors signifies "complete agreement" or "complete compliance" with the divinatory verdict. It is a cool color, which indicates that "he is doing this thing in his belly"—he agrees, in other words, that he has done wrong and that he is not merely going along with the verdict or being coerced into making sacrificial retribution.

Since Benie was too ill to perform the piacular rites, he authorized his younger brother, Dambugu, to do it on his behalf. Dambugu collected sixty white cowrie shells and a white chicken, which cost 1.30 cedies (about one dollar). He approached Kazaar and the lineage elders, who had assembled before the lineage *lɛlɛɛ* shrine. He presented them with the sixty white cowries. On behalf of his elder brother, he said, "What I have done by refusing to go to the farm is wrong. Now I am reaching out to the ancestors to tell them that I agree with them. Whatever they say, or whatever my father says, I will do it." Then he handed over the white chicken to his father, who gave it to the headman, who had it sacrificed on the shrine. It died on its back, signifying that the ancestors had willingly accepted the offering. A fire was built, and the chicken was roasted and eaten by all present. Dambugu then took some of the white ash from the fire and rubbed it on the father's *tomuŋ* shrine. This symbolized that an apology (*a chuala*) had been made. *A chuala* signifies a desire to "cool" a quarrel. At the same time, Dambugu promised the shrine a colored chicken if it would permit Benie to become well. He repeated the apology he had previously made to the *lɛlɛɛ* shrine.

Benie eventually became well enough to begin farming with his father again. Once he was well, he gave another chicken to the ancestors in thanks and promised a chicken to the *tomuŋ* shrine. As of the summer of 1977, six years after his illness, he was still unmarried and working for his father.

What emerges upon comparing the case of Wengkuoro (case 6) with that of Benie (case 7) is that their structural positions, and hence their relative independence from the group, differed. While Wengkuoro was a man of middle age, a nonheir to the patrimony, a married man with two wives and children, Benie was an unmarried and dependent child. As the eldest son, Benie stood to inherit his father's position and wealth. Moreover, he had no opportunities beyond the limits of dependence on his father. He had no skills to sell in the larger economy, nor did he know farming well enough to start his own farm. Wengkuoro had more freedom to start a new life apart from his natal lineage. For Benie to have left would have meant foregoing the inheritance of the patrimony, or at least it would have made the inheritance picture confusing. Thus, there are both push and pull factors to consider in these cases. The major push factor is the structural position of the subordinate. In Wengkuoro's case, he was disinherited, and he did not get along with his elder brother, who did inherit. Benie, however, stood to inherit. Wengkuoro was a good farmer who already had a private plot while working on his father's farm. It was a simple matter for him to expand that plot into a farm and become economically independent of his elder brother once the father had died. The were no pull factors for Benie; in fact, the only time he ever got away from home was when he was arrested and sent to prison. Thus, the relative dependency of Benie gave the piacular sacrifice the appearance of effectiveness, yet in Wengkuoro's case, a similar sacrifice failed to prevent fission of the lineage.

In summary, then, the divinatory process contains two institutional complexes: *vuguŋ* divination and piacular sacrifice. *Vuguŋ* is a diagnostic device used when medicine fails to cure an illness or when medicine is deemed inappropriate. *Waasɛ wiaa*, or piacular sacrifice, is a curative episode in the process. It appears that *waasɛ wiaa* may have some psychotherapeutic functions for the individual, and this may provide social functions for the group, at least on a temporary basis. Thus, one could say that these institutions have functions, but one must not mistake functions for causes and assume that the institutions exist because of the functions or that their main contribution is to the maintenance of group solidarity and harmony. In the following chapter I will present data to support the hypothesis that divination has three main functions relative to dispute settlement. First, it is an institutional framework that provides incentives and constraints to the disputing parties while at the same time masking group conflict. Second, divination also allows people to cope with the indeterminate and conflictual nature of social life by focusing attention in crisis situations on one set of system principles and procedures.

Third, divination functions to update or rework the rules as they are situationally applied.

Viewed as a communicative device, the divinatory process may communicate those phenomena that are difficult for people to confront directly. It airs both harmony and conflict, instances of unity and difference. It may unite the group, or it may sharpen the differences between factions within it. We cannot assume that the process contributes to lineage solidarity every time. It may serve to clarify for participants some unresolvable problems and thereby strengthen their determination to leave the group. In those situations where the push-pull factors favor unity, the rites may give the appearance of providing a positive function; but where the the push-pull factors do not favor unity, the rites may clarify the situation so as to facilitate the division of the group. Let me be clear on this point. I consider the main push factor to be structural; in other words, where there are structural cleavages and contradictions, fission will likely occur in spite of the divinatory rites. The main pull factors are economic opportunities beyond the corporate group. Divinatory rituals are dramas that highlight all such factors, not just ideals, while masking conflict.

6
The Labeling of
Deviance and
Social Control

I We have seen how instances of misfortune become tied to deviant behavior
in the divinatory process. Piacular sacrifice is overtly an attempt to make
retribution for the deviant act in order to redress the situation and ameliorate
the misfortune. In the last chapter I described this process in terms of a
therapeutic model. I shall now turn to the social control aspects of the
divinatory process. I intend to show that divination allows authorities and
powerful men to enforce their particularistic wills in life-crisis situations,
though not absolutely, while ostensibly pursuing universalistic goals.

The divinatory process is a political process wherein the elders and
influential persons manipulate divining sessions and influence rites so as to
label an individual or a particular faction within the group as the party
responsible for the group's misfortune. The definition of deviance and the
consequent labeling of a deviant emerge from the interaction, maneuvering,
and political struggle among authorities, opinion setters, and the concerned
public.

The native model of the divinatory process purports that it is an effective
social control instrument because its directives come, not from living human
beings, but from the ancestors. The process is seen as one of determining the
deviant person or group that has caused the ancestors to withdraw their veil of
protection from the lineage, thus allowing a misfortune to befall one or more
lineage members. The labeling of a deviant is sanctified and given solemnity by
the use of the institutions of divination and ancestral sacrifice to link proclama-
tions with life-and-death situations. It is thought that unless the deviant

makes retribution for his misdeeds, further misfortune will affect the lineage, because the ancestors continue to withold their protection until they are satisfied that an apology has been made and retribution effected.

Ideally, the lineage headman acts on behalf of the group in punishing the deviant act. He can do so with impunity because of the authority (*hiesaŋ*) of his office and the institutions at his disposal. Ideally, he plays his role for the good of the group as a whole, without any particularistic interests or goals. I shall show that this ideal is not always met. These official rights are supposed to provide the elder with the institutional tools whereby he can control the behavior of his subordinates. Ideally he should be able to do this with all wayward persons and factions within the group, regardless of their wealth or power. I shall show that this ideal is modified by two important variables: the structural relations between the elder and the accused, and the opportunities perceived by the labeled deviant beyond the limits of the elder's authority.

I do not view the institutions of the divinatory process as effective social control devices as defined by both the native model and the consensus theorists. I present the following data in an effort to show that the divinatory process appears to function to control behavior but that there is probably more appearance than fact involved. Of the fifty-three cases of divination rites on which I have sufficient ethnographic facts, only 32 percent appear to have been effective in maintaining group unity, or conformity by the deviant. The data in table 6.1 indicate that the divinatory process is problematic as a social control device. I was able to check on many of these cases over a seven-year period, in three separate field trips to Sisala-land, and I feel confident they adequately demonstrate that the rites of the divinatory process are ineffective as a social control measure. These data remain subjective, however, because in analyzing the cases I sometimes had to make arbitrary decisions regarding whether a case demonstrated effective social control. The problem is this: When does one decide that a case is finished? How long does the anthropologist need to wait

TABLE 6.1   A Subjective Evaluation of Ritual's Social Control Function

	N	%
Divination appeared to provide unity or conformity by the deviant	17	32
Divination did not appear to provide unity or conformity by the deviant	29	55
Subject could not make a determination	7	13
Total	53	100

before he can be sure that sufficient time has elapsed for the rite to be effective? There is no definitive answer, but it seems to me that following the cases as I did provides at least tentative confirmation of the hypothesis that divinatory rites are ineffective regulators of human behavior and that they do not maintain the unity of the group through time.

II   The approach I am using here has many precedents and a variety of names. It is best called the interactionist approach. The basic premise is that reality is socially constructed as people use symbols to interact (Berger and Luckmann 1967; Blumer 1969, 1972). It also shares some characteristics with ethnomethodology, which states that behavior is to be evaluated in terms of the intentions of actors; actors are not viewed as strict rule followers (Hawkins and Tiedeman 1975; Turner 1974). Essentially this perspective claims that it is necessary to consider the meanings actors apply to symbols used in any social situation. These meanings are not seen as fixed or wholly derived from a cultural code; rather, as individuals interact with each other, their definitions of the situation emerge. This is not to say that cultural codes, rules, and structures do not exist or influence meanings—they certainly do; but real life is more fluid than a structural perspective implies. Rules are not preestablished molds into which behavior is poured; individuals take into account all kinds of symbolic meanings when deciding on a given course of action. A complete theory of human behavior must include a consideration of the decision-making process. As I view it, the interactionist perspective does this while retaining the structuralist view of a sui generis sociocultural order—that is, cultural codes precede the individual, but the individual has a whole array of codes to choose from and therefore must make decisions about how to behave. Cultural ideals and social structures are one kind of influence on such decisions, but there are others as well: the makeup of the audience, the relative power of persons involved in interaction (regardless of their official roles), and real or imagined opportunities to escape the situation, which exist in the mind of a participant, to name just a few nonstructural influences on the decision-making process of the client in the divinatory process.

Blumer (1972:66—67) sets out the basic premises of the symbolic interactionist perspective: first, that human beings act toward things (phenomena) according to the meanings that the things have for them; second, that the meanings are derived from or arise out of the social interaction one has with one's fellows; and, finally, that these meanings are handled in and are modified through a process of interpretation used by the person in dealing with things. In my consideration of the divinatory process, I contend that the institutions of divination and piacular sacrifice serve as formal structures within which group members define deviance and make decisions to act based on the definitions which emerge from their interaction. In so doing, they take into account the ancestral code, group interests, and personal interests. Final action is the result of participants' efforts to fit their different views and lines of action together. This is a process whereby the various meanings and intentions of discrete individuals and factions are interlinked, and it provides the divinatory process with its fluidity and vitality as a mechanism for labeling deviant behavior. It not only allows elders to couch such accusations in terms of the ancestral code but also permits input into the decision-making process from influential people and other group members. I believe that this is why the divinatory process has remained such a viable part of everyday life in Sisala-land: it provides an acceptable forum wherein individuals with variant views can interact and participate in the formative process of defining and constructing their social reality. Since divination and sacrifice are sacred institutions, they provide a safe and acceptable political arena for individuals, factions, and groups to work out their problems. The results of this political struggle are not always based solely on sacred codes, but they are always symbolically clothed so as to appear to be.

The view that actual social reality is more than structure is not limited to symbolic interactionism. British structural-functionalists have also seen the need to move beyond the mere statement of rules as a determinant of human behavior. Firth (1963:211), for example, has said, "The fulfillment of the moral obligations laid down by structural requirements is conditioned by individual interests." Leach (1962:133–134) has also chafed against the constraints of the pure structuralist approach. While pointing out that all social systems have structured relationships, he goes on to say that not all human behavior is determined by structure. All systems allow enough latitude so that the individual can make personal choices and can manipulate the system to obtain his own ends, even if those ends may be in conflict with system rules. He reminds us that although roles and jural rules exist everywhere, so does the "calculating man" who uses strategy to bend the rules in his favor.

I am not saying that rules and institutions do not exist or influence thought and behavior. It is not a matter of *either* normative causation *or* interactionism. Evens (1977:593) makes a good point while contrasting the interactionist approach of Barth (not Blumer) with that of structural-functionalism. He says that the structural-functionalist needs to alter his model, radically, by bringing into his account the concept of choice in such a way that institutions may be seen as being affected by people making choices. The interactionist needs to alter his model, also radically, by bringing into his account the fact that the choices people make about their own separate concerns are fundamentally conditioned by choices of another kind, ones that entail and imply institutions and formally normative phenomena. Taking the inter- actionist view of the divinatory process allows us to see deviance as a definition of the situation which is worked out as a political process between competing actors and group representatives. A deviant is labeled as such when the actors interact to define the misdeed, the perpetrator, and what steps should be taken to rectify the deviance. Inherent in this view is the claim that the actors, including the labeled deviant and/or his backers, are not passive. They struggle with each other to sway minds and to swing the decision in their favor. As they do so, each ritual participant cites reasons why a given action should be taken. He may have a purely selfish reason for wanting this choice made, but he cannot come out and say so. He must couch his reasoning in culturally acceptable symbols. He must convince others that his way is the morally correct way. To do so he must use cultural codes and structural rules to his advantage.

In thinking about cultural symbols I would suggest using the analogy of a box of building blocks. Codes and rules—or symbols, for short—are build- ing blocks used by goal-oriented actors to construct social reality in a given situation. The box contains the sum of a given society's codes. There are many sizes and shapes of blocks, which can be fit together in many ways to construct just about anything, but some don't fit with others. Some persons are more skillful than others at using symbols to make a point or influence the group. As actors struggle with each other within the divinatory process, they use symbols and rules as the building blocks of their view of what course of action should be taken. The social construction can take almost any form, given the cultural stereotypes of others and the contingencies of the current situation.

Within the divinatory process, actors use cultural symbols to label persons formally as deviants. The labeling process is a series of classifications that are made according to etiological and cosmological beliefs. As the diviner takes his code objects out of the skin bag, one informational item guides the placement and interpretation of the next in the sequence. As the divining session proceeds, more and more items are added, until the participants arrive at a definition of the situation. A deviant individual is labeled in a series of formal steps that build up to a cumulative public definition about the actions of the deviant. One cannot ignore, however, the fact that elders who go to the diviner sometimes already know who the deviant is and wish to label him as such. They have arrived at this decision by a series of informal classifications based on their experience in everyday life. A point is reached in the informal process of labeling at which the individual is sufficiently defined as deviant to be formally labeled as such. Divination provides the formal mechanism whereby this is accomplished.

Werbner (1972:229) defines four ways in which accusations of deviance can be made: (1) by the private baiting of the deviant, (2) by insinuation in gossip, (3) by denunciation in public, and (4) by the legal charging of the deviant. In Sisala-land, open baiting or charges are rare. Rather, informal labeling of deviance is accomplished through gossip (*hari-gaariŋ*), aggressive thoughts and feelings on the part of group members, and, sometimes, through direct insults; but formal labeling takes place by means of several customary procedures, of which divination is one. According to this view, deviance definitions are a public reaction to deviation on the part of an individual. Deviation is noticed and labeled informally, while the public acknowledgment and labeling of deviance is carried out through formal, institutionalized procedures.

The labeling of deviance is obviously only a subcategory of the human capacity to produce stereotypes and classifications. "Labeling can be defined as simply the process of placing some act or event into a larger category as a means of classification," wrote Hawkins and Tiedeman (1975:63). We create such ordered patterns in order to understand the world. The labeling of deviance with regard to misfortunes within the group provides a double-barreled explanation to the questions, Why does misfortune occur? and Why does conflict occur in a perfect social order? Deviance and misfortune are linked to one another and explained in Sisala lore. The Sisala answer to both questions is that the system is perfect but individuals break the rules, which causes misfortunes to occur. The labeling of deviance is therefore necessary to ensure the safety of the group.

Hawkins and Tiedeman (1975:64–65) define the labeling process as a series of steps, which are not necessarily sequential. They are:

1. Observation: the act or acts become known.

2. Recognition: the act or acts are defined as rule violation.

3. Imputed cause: the act or acts are categorized as to cause.

4. Motive: the act or acts are categorized as to motive.

5. Potential reactions: those reacting to the deviation list their possible reactions.

6. Reaction is chosen: a reaction is chosen from a possible range of choices.

7. Impact of reactions: reactions take effect on the deviant and his behavior.

This model is a useful way to view the labeling process of deviance, but in Sisala culture the process differs from that of Western society. In the first place, intent is not necessarily used as a criterion of classification. A deviant may perform a misdeed that leads to trouble for the group and be unaware of that misdeed. (In the extreme case, a witch may be a witch without knowing it.) Second, there is no decision about the deviant's true nature. It is considered human nature to deviate. It is only when that deviation causes trouble for the group that informal knowledge about deviation gets transformed into a public statement about deviance. Since deviants are not considered inherently evil, they are given a chance to admit their deviance and atone for it through public confession and ritual retribution.

III The definition of deviance emerges, then, from the interaction of concerned individuals—the elders, influential big men, the deviant and his family, and other group members. It is important to make the distinction between deviation and deviance clear. On a given day in a lineage there are many misdeeds that never come to be formally labeled as deviance. They are deviations from the commonly accepted norms. Sometimes, however, such misdeeds are dealt with officially through the divinatory process or other judicial institutions and thus become labeled as deviance. Each division of the kinship system has an official who is responsible to select some misdeeds with which they will deal formally. In the lineage, this officer is the headman (*jachikiŋ-tiina*). It is his responsibility to monitor the actions of his charges and to punish those deviations he chooses to define as deviance. From the multiple deviations that occur in his term of office, he is expected to use the institution of divination to determine precisely which deviations are the cause of trouble and therefore should be considered deviance. Divination provides the means whereby the elder can link a deviation with a group misfortune, thereby transforming a deviation into trouble-causing deviance. Defining deviance, then, involves a representative of the society selecting those misdeeds that are thought to be a threat to the group for which he is responsible. It is crucial to see that his process has both informal and formal labeling phases. In the informal phase, the elder is influenced to select some deviations and ignore others. He is influenced by the moral code as it is interpreted by him and as it is presented to him by other persons and factions within the lineage through gossip and persuasion. In other words, the elder has in his mind knowledge about everyday behavior which he comes to define as deviation through his own thought process and through the influence of others. It is in this informal stage of labeling that the particular interests of the elder or of his faction may influence his selection of one person or faction as the deviant. If he is thoroughly determined to label a specific person or faction as the deviant, even on the basis of selfish reasoning, he can easily do so by manipulating the divination. This is done all the time. Elders admit it. Why? Because in their system of thought, the elder is not wrong in presenting any alternative to the ancestors. The ancestors cannot choose the wrong man as deviant.

Gossip (*hari-gaariŋ*) is a frequent form of arriving at an informal definition of deviation. Through gossip the community becomes aware of a deviant (*haachε-diire*) and his wayward ways. This gossip is always influenced by the moral order as it exists in the commonly held values and attitudes of community members. In any Sisala community, at any given time, the local gossip is replete with cases of deviants who have not yet been officially labeled or punished. Indeed, many will never be officially labeled as deviants. This corresponds to Denzin's claim (1970:121) that only a small percentage of any group of deviants ever comes to the attention of the formal social control agencies. If, however, public opinion builds to such a point that the headman must act officially on the matter, the labeling process moves into its formal phase, although informal pressure on actors in the drama continues throughout the entire divinatory process as well as during the sequence of events that lead to a deviant being officially selected, punished, and forgiven. The headman is constantly influenced by his awareness of the need to make his behavior conform to the accepted code of ethics and to public opinion. Nevertheless, when he selects a deviant through divination, the formal machinery of social control is set in motion.

Besides general gossip, the elder is influenced by interested parties. These include persons and factions who wish to influence the outcome. Thus, the definition of deviance may be affected by powerful groups or factions whose reputations in the community provide them with political leverage and the ability to arouse the community against a rule breaker. Such influential men are often ones with extensive social networks and/or personal shrines and medicines. They manipulate the outcome of the divinatory process by manipulating the headman and other officials. Generally it is not a simple matter of either public opinion or a "moral entrepreneur" or the action of an official; rather, the definition of deviance emerges as a result of the interaction of influential persons in the context of a community setting. The definition is not pre-ordained by the moral code, though it is influenced by it at every level. Instead, deviance definitions arise out of the symbolic communication and interaction of individuals and factions of varying degrees of power. The following case illustrates how the deft arbitration of an influential person, or opinion setter, imposed his will upon the family but at the same time buttressed the authority of the lineage headman.

CASE 8.

Ali-Seki is a man of forty who has achieved great power in his community, although he has an elder brother, Kening, who holds the formal title of *jachikiŋ-tiina*. While Kening is old, blind, and unable to feed himself and his wife, Ali-Seki is is young, able, and completely supports his elder brother and a large part of the lineage family. The youth of the family look up to Ali-Seki. Several have even attached the name "Seki" to their names in obvious identification with this prestigious man. Not only is Ali-Seki well known in his small village, but he has made his mark in a larger arena. He is a famous big-game hunter who is known throughout Sisala-land and northern Ghana. He has a motorcycle, a double-barreled shotgun, five wives (at last count), and a large and growing family. He has three houses, one near Wa, one in Tumu, and another in his natal village. During the dry season he is away hunting, and during the rainy season he directs the work on the family farm in addition to that on his cash crop farm near Tumu. Because of his informal status as a big man, he is able to attract many young men willing to work for him on these farms.

Ali-Seki operates well in all worlds. He has attached a Moslem prefix to his name, which makes him more acceptable to them, although he is a practicing pagan. He speaks good English, encourages education in the area, and therefore has earned the respect of the local Christians. Al-though not educated through formal schooling, he associates with school-teachers and government officials. He is equally at home with the humble people of his home village, where he is a real hero since he frequently returns home bearing money, kola nuts, and animals to be used in sacri-fices at the lineage shrines as well as at his many personal shrines. His return is seen by members of his lineage as a time for great celebration and rejoicing. It is at this time that the drums are taken out and dusted off, and the dancing and singing can be heard far into the night. He provides money for brewing native beer and sacrificial meat for all. He is seen as a true leader and influence in the community, although he holds no formal office in the lineage hierarchy.

One day, while Ali-Seki was away from his natal lineage, a younger brother named Marifa went to a certain distant village and wrongly informed a lineage headman there that he had been sent by Kening (his lineage headman) to collect the bridewealth (*ha-jaari-kiaa*) for their sister, who had married into that lineage. He collected twenty pounds (about thirty-five dollars) from them and spent the money on himself. About three months later, Kening sent a messenger to that same lineage to collect the bridewealth, but he was told that Marifa had already collected it. When the messenger returned and informed Kening of this fact, he called Marifa before him, and Marifa confessed that he had indeed lied to get the money. He had spent the money on a bicycle, which he kept at a friend's house nearby. Anytime that he was seen on the bike, he told people that he had just borrowed it from a friend.

Kening, who is old and cantankerous, exploded with anger upon hearing Marifa's confession. A terrible scene ensued, leading to harsh words on both sides. Marifa said that he was leaving the lineage and actually did move his wife and young child out of the compound to a temporary residence at his yam farm. He informed the family that he planned to expand his farm in the following year in order to be independent of Kening. Upon hearing this, Kening said that if he saw Marifa again, he would place a formal curse on him. This is a sign of real trouble in the family. Fortunately for the family, Ali-Seki returned from a hunting trip at this point. He heard the story from gossipers and talked the matter over with his elder brother, Kening. He then sent word to Marifa, his younger brother, that he desired to speak with him, but Marifa refused to come.

After some time, one of Ali-Seki's wives fell ill. He asked Kening to consult on his behalf. Together they went to a local diviner. All three actors in the drama, the diviner, Ali-Seki, and Kening, were aware of the gossip about Marifa and the argument. The divination revealed that the behavior of Marifa was responsible for the illness. It was disclosed that the dead father of all three principals was greatly displeased with the family dissension; the illness would abate only if Marifa performed a piacular sacrifice (*waase wiaa*) on the dead father's blacksmith shrine (now under the control of Kening).

After the divination, Ali-Seki sent word of the diviner's verdict to Marifa and informed him that he would hold him personally responsible if his wife died. He instructed Marifa to return from the farm to perform the necessary rites and further reminded him that since the ancestors were angry with him, Marifa and his family were in danger too.

Marifa returned and performed the expiatory rite. At the ceremony he confessed that he had done wrong and promised to right his ways. Kening used the occasion to harangue Marifa and demand a repayment of the twenty pounds. Clearly Marifa would have been hard pressed to come up with such a sum of money, and the matter seemed to be taking a turn for the worse. Then Ali-Seki spoke up, saying that another bicycle was needed in the family and that he intended to buy it from Marifa for twenty pounds. This was said in front of the entire membership of the lineage, which had assembled for the rite. By this device Marifa was pardoned, the headman received the bridewealth, and Ali-Seki gained further stature in the family as a deft arbitrator.

After the ceremony Ali-Seki bought the bicycle and gave it to Kening for use by the lineage. Marifa gave the twenty pounds to Kening, but since Marifa was the only person in the lineage in great need of a bicycle, Kening placed him in charge of it. Everyone seemed pleased with the outcome. Family unity had cost Ali-Seki only twenty pounds, and his prestige had grown considerably as a result of his skillful arbitration.

Not long afterward, however, Marifa's child fell seriously ill. His parents tried several herbalists and finally took him to the government health center in Tumu for treatment. As they were bringing him back, he died. The lineage elders consulted a diviner and determined that the ancestors were still angry because Marifa was still harboring resentment against Kening over the palaver. Therefore, Marifa was once again required to bring a sheep and several chickens to sacrifice on the lineage *lelɛ* shrine, lest the string of maladies be extended. He did so, and the case was again considered closed.

Often a big man will use his influence in just this way to arbitrate matters in the family or community. He is able to do so because of his influence (*doluŋ*) rather than his authority (*hiɛsaŋ*). Nevertheless, such power is often the militating factor in a palaver that threatens to split the group. Influence and skillful arbitration are qualities that ideally accompany the occupant of office, but, lacking that, it is a fortunate family that has a person of influence around to aid an incompetent elder such as Kening. As of the summer of 1977, Marifa was still farming for the lineage.

The definition of deviance emerges from the interaction of a variety of actors: the deviant, his community members, influential persons, and officials. As the above case shows, when the deviance is linked to some trouble concerning the entire family, the headman exercises his authority and consults the ancestors about the matter. A person who repeatedly breaks rules is, therefore, liable to be labeled as a deviant. This definition may first exist in the minds of individuals, but it becomes shared through symbolic interaction with others via gossip and informal conversations about the deviant and his deeds. The labeling process may stop here. The person may continue to live a normal life. The gossip may consider him only "odd" or "mischievous." The odd man out tends to attract further, more formal, attention, however. Odd persons are frequently pointed out as deviants. The degree to which the labeling process is formalized and the point at which the deviant is brought before a formal tribunal can be seen as the result of his or her visibility, the perceived threat to the authorities, and the power-dependence relations that exist between the lineage elders and the deviant. Sagarin (1975:129) puts it this way:

> In short, deviance is manufactured by the hostile reaction of rule-makers. Not all rule-breakers are reacted to in a hostile manner. It depends on who you are, what you do, and to some extent on the visibility of the act; for the labelists, this proves that breaking a rule is not enough to establish a deviant role or deviant identity. If society did not manufacture deviance, it would not exist. Furthermore, the label perpetuates and aggravates the deviance.

Deviance, therefore, is an emergent property of the interaction that occurs between the deviant and members of society, especially those who make and enforce the rules. Moral codes guide this process, but individuals select which actions to label and which actions call for severe punishment through institutional mechanisms.

When the lineage experiences trouble, an opportunity arises for the elder to connect that trouble with the misdeed(s) of a group member. Only he controls the presentation of the names of potential culprits to the oracle. It is clear that any given elder is aware of more cases of rule violation than he can effectively punish. Edgerton (1976) points out that some rule violation is always ignored, while some is always brought before the public. Becker (1963:13) makes a similar point when he says, "Some rules are enforced only when they result in certain consequences." We must ask ourselves several questions about the nature of these consequences: Consequences for whom? How are these consequences defined? Who is responsible for making such a determination? Is there room for manipulation of this selection process by officers who wish to further their own goals or act on the basis of personal definitions of the situation? Can particularistic interests replace universalistic ones?

Thus, while deviants are presented to the community as having violated the moral code, they may be selected for entirely different reasons. Two identical acts of deviation may be treated in a different manner by the same community, depending on whether one deviation is made public in a formal manner and the other is not. It may be in the private interest of certain individuals to bring a deviation to public attention. The lineage headman is especially well placed to see to the interests of the whole lineage in this regard; but he is also a private individual who has self-interest and who is a member of one faction or segment within the whole lineage. We must evaluate the behavior of the elder in terms of both the stated norms of his office and the possible intended consequences of his role playing. I am not saying that social and private interests are mutually exclusive categories. In point of fact, I am saying that the divinatory process allows the elder to label and publicly punish a deviant while at the same time pursuing his own interests. The rites of the divinatory process become a sanctified cloak of public interests, under which much manipulation of the rules takes place. The outcome of the elder's actions, however, always has the appearance of altruism and, therefore, receives public approval. In short, every public act has both public and private consequences.

While the Sisala see divination as perfect, in the sense that the ancestors cannot give a wrong verdict, it is imperfect in the hands of humans, who may use it improperly. They realize that it is subject to human error, which can affect the outcome. Wilson (1970:710) accurately describes such an interpretative paradigm as "definitions of situations and actions which are not explicitly or implicitly assumed to be settled once and for all by literal application of a preexisting culturally established system of symbols." The Sisala explain this imperfection by a variety of rationalizations: they say that some diviners tell lies, for example, or that many actions on the part of the diviner can render him ineffective on any given day, or that the client has not used divination properly. Hence, it is always considered best to get more than one divinatory opinion. In the native model, though, one thing that cannot disrupt the divinatory process is personal manipulation. If the diviner has connected the living with the ancestors, the client may try to fool them with a variety of maneuvers and manipulations, but they will always reject these and tell the truth. The client is thought to be acting properly if he tries to fool them, even if he tries to influence the outcome to his own advantage. Since he cannot get a wrong decision because of his conscious attempts to manipulate divination, he cannot err. He may avoid being labeled at fault himself, try to prevent any of his close relatives from being accused, try to implicate a personal enemy, attempt to implicate anyone attending the seance. Or, if he or a close relative does get definitively labeled as the deviant, he can legally try to reduce the cost of the sacrificial animals to the lowest possible amount.

Thus, the client who consults a diviner may use the situation to further his own interest or the interest of his segment of the extended family. From this perspective, rules are followed when it is to the advantage of one who is in authority. This authoritative position allows him to ignore some deviations and select others to be labeled as deviance. In Sisala-land, elders continually consult diviners about family matters, and hence they are in a powerful position with regard to those family members who do not have access to diviners. They are able to filter through all the deviations that they are aware of in order to punish those acts that they define as particularly threatening to them, those that are openly trouble causing to men of influence, or those to which public opinion demands attention be given.

Nonelders are generally barred from consulting diviners by their lack of knowledge of the procedures involved. A woman may not consult a diviner alone. She must be accompanied by a man, who consults on her behalf. A young man may go to a distant diviner to consult if he knows the techniques. If he does not, he may consult, but it is unlikely that he will get much out of the divination. Usually young men go to a diviner with an experienced elder who consults on their behalf, and in this way they learn the techniques. Men begin to do this when they start their families and must face the fact of illness in their young families. Once a male nonelder has the knowledge of divinatory techniques, he may consult for himself, although it is thought better that he ask his jural guardian to accompany him.

Viewed as a labeling process, divination may result in an outcome that reflects deviance definitions of either the consulting elder(s) or the community at large or both. Certainly the elder cannot make accusations that to any great degree are contrary to public opinion. For instance, Gluckman (1973:38) points out that the king's subjects may rebel against him if he fails to live up to the ideal view of a king. They also become dissatisfied, however, when "he does not appear to take the action which suits them, even when in fact he does live up to the ideal."

Divination is a guise under which private and public accusations can be made. It is a legitimate labeling device that requires the accused to make a public confession and compensate for his misdeed. Although private motivations may initiate the process, the official labeling of a deviant must proceed according to a formal procedure in order to give those particularistic motivations the appearance of legitimacy. The following case illustrates how selfish motives can be disguised with formal procedures.

CASE 9.

The village gossips said that Haluri was an adulteress. Her husband, Dima, eventually got wind of the gossip but could do nothing directly against his wife because he feared that she would leave him if he beat her. He had done this once before, and she had returned to her natal village. It had taken Dima several weeks to get her back again, and he had had to pay another installment of the bridewealth payments (*haala-kiaa*) to get her father to influence her return. He wanted to avoid a repeat of that, if possible.

One night he sent a small boy to summon Haluri from her room, but she could not be found. Someone said that they had seen her going to defecate in the bush at dark. Dima stood guard at the lineage entrance, waiting for her to return. Later that night his brother joined him in the vigil. About four o'clock in the morning they spotted her attempting to sneak back into the compound. They confronted her, and she confessed that she had a lover. Dima did not beat her but warned her to stop the behavior and sent her to her room. The next morning, though, he went to the house of the lineage headman and asked him to consult a diviner about the illness of his daughter. She had been sick for weeks, but no divination had yet been performed. Together they went to the diviner and determined that the illness was due to a wrongdoing on the part of a woman. Upon further questioning, the oracle revealed that it was Haluri's adultery that had caused the trouble. Later that day they summoned Haluri to the headman's house. Several of the lineage elders were there, along with Dima. She was informed of the divinatory verdict and was told the oracle had instructed them to inform her that she must sacrifice two chickens and a sheep upon the lineage ancestor shrine. She noted that she had no money of her own, so she was told to get it from her natal kin.

She returned to her natal village but did not return in a reasonable time. The child grew worse, so Dima sent a message to Haluri's father to inform him that the oracle had revealed that Haluri's clan had been implicated through the oracle and therefore stood to suffer a calamity if the sheep was not paid and she did not return to take up her wifely duties. Furthermore, the message said, should the daughter die, Dima would consider the death to be on the heads of Haluri's people. She had been gone about six weeks at this point. She apparently had made up her mind to leave her husband. She had begun to sell groundnuts in the daily market and had entered into a sexual union with a wealthy merchant in the town. She refused to obey her husband or her father.

The matter hung in limbo for another four weeks, and the daughter died. Shortly thereafter, Haluri's father fell ill. Upon consulting a diviner he determined that his malady was due to the fact that he had not enforced the duties of his daughter's marriage. He summoned his daughter and informed her that she must obey him and return to her husband. He gave her a sum of money, two chickens, and a sheep and sent her brother to accompany her back to her husband's village. When they arrived they gave the money to the lineage headman with the instructions that he should purchase native beer to be enjoyed by the elders. They did so and sacrificed the animals on the lineage ancestor shrine. Haluri was required to attend along with her brother. The brother handed each of the animals in turn to Haluri, who handed them to her husband, who handed them to the headman. Neither Haluri nor her brother ate any of the sacrificial meat.

When the sheep was about to be slaughtered, the brother said as he handed the sheep to Haluri: "See this sheep. It is to be given to your husband. He has paid the bridewealth [*haala-kiaa*] for you, and you should obey him. Do not shame our people. Show proper respect for your husband and his people."

Upon taking the lead rope, Haluri said: "I understand that I did a wrong thing that caused a great deal of trouble. Therefore, I am this day giving up these things. A woman should obey her husband and respect his people. That is why I am giving up these things."

The officiating elder has a great deal of latitude, within the parameters of the cultural code and public opinion, to manage or manipulate divinatory process. The seance is structured so as to allow this. The client's role dictates that he must determine the behavior responsible for the ancestral anger, find the enraged ancestor, and ascertain the nature of the retribution; but he may select from a wide range of persons, ancestors, and social groups when placing possibilities before the oracle. These selection decisions lie solely with the client.

Gluckman (1973:73) has pointed out that accusations of witchcraft are often made by persons against their personal enemies. So it is with accusation of deviance made under the auspices of divination in Sisala-land. Gluckman (1973:87 – 88) goes on to describe this process among the Azande:

> More usually the sufferer puts the names of his personal enemies to the diviner or apparatus, in order to select from them that enemy who has the power of witchcraft and who had used this power to cause the misfortune under investigation. The consultant in fact believes that all the persons whose names he submits to the oracle want to harm him: he wants to know which of them is working maleficently against him at the moment.

IV   In the ideal native model, the elder has absolute control over his subordinates in the lineage. I shall attempt to show that this ideal is affected by the fact that the structural contradictions inherent in the segmentary lineage create tensions and conflicts that eventually lead to fission. When fission occurs, the headman loses control over a number of his subordinates, and a new lineage comes into being (Mendonsa 1979).

I see these contradictions as being inherent in the social structure of the lineage. The contradiction exists between two principles of the system, namely, polygynous marriage and the unity of the lineage through time.

Polygyny creates matricentral cells, siblings who share one mother. These siblings are fed apart from others, sleep with their mother, and have a strong sense of unity—stronger, for example, than the unity that exists among siblings of the same father by different mothers. Thus, children have conflicting loyalties. On the one hand they are united by the fact of descent through their father, but on the other they are set apart from siblings with different mothers by the fact that they share different lines of matrilineal descent (Fortes 1970). Such matricentral cells are at once linked together and alienated from one another, or, put another way, the ties uniting siblings of one mother are stronger than those uniting the siblings of one father.

Although this conflict does not manifest itself behaviorally in most daily life situations, it may surface at times of life crisis or during succession. Since the headmanship of the lineage can only devolve to one person upon the death of the family head, one sibling of the dead man will succeed, and the others will become subordinate to him. When there are only one father and one mother, the sibling group is united by two lines of descent and separated only by normal interpersonal rivalries. When the dead man has multiple wives, however, structural cleavage weakens the unity of the patrilineal group, yet this cleavage is created by ideal normative behavior—the marriage of one man to many wives.

Once succession takes place under such divided conditions, there arises the problem of whether the new headman can control other sibling groups who have different allegiances. By law, the headmanship devolves to the senior son if there are no surviving younger brothers of the dead headman. The very fact of succession sometimes sets off the process of fission, because sibling groups owe less allegiance to the new headman than to the last one. They may consider him unfit, or there may be overt animosity of a long-standing nature between the groups. When such a situation occurs, it is likely that the lineage will undergo fission, especially if the group that wishes to leave has economic opportunities beyond their dependence on the parent group. If not, the lineage may experience only more internal segmentation as the dissatisfied group merely creates a separate living space within the lineage compound and possibly expands its private farm but still remains within the overall framework of the headman's authority. Thus, factionalism is inherent in the theory and practice of polygyny within the structural context of a unilineal descent system, a fact we must keep in mind when discussing the political nature of ritual in general and the divinatory process specifically, because it is the headman who can determine the outcome, and this outcome will likely not affect all segments of the lineage equally.

In general, then, I view daily life in a Sisala lineage as potentially conflictual because different factions or segments with different allegiances exist. Moreover, these factions struggle for scarce resources, such as women, food, and money. One cannot discuss these political struggles outside of the ritual context because ritual authority is the bottom line in this system. Because they are physically and materially weak, members of the senior generation jealously guard the right to accuse and punish wayward subordinates through ritual means, while the subordinates are strong and may leave the group to seek their fortunes elsewhere. The elders' power derives from positions in the kinship system and their control of ritual. The power of subordinates derives from their youthful strength and options they have beyond the limits of lineage authority.

The keystone of lineage authority is the right of the headman to consult diviners about illness and misfortune. Through these divinatory rites they hope to try to control the behavior of their subordinates, both men and women. Exclusive access to the ancestors through diviners and shrines provides the elders with power in times of life crises, as long as the subordinates believe in the system and continue to support it. Therefore, the ritual system of social control must appear to be fair and indiscriminate. It must appear to treat all individuals and factions equally. It must appear to be closed to manipulation by the elders. The system rests on the assumption that the dead members of the lineage hold absolute control over its institution and that the living are merely stewards who carry out the wishes of the omnipotent and omniscient ancestors. Since the ancestors are symbols of lineage unity and continuity, they are not interested in furthering the political cause of any segment of the group, and they are thought to guard against any attempt on the part of living elders to manipulate the divinatory process to their own advantage. Of course, from the viewpoint of the elder, since he can in no way influence the outcome without ancestral approval, he is free to try.

In the lineage there are three distinct categories of person who, in the native model, are ranked into two levels of power: male elders and their subordinate men and women. In this model, women are the least powerful category. They are never allowed to consult diviners or sacrifice at shrines, except through a male guardian. They are thought to lack jural authority (*hiesaŋ*), although it is recognized that some women become wealthy (*jigi*) through entrepreneurial activities or gain power (*doluŋ*) by attaining rank in the hierarchy of females within the family. While they lack authority women have a lot of potential power because the practice of polygyny keeps women in short supply. Men struggle to get and keep wives because no man can attain full adult status without a wife and legitimate children. Women can leave a marriage, however, and remarry rather easily. If a woman's husband does not treat her well, she will leave him. In theory, her kin support the marriage because they have an interest in its success, but that arrangement sometimes does not work as it should. If a runaway wife does not return to her natal village, it is difficult for her people to control her. Nowadays a woman has the option of going to a town to work or remarry because of the existence of new towns with many resident strangers, which creates a demand for females and female labor. In the case of Haluri (case 9), she easily found another sexual union upon leaving her husband, one that could have been legitimized in time if her father had not fallen ill and demanded that she honor her commitment to her husband. In the normal course of everyday life, women perform female tasks primarily under the direction of other females. Men do, however, give orders to such senior women. The potential power of women to rebel against men is realized only through divorce, but this threat lies latent in most husband-wife interactions. This threat gives women a certain degree of leverage, enabling them to negotiate with and manipulate their husbands in private. In public the man appears all-powerful. When a girl marries, she leaves her father's authority for that of her husband, who then becomes responsible for her health and well-being. This is his ultimate weapon: disrespect against a husband or senior male is thought to cause illness or misfortune.

Young men and elders whose fathers are still alive constitute another class of subordinates. While a man can be quite advanced in age, if his father is still alive he is considered to be a jural minor who must defer to his father in all matters. That the father-son relationship creates interpersonal tension is well documented in the anthropological literature (Fortes 1959; Goody 1970). What a jural minor lacks in authority is compensated, however, by his physical power and his economic potential beyond the authority of his father. Most men stay in their natal household and work for their fathers until the latter dies, but the elder must always take into account the fact that some sons do leave. In almost every village there are sad examples of elders who have no offspring to care for them, and these cases serve as a constant reminder to other elders of the economic importance of youth. These able-bodied men have power because of two facts. First, the population density in Sisala-land is between ten and twenty-five persons per square mile. This makes it very easy for anyone wishing to clear a separate farm to do so. Land is plentiful. Most young men have such farms, but they are usually near or attached to the family farms where they work for their fathers. The family farm grows millet and other staples, while young men grow either yams or cash crops to supplement their share from the family farm. If a young man chooses to become free of his father's domination, he can plant his own millet and stop contributing to the family granary (*virebaliŋ*). This potential is recognized and feared by the senior generation because their well-being is directly dependent on the labor of their subordinates. Most men look forward to the day when their sons will support them. It is one of the stated reasons for having many children (Mendonsa 1977*b*).

The second fact that affords a young man power, if he chooses to exercise it, derives from the opportunities to work in the nonfarming sector. The opportunities increased during colonial times, when a certain degree of modernization created a demand for unskilled labor, especially in the cacao farms to the south of Sisala-land. The expansion in the government has also created many jobs in towns throughout northern Ghana. Also, a good number of youths got some education during the colonial period and early years of independence, which enabled some to obtain semiskilled jobs. These opportunities have tended to afford the youth more spatial mobility and the chance to gain wealth independent of family labor.

It is important to keep in mind that the limiting factor to a family's economic well-being is not land but labor. The more workers an elder is able to assemble, the greater the size and output of his farm (Mendonsa 1977*b*). Since a worker can produce more than he eats, an elder can support a large family through the labor of a few strong men. If he loses their labor, however, it is difficult to replace it, since wage labor in farming is virtually unknown in Sisala-land. Only the rare big man, who has wealth from a nonfarming source, can attract client workers in sufficient quantity to work his farms and produce wealth beyond the capacity of his offspring. The average farmer is dependent solely on family labor for the major part of his farm work.

The power of the elders to direct the activities of others derives from jural authority (*hiesaŋ*). It is essential that the youth respect that authority so that the elders can control their labor. The big man attracts clients because of his prestige, but the average farmer relies on the good faith of his sons. One who occupies an office in the gerontocratic kinship structure has the jural responsibility (*bene*) to control the behavior of his subordinates for the good of the family. As an officeholder (*-tiina*) it is his duty to punish (*dɔgisɛ*) anyone under his authority who violates the customs, or who disobeys (*digeliŋ*) or is disrespectful (*siiduoŋ*) to an elder. The ability of the elder to control his subordinates rests squarely on his occupancy of office, and his ritual control of food and the curing of illness, and his ability to control the marriage payments of his subordinate males.

Control of food is symbolized by the ritual prohibition against the growing of millet (*miaa*) by subordinates. The production and control of the distribution of *miaa* is institutionalized as a right of the lineage elder (*jachikiŋ-tiina*). He governs the production of *miaa* on the family farm. He allocates portions of the harvest to the various component households of the lineage. He stores the excess in the lineage granary (*virebaliŋ*). The *virebaliŋ* is a shrine (*vene*), and no one may place a hand into the granary without the permission of the *jachikiŋ-tiina*. Should someone steal millet from this granary, it is thought that the ancestors will kill him. The lineage headman controls the excess millet until the "starvation" period (roughly May through July), when stores run low, and he then doles it out to each family in the lineage. This control is one of the rights vested in the office of headman.

Another right is that of sacrificing on behalf of lineage members. The *jachikiŋ-tiina* is the custodian of the lineage shrines. The power to cure illness and ameliorate misfortune is a right and duty of this custodianship. If a subordinate wishes to appeal to the lineage ancestors at one of the shrines, he must do so through the auspices of the *jachikiŋ-tiina*. Thus, one's relationship with this elder is crucial to one's well-being. The same is true of the father-son relationship within each household in the lineage. Indeed, anger or vexation on the part of any authority may bring affliction to his subordinates, though the reverse is not true. It is thought that the ancestors will see this rightful indignation and punish the subordinate (see also Middleton 1960).

Meillassoux (1972) has said that the control of the elders is largely due to their control over the marriage payments of their subordinates. This is true to some extent, but I feel that he has distorted the facts to a certain degree. I would say that the control over marriage payments is an epiphenomenon of the elders' jural role. Rather than merely controlling the material payments to secure a wife—which, by the way, are quite minimal in Sisala-land—the elder controls a bundle of rights over subordinates, of which this is merely one (Mendonsa 1976*b*). These rights and duties are underpinned by the ritual system and the elder's exclusive right to intercede with the ancestors on behalf of his subordinates. Each marriage payment has a ritual counterpart. The gifts are not just given—they are sanctified on the lineage shrines. Before giving the marriage gifts, a young man must have the good wishes of his jural guardians, his father, the *jachikiŋ-tiina*, and the ancestors. It is not merely the control of material goods that limits the behavior of the youth. Any young man can muster enough money to purchase the consumables presented to the bride's father (*haala-kiaa*); these are relatively inexpensive. What he cannot do on his own is present these gifts with the approval of his lineage elders and ancestors. If he tries to acquire a wife on his own, he stands to suffer a withdrawal of ancestral protection and a probable misfortune. Thus, the control of matrimonial prestations is one aspect or an epiphenomenon of the elders' control of a total bundle of rights and duties relative to subordinates which is underpinned by ritual authority.

Elder-subordinate conflict derives in part from the pattern of inheritance and succession (Goody 1958; 1970). Where there is a relationship of holder-heir and disciplinarian-subordinate, there is often interpersonal tension. In the dialectical struggle between the holder of the rights over offices and property and the heir, each utilizes a variety of strategies, but the holder has the weight of authority and public opinion on his side. This tension is highest where a subordinate is likely to succeed—for example, in a father—eldest son relationship—but it is also an aspect of all superordinate-subordinate relations in the gerontocracy. The reader should not get the impression that elders frequently need to resort to the use of formal sanctions against subordinates, because usually the elder is obeyed or uses friendly persuasion. Public opinion and the weight of tradition are on his side. To disobey an elder is a public shame (*hiise*). The threat of this shame is ever present in this rural African society where almost no part of daily life is private. Should the elder wish to punish a recalcitrant deviant, however, the least disruptive and most effective method is ritual accusation. In so doing, he buttresses public opinion with ancestral omnipotence. Middleton and Winter (1963:15–16) conclude that African accusations of deviance are tied up with property relations. In tribes where each wife is the center of a separate estate within her husband's property complex, misfortunes are frequently ascribed to witchcraft. Gluckman (1972:28) says in this regard:

> It seems indeed possible that, where one man is responsible for administering a whole estate in his and all his kinsmen's interests, occult fears are more likely to focus directly on relationships between the males rather than indirectly *via* wives and mother into those relationships between men. Occult fears focus on women where property interests center on women.

In other words, since Sisala women are in no way involved in the inheritance of property or succession to office, ritual sanctions are limited to men, especially office holders. Since all males in the group are potential office holders, some tension exists in all vertical relations between proximate generations, but these are intensified in direct holder-heir relations.

According to this view, we can see the absence of tension among women in Sisala-land, and the low incidence of witchcraft accusations between them, as a result of the fact that they are not directly involved in inheritance. Authority and control of the patrimony passes from man to man within the patrilineal descent group. What conflicts do exist between women are petty squabbles concerning children, food, or chores. Witchcraft is not the main explanatory paradigm of misfortune, because misfortune is adequately handled by the dominant paradigm of ancestral anger over such squabbles. If a woman becomes ill over a squabble with another woman, it is not thought that the woman bewitched her but that the anger and conflict between them is deviance punished by the ancestors through the illness. This is true of all kinship and affinal relations. They are governed by ancestral codes and are thus subject to ancestral punishment.

Lewis (1971:116) shows that accusations of witchcraft tend to take place between equals or are directed from inferiors toward superiors with the intent of dethroning them. Accusations through possession tend to be made by inferiors against superiors. In other words, persons peripheral to the authority system use possession as a means of protest against their leaders.

In Sisala-land I found no such formalized protests against the leadership. The Sisala have no theory of possession as such. Within their main explanatory paradigm there exists the explicit belief that anger on the part of subordinates cannot harm the elders, only the reverse. Protest is reduced to the individual level and is considered personal deviance, which is threatening to the health (*duoruŋ*) of the group. Thus, their etiological explanations of deviance and illness are formulated so as to reinforce the position and authority of the elders. The ancestor cult protects the authority of the elders and the unity of the group by defining protest as deviance and therefore wrong. Lewis (1971:116) says that "what we find over and over again in a wide range of different cultures and places is the special endowment of mystical power given to the weak." This is certainly true in Sisala-land if we view the elders as weak. The ancestors provide the elders with mystical power and an authoritative cloak of sanctity *because* they are materially and physically weak. By virtue of the gerontocratic rule of succession by the eldest, the elders are the oldest persons in their respective groups. In this harsh land they are usually bent with age and afflicted by a wide range of illnesses, especially blindness. During my fieldwork in the village of Bujan, seven of the eight lineage headmen were blind, and the eighth was too feeble to farm for himself. Their power lies in a bundle of rights and duties vested in them as group authorities. This authority rests on its perceived and continued legitimacy on the part of group members. The mystical sanctions of the ancestor cult reinforce the dictates of the elders; such commands are beyond question. Anyone who denies this authority becomes labeled as a deviant and is dealt with in such a way as to remind him, and the members of the group, of the need to work together as a group and of the need to obey the elders.

Today the Sisala live in a remote part of Africa that has been influenced by colonialism, modern technology, and the world economy (Grindal 1972; Mendonsa 1975*b*, 1980). Any analysis of the process of social control must take this culture contact into account. Social scientists generally offer three kinds of explanations for deviance and conflict in non-Western societies (Sellin 1938:83). First, there is the conflict that arises between the acceptable standards held by the older generation and those of the younger generation. Second, there is the conflict between the traditional culture and the modern one, which impinges on it from without. And third, there are general theories about a shift from a well-organized, homogenous society to a less well-organized, complex society. With each of these explanations a dialectic is created between the norms of the traditional authority system and behavior as it is influenced by new ideas and opportunities deriving from industrial society. These new ideas and opportunities are grasped differently by different age groups in society. The differences are seen as causing conflict between generations and as leading to increased deviancy by the young as they respond more positively than their elders to such new phenomena.

Grindal (1972) has described the Sisala as a people caught between two worlds. He says that the younger generation has been exposed to the ethos of "progress," which is a result of the colonial experience, modern education, Western religion, and ideas supported by the present-day national government. Grindal did his fieldwork in the mid-1960s, when this theme of progress was certainly prevalent among the educated Sisala and the youth in general. It was a time of hope and naiveté. Since that time Ghana has slowly lost power in the world economic arena, and the dreams of yesterday have become tempered by the harsh economic realities that persist in many Third World countries today. In Sisala-land, the educational system has been sharply reduced, mechanized agriculture has been a dismal failure, planned roads and communication systems have failed to materialize, health care remains extremely primitive, and periodic starvation is not unknown. National governments seem to come and go without altering significantly the daily lives of the people. They receive few modern benefits, either social or material. The hopes and promises of the sixties went beyond the capacity of the nation to produce, given its dependent position in the world economic structure (Mendonsa 1980).

This ideal of "progress" and modernity affected, I feel, the level of deviance in Sisala-land and the effectiveness of the ancestor cult as a social control mechanism. In the beginning there were more opportunities for youth. There was education, and there were jobs. Above all there was hope, and the average primary-school leaver could expect to be employed. The raised expectations and real opportunities influenced the youth. Even the youth who did not go to school could expect to get employment in the wage sector or to benefit from the economic prosperity and abundance of industrial goods that flowed into Ghana after the Second World War. For the first time in history, Sisala youth had significant avenues for social mobility beyond the capacity of indigenous horticulture or the authority of their fathers. Youth could get cash, through cash crop farming on their own or through wage labor, and this enabled them to acquire the symbols of modernity and adult status earlier than and independently of their elders. Young men sought cash for tin-roofed houses, bicycles, modern clothes, sunglasses, transistor radios, even early marriage. There were plenty of successful role models around, migrants or the educated who had "made it" and who ostentatiously displayed their newfound wealth to the envy of the youth. This culture change weakened the power and authority of the elders and of their use of ritual to control the youth. The most significant factor was the increase in spatial mobility, because youth could move hundreds of miles away and find new lives in the growing urban areas to the south.

During my first fieldwork in 1971—1972, the dream of progress was still alive, and the economy seemed to be growing. Industrial goods and exotic foods were plentiful and cheap in local marketplaces. Transportation and communications were good. Many schools had already closed, but those who left school still had high expectations. Tractors and modern fertilizers were transforming the Sisala system of hoe horticulture into a cash crop agricultural system, with the government acting as the buyer and broker for local farmers. But by my second field trip, during the summer of 1975, things had become much worse. Most schools had closed, morale was low among the youth, there were few industrial goods and little food to be had in local markets. Above all, agriculture had come to a standstill because of the lack of petrol and petro-chemical fertilizers. By my third trip, during the summer of 1977, the area had reverted to pre-"progress" times. There was widespread starvation, due in part to the conversion to the cash crop system and in part to the Sahelian drought, which had begun to affect northern Ghana (Mendonsa 1980). Young men still clung to the belief that they could get independent wealth through cash crop farming, and many tilled small plots in their spare time in hopes of obtaining some prestige item such as a radio or a tin roof for their rooms. By then, however, most people could see that Sisala-land would not immediately benefit directly from modernity in quite the naive ways hoped before.

For females modernity meant fewer opportunities than for men because they tend to marry in their early teens and are not involved in holder-heir relations or directly in farming. The development of nearby towns, such as Tumu, did provide some unmarried or divorced women with new employment possibilities. The influx of non-Sisala men to work in the town created a demand for beer halls and prostitution. Yet since polygyny has always caused a shortage of women, they have been in demand and have had some measure of power based on this scarcity: a woman has always been able to move quickly out of one marriage into another if her husband did not treat her well. In general, then, modernity and expanded economic conditions in Ghana during the fifties and sixties probably provided youth with increased power relative to their elders. The following case illustrates the type of conflict that resulted from this change.

CASE 10.

Tia had luckily landed a government job in the nearby town of Tumu as a latrine attendant. This led him to be away from the village a great deal and to become accustomed to the ways of town folk. His elders complained that he was frequenting bars and chasing women, but such complaints were only gossip until his father died. Tia was at work at the time, but his elder brother Viiri sent him a message that his father was gravely ill, although he had already died. This is because it is forbidden to send a death message to someone who is away from home. Tia responded, saying that he could not return home (only three miles) because he had to work. Viiri was ill in bed himself and could not see to the burial. The body lay stinking for several days before Viiri could arrange for the burial. Finally Tia returned, and a violent argument ensued between Tia and Viiri. Later, after the heat of the argument had died down, Tia went to see the village *nihiaŋ nihiaŋ*. This is the oldest man in the village, who often acts as a go-between in disputes. He asked the *nihiaŋ nihiaŋ* (literally "eldest elder") to arbitrate the dispute between himself and his elder brother. Together they went to Viiri's house. Tia spoke first, saying: "I realize that I have done wrong, and if a person does wrong, even to his wife, he should admit it, how much less to an elder. When our father died I was at the funeral of the mother of the chief of Tumu. My brother [Viiri] called me and told me that our father was seriously ill, but I did not come, so they had to send another man to tell me that he was dead. Since I work for the government I had to ask permission to leave, but they told me that I was needed because of the chief's mother's funeral. This made my brother very mad because I didn't come. So some other people had to bury the corpse. Now I am giving these twenty white cowries to you [the *nihiaŋ nihiaŋ*] to confess that I wronged my elder brother and to show that I realize my wrongdoing."

The *nihiaŋ nihiaŋ* then said: "I now greet you, chief [Viiri was also the village chief]. I did not do so before because Tia called me to come here. Tia now realizes that he has done a very bad thing by leaving the body to lie for four days without burial. Our forefathers always used twenty cowries to confess a bad deed against an elder, so this is why Tia has brought these cowries to you today. To go on without an apology would be a further offense, so he has asked me to give you these twenty white cowries. This is what brought me out of my house and to your place today."

Then Viiri said: "This affair has not made me happy at all. This man never even came to our father's burial, but I am accepting these cowries. You can't stop people from going to the towns, but these young people today don't even understand our language when we speak. As our father died and lay for four days, he became rotten and smelled up the whole compound. I could do nothing, being confined to my bed, not able to walk. Of all the dead people in the past, have you ever seen such a thing as a lineage having to bury their own dead? So I sent a message to the Tumu chief asking his permission to allow us to bury our own body, and he sent the message back telling us to go ahead. Now Tia should tell the chief that he and the other gravediggers refused to bury the body. Then if the chief wants to punish them he can. Now I wait to hear from Tia. As I am confined to my bed, I am very dependent on him. If there is any sickness in the compound Tia won't come on his own, even if he hears of it. But soon I will not be alive and he will succeed me as lineage headman, and then he will see how hard it is. Very soon matters of our own lineage will rest on him, and he will see. Now the young men of the lineage should decide when the funeral should be. The dead man has not told us [through divination] that he wants his funeral to be performed immediately, so if the young men want to wait for the moon, they can [with the coming of the moon they can dance]. Since Tia did not come to inquire about my health and did not set a date for our father's funeral, he is waiting for me to die so that the funerals can be held together. If not, he should set a date. I called Tia to come and collect our daughter's bridewealth because we have no money to perform the funeral. He refused to come, and we still have no money for the funeral. If he had come when I called him he would have had the money by now, but we do not have it. They say that I am the custodian of things, but these younger men all work for money on the farm, and I am left here alone. Yet they give me nothing, and what do I have but my daughter's bridewealth to draw upon? Since our ancestors used twenty white cowries to apologize, I must accept them, but if it were left up to me, I would demand an animal. But since our forefathers did not do it this way, I am forced to accept his apology with these twenty white cowries. I am speaking not only to Tia but to all the young men of our lineage that when I die I am afraid that you will also let me rot like our father. It would be better if I didn't have any kinsmen and that I be eaten by vultures than to die and have my kinsmen let me rot and stink."

The *nihiaŋ nihiaŋ* then spoke, saying, "May God take this quarrel to a far place so that when you [Viiri] die this affair will not be repeated." A discussion about the the date of the funeral followed. Tia wanted to put off the funeral until after the harvest was completed. Viiri said, in a somewhat conciliatory manner, that it was all right with him because he did not have the money to perform the funeral anyway. He explained that his daughter had just informed him she was pregnant, and it is forbidden by custom to ask for a daughter's bridewealth during her pregnancy. Tia, being equally conciliatory at this point, said that when the harvest was over he would provide the money for the funeral. The discussion then ended.

Clearly, this method of dispute settlement brings the disputants together in a formal situation of arbitration under the authority of the senior village elder, who acts as mediator. It serves to "clear the air," but it rarely settles the matter finally because future divination can reveal complications. In this case, the divination held immediately after death showed no complications, but the divination held at the funeral indicated that some calamity awaited if Tia did not make a piacular sacrifice of a sheep on the lineage ancestor shrine. This he eventually did, and they proceeded with the funeral. Viiri, the elder brother and lineage headman, was the one who conducted the funeral divination. Thus, an apology was made and a piacular sacrifice performed by Tia, but such rites do not completely remove the tension inherent in structural relations and life conditions. The holder-heir relation between Viiri and Tia still obtained, as did the fact that Tia had a government job in town, which rankled Viiri. Not only did the job keep him from his family duties, but it provided him with an independent source of income and thus enough security so that he rarely helped out on the family farm. Such issues were behind the conflict over the failure to bury the body, but they were not directly addressed or resolved by either the apology or the postdivinatory sacrifice. This case has an element of modernity about it, but the structural relation between holder and heir is fraught with tension. Tia's government job, money, and freedom only added new aspects to an old plot. Perhaps social change has exacerbated this inherent structural conflict, but the conflict does not arise solely from social change or culture contact.

Anger (*baaniŋ*) should not be expressed openly in a violent manner, but it should also not be kept hidden. Thus, the Sisala find themselves in a double bind (Bateson 1936, 1949). Their cultural ethos is nonviolent. All forms of physical aggression are rare. Even if one is extremely angry at a person, it is not acceptable to express that anger outwardly, either verbally or physically. Their culture stresses the preference of a "cool," rational discussion, but of course this is hard to conduct in an angered state. Divination is an institution designed to reveal "hidden things," such as unexpressed anger. The Sisala use the verb *bε*, meaning "to wrap something up" when referring to treacherous thoughts, feelings, or action taken behind someone's back. They say, *U bε zεnbe*, "He behaved treacherously." The implication is that he did it under wraps. Good behavior or feelings are those that can be aired openly. For instance, the Sisala say, *U zɔmɔ nɛ lii chiŋ*, "It is good to stand out in the open," or *U zɔmɔ nɛ chaasa bul*, "It is good to speak frankly." The verb *chaasa* carries the connotation of "straightness" or moral goodness. A moral person is one who is open and frank but who never quarrels or expresses hostility. Open hostility is thought to cause trouble (*wii-juuluŋ*), but so does hidden hostility.

The following case illustrates how hostility and trouble can be generated by a clash between the new and the old orders in Sisala-land and how the divinatory process provides a means of indirectly dealing with the tension and latent hostility inherent in intralineage relations.

CASE 11.

Baadi, a lineage headman, created a great deal of conflict within his lineage through his open hostility to others. He was about eighty years old and blind. He lay all day on his sleeping mat in his room. He was cranky toward his family members and made such undo demands on those who came near him that whenever possible people avoided going near his room.

The Cotton Development Board (a national agency) had recently begun a campaign in the village to convince the farmers to plant more cotton, which would be purchased by the government at a controlled price. The young men of Baadi's lineage were excited by the prospect because extra cash meant that they could purchase some prestige items—a zinc roof for their rooms, for example, or a radio, or a shotgun, or a bicycle. Baadi was earnestly against the production of any cash crop. He forbade any of the younger men to grow cotton, saying that the ancestors had not grown it and that they should stick to the production of cereal crops.

This arbitrary decision created much dissension among the younger members of the lineage. Two of them started secret cotton farms some distance from the family farm. They cleared these farms near the road to Tumu so that they could easily transport the cotton to town, without having to parade it past the villagers, although it was common knowledge among the villagers that they were cash-cropping. Another young man eventually left the village altogether to farm with his mother's brother, and another emigrated in search of wage labor. Those who remained in the lineage continually grumbled about the fact that Baadi was "spoiling the lineage." The heir to Baadi's custodianship vigorously tried to persuade Baadi to allow the younger men to plant at least some cotton "so that they will not all run south." But Baadi shouted at the heir and raved on about not being respected by the youth. Every chance he got he yelled at someone.

During this conflict, the wife of one of the younger men became seriously ill, and he approached Baadi to consult a diviner on his behalf. Since Baadi was immobilized, he sent a small boy to fetch a diviner. During the course of the divination it was revealed to Baadi that the younger men were spoiling the lineage. He claimed that the ancestors were angry because they had disobeyed him. The divination revealed that Baadi's deceased father was the offended ancestor and that one young man named Ali was the culprit. Ali was required to present some fowls and a goat. During the postdivinatory sacrifice, all the lineage men gathered at the ancestor shrine. Baadi conducted the ceremony. Ali presented the animals by giving them to the senior man of the village (*nihian nihian*), who in turn passed them on to Baadi. Ali apologized for his deviant acts and promised to change his ways in the future. He pledged his support for the lineage and said that he would obey the directions of Baadi in the future. The *nihian nihian* repeated Ali's words to Baadi, who then began the sacrifice with an invocation of the ancestors. He repeated the call for all the family members to unite and show proper respect for those in charge. He rambled at some length about how the present was not as good as the past and how the youth no longer showed respect for age and authority. He reprimanded Ali specifically and all young men in general for their disrespect and exhorted them to conform in the future. Then the sacrifice was completed, and all partook of the sacrificial meat.

Several months later Baadi died. The initial preburial divination revealed that the death was a "troublesome" one. After the funeral, a second divination conducted by the heir disclosed that no one specific individual was at fault in the death of Baadi; the general disrespect of the young men was the reason behind it. The divination showed that a small sacrifice of three chickens on the ancestor shrine would suffice to appease the ancestors. One chicken was to come from each of the three *kaalaa* (compounds) of the lineage. After this sacrifice the new officer holder informed the young men that he had consulted "several" diviners and that it had been revealed to him that it was now all right to plant cotton, as long as they also continued to work on the family farm.

V   The above case illustrates the fact that divination, while it does have some social control functions, does not always act as an effective social control mechanism except in the symbolic sense. While Ali was forced to make a symbolic gesture, two disgruntled young men left the lineage, and eventually the youth began to grow cash crops anyway. In fact, divination was used by the new headman to open the way for this innovation. In other words, divination provides a symbolic statement of the wishes of the lineage authorities. When this is in substantial agreement with the majority opinion, divination appears to direct action, but when it is not in line with the opinions of those who have alternatives to conformity, they may choose to exercise those options. The divinatory drama is a symbolic statement that affects different persons in different ways, and the outcome of a divinatory case is methodologically difficult to determine because it is open-ended. When I returned to Sisala-land on my last field trip, for instance, I found that Haluri (case 9) had again left her husband and moved back into town, where she had taken work as a prostitute in a beer bar.

The rites of the divinatory process often give the impression that order has been restored, that the problem has been solved. The anthropologist who limits his ethnography to a one- or two-year "synchronic snapshot" may be lulled into believing in the efficacy of retributive rites. When one has a longer association with a group, however, it is possible to follow the progress of cases over an extended period (Van Velsen 1967). What emerges from extended cases is that, in time, the trouble-causing behavior sometimes reemerges, or conflict causes an irreparable breach in relations in spite of the rites. When such a breach occurs, it usually has a long history of conflict and tension, as in the following case.

CASE 12.

Tiibie and Basugolo were brothers of the same father by different mothers. The eldest, Tiibie, was seven years senior to Basugolo. Both worked on their father's farm, but because he was the eldest, Tiibie was put in charge by the father. Throughout their life together Basugolo resented this. The crisis came when Tiibie succeeded his father at the age of thirty-eight. There had been a long history of conflict between them—Basugolo had wanted to take a second wife, for example, but Tiibie had also wanted a second wife. They had argued their cases before the father. Basugolo had claimed that he should take preference because apparently his first wife was barren, but Tiibie had won out and taken a second wife. His father had told Basugolo that he would be able to marry another wife as soon as he found a suitable woman. Shortly afterward the brothers had had a violent quarrel when Basugolo's wife was accused of beating one of Tiibie's children unjustly. Basugolo had shouted many angry words at his elder brother, but the argument was stopped through the intervention of family members. Subsequently, another one of Tiibie's children had fallen ill and died. The divination revealed that the cause of death was the anger of Basugolo over the marriage arrangements and the quarrel. The father presided at the divination and informed him that he would have to sacrifice a sheep on the lineage medicine shrine (*vene*). He begrudgingly did so, and the matter seemed settled.

Five years after this incident occurred, their father died, and Basugolo refused to farm anymore for his elder brother. He had long cultivated his own farm, but had also worked on the family farm. When the father died, Basugolo finished out the season on the family farm, but during the dry season he built a separate house away from the lineage compound. He moved his two wives and one child into this new structure, and he also stopped farming for the brother.

The following year Tiibie lost much of his harvest when the rains spoiled them. Basugolo had luckily harvested his just before the storm struck. According to the norms of the Sisala, Basugolo should have shared his harvest with his brother, but he did not. This action was the subject of much gossip in the village. Tiibie consulted a diviner to find out the cause of his bad harvest and found out that his junior brother's disrespect had brought about the disaster. He informed Basugolo of the divinatory directive that he he apologize through sacrifice of a sheep and a goat on the lineage ancestor shrine. Basugolo refused. He said that he no longer recognized the authority of his elder brother and no longer wished to participate in lineage affairs. Instead, Tiibie sacrified the animals to the ancestors and survived through the next year on stored food and the proceeds of two cattle that he sold to traders. To this day there is a rift between the brothers; it had lasted fourteen years at the time of my fieldwork.

If the anthropologist had recorded the case after Basugolo begrudgingly performed the piacular sacrifice on the behest of his father, the case would support the thesis that piacular rites do function to restore the social order. When the case is recorded later, though, it becomes obvious that Basugolo had made that concession only because he was still in a dependent position and was therefore unwilling to defy his father. The piacular rite gave the appearance of unity where there actually existed strife and conflict that eventually led to group fission.

From the cases presented, it appears that there are two significant variables that condition whether a person who is labeled as a deviant will be coerced by divinatory directives: first, his position in the social structure of the lineage, and second, his opportunities and options outside the lineage. The first arises from the tendency inherent in the segmentary lineage system to differentiate groups of siblings according to their relationship to the various wives of one man. The second arises from the fact that the headman cannot control the means of production available to group members, such as tools and land, and he cannot prevent young men from emigrating in search of wage labor. This allows the subordinate youth to pursue economic independence if he is willing to disregard the norms that emphasize unity of the lineage. Of course, labor is the critical factor limiting production in Sisala horticulture. Thus, it may be thought that those who wish to leave to start their own farms will be limited by the lack of labor, but this is not usually the case if the man is married. One man working alone can produce enough food for a wife and small children. As he establishes ties of friendship with neighbors, he can marshal cooperative labor when necessary. The critical labor needed by the man, however, is female labor, for it is very difficult for a single man to get along without a mother or a wife to do his domestic chores. As a man's children begin to grow up, he is on his way to producing his own labor pool, and it behooves him to control that labor as long as possible in order to ensure his security in old age. The main hold a father has over this labor is his children's acceptance of the norms supporting his authority over them until his death. This authority is backed by a variety of ritual sanctions that exist in the institutions of divination and ancestral sacrifice. Such authority can be viewed as a bundle of rights and duties that inhere in an office holder's role, whether he be the father of a nuclear family or the headman of the lineage.

Goody (1962:328) has pointed out that "the whole system of sacrifice to one's forebears is linked, by the LoDagaa themselves, to the perpetual nature of claims upon property." *Property* must be understood in the broadest sense of the term. It is more than merely the control of the means of production or its products. It is also the control of behavior, especially that which has economic ramifications. Where such concerns over inheritance, succession, and discipline exist, there also exists interpersonal tension; that is to say, the interpersonal tension arises out of the structural relation of holder-heir and/or authority-subordinate. In these close kinship relations, tension and conflict should not occur, but they do. In the personalistic cosmology of the Sisala, the occurrence of conflict between the holder and the heir results from personal deviance from the normative structure rather than from the structural relation itself.

Functional theorists have noted a variety of institutions that serve to reduce or avoid this structural tension, including accusations of witchcraft, spirit possession, avoidance procedures, prohibitions on interaction between holder and heir, and rituals of rebellion. Theory states that structural tension exists but cannot be expressed in direct forms of rebellion; it must be dissipated or projected elsewhere. In Sisala-land there are institutionalized prohibitions on behavior between holder and heir, especially between father and eldest son, and also the projection of tension to an ancestral plane through a personalistic etiology and a theory of ancestral retribution. The institutions of divination and piacular sacrifice are devices that can be used by elders to control the behavior of heirs and subordinates. This is an emic fact, but we should be careful in assuming that such stated functionality is a behavioral reality; rather, I would view such institutions as symbolic statements or ritual dramas that emphasize group unity and obedience to authority. The effect of such dramas is tempered by the two structural and economic facts mentioned above: the nature of the relationship between the accused and the authorities and the nature of his external economic options. Where these variables support the social control functions of ritual institutions, they will have the appearance of providing social control. Where they run counter, such institutions may have very little social control effectiveness over time. Over an extended period, such rites and institutions may not prevent group disunity. Moreover, by focusing on the stated function, we may wrongly conclude that the Sisala, and preindustrial peoples in general, live highly structured lives that are neatly, almost perfectly, ordered by structural rules. Such a view denies the reality of deviance and of the fact that role players use a variety of tactics to control each other, including manipulation of rules. In this view, institutions are to be seen not so much as functional realities but more as dramatic arenas in which political battles are fought among antagonists who use cultural ideas, including rules, as weapons. In other words, they cite rules and precedents that they see as supporting and implementing the outcome they desire.

VI When conflict arises, elders solve the problem in a variety of ways, using persuasion through discussion and palaver. Yet the institution of divination also serves to adjudicate in times of life crises. Why is it that some conflicts are dealt with in nonritual ways and others are handled within the divinatory process? I do not think there is a simple answer to this question. There are many reasons why individual elders choose to consult diviners. Culturally, however, Sisala etiology is clear on this point: the presence of misfortune is no accident. It has been caused by a sentient being. If it is ignored, more misfortune will follow. In general, elders first try to solve intralineage arguments and squabbles through persuasion, but the simultaneous occurrence of conflict and misfortune in the lineage sets the stage for the linkage of the two events through divination. The headman's role includes the responsibility to consult a diviner to cure illness for his family. In the performance of that role, illness becomes linked to deviance because of the internal structure of the ideas and techniques of divination itself. That is, divination is structured so that it almost always links deviance and misfortune and directs the client toward ancestral sacrifice as the solution.

A basic assumption of functional theory is that institutions arise in response to societal needs. This is not an automatic process. Society is not a sentient being; rather, social rules and ideas are carried in the minds of human beings, who think and act on the basis of those ideas in response to the problems that arise in their lives over time. They pass these ideas and rules on to their children as codes and institutions. If divination evolved in such a manner, it must be useful in some way to those actors, given the structure of Sisala society. I submit that within the group, divination serves to handle troubles and conflicts that are insoluble through reason and persuasion. These problems arise mainly from the interplay of contradictory structural principles (Kelly 1977). Divination provides an authoritative way of making decisions in cases where decision based on reason and persuasion is difficult. It gives the authorities a mechanism whereby an arbitrary decision can be made to have the appearance of an authoritative one, one that, since it comes from the ancestors themselves, is beyond question. This is a double-barreled function, as divination protects living authorities who need to control the behavior of group members and also protects the cultural system that constitutes and supports that authority but is filled with contradictions and ambiguities.

When trouble results from an insoluble conflict in principles, blame is deflected away from the social order and toward an individual deviant actor. Again, it is important to understand that this happens because it is in the interest of the actors who constitute the system's authorities. They, as elders, have a need to control their subordinates for a variety of social and material reasons. If they do not, they lose face and credibility as leaders, and they lose control of the right to direct the economic activities of their subordinates. As a constituted system, divination and the ancestor cult provide elders with credible answers to troubles that emerge because of imperfections within the social system, but rather than redressing these structural contradictions, ritual covers them up and pins the blame on a person. Through divinatory implementation of their personalistic etiology, elders are able to deflect attention away from the system's imperfection, about which nothing can be done because the system is defined as axiomatic, and toward individual deviance, about which something *can* be done.

Divination is a technique whereby the headman and authorities can search for evidence to confirm personal or public suspicions. This is a system of typification that enables them to make sense out of an ambiguous situation, allowing the group to "deal effectively with an environment that carries with it ambiguity and gaps in 'directions to concrete action' because the typical is rendered homogeneous, nonproblematical, and, therefore, taken for granted" (Cicourel 1972:255). Following from this view, deviance would appear to be not so much a quality of the act a person commits as a societal creation and a consequence of the process of group labeling (Becker 1963). Accusations of deviance may have little to do with the real causes of conflict within the group; rather, it is what people define as real that counts (Thomas 1928). Divination provides a technique by which elders can define the situation for the lineage public in such a way as to direct the nature of the investigation and adjudication. Divination enables them to select a plausible answer through what Sacks (1972) calls the "economy rule" and Douglas (1971) calls the "primary effect." In this process, the situation is interpreted by means of the first plausible idea; the result is an acceptable definition based on incomplete evidence. Once this classification is made, the rest of the investigation involves a search for information demonstrating that that classification is the correct one. In divination, the client presents to the oracle several possibilities he has in his mind. Once the oracle selects one of these, the rest of the divination is a process of expansion on that specific definition of the situation.

Divination is not the only formal labeling procedure at the disposal of an elder. He may also use the scorpion ordeal, or he may require that suspects swear an oath on a shrine, or, in cases of death, the corpse of the deceased may be used to reveal the identity of the person who caused his death, though this is rare. The scorpion ordeal is a labeling procedure used when a crime has been discovered but has not caused apparent misfortune, though it has the potential to do so if the deviant is not found. Case 13 illustrates this technique.

CASE 13.

One day, upon his return from the farm, Dasuki noticed some millet grains near the lineage granary (*virebaliŋ*). It is forbidden for anyone to remove millet from this granary without the headman's permission, so he, as headman, called all the women of the lineage together and asked who had stolen the grain. None spoke, so he ordered a scorpion ordeal. Dasuki instructed the children of the lineage to look for a scorpion. When one was found, Dasuki again assembled the women and asked if anyone had anything to say. Since none did, he placed the scorpion on the arm of the first woman. It did not sting her, so he placed it on the arm of the second, with the same result. When he approached the third woman in line, she began to cry. He asked her why, and she confessed to the crime. It is thought that such theft is punishable by death through ancestral anger, so her husband, Babgadere, was required to sacrifice a goat, two hens, a guinea fowl, and a fine of 100 cowries. There was no need to consult a diviner in this case because the rule is unambiguous, as is the result.

When matters are less well defined, the headman may resort to divination to sort matters out, as case 14 illustrates. It also demonstrates how a headman may use divination to accuse a deviant when direct accusation is made difficult by the elder's dependence on the accused.

CASE 14.

Dubie was a lineage headman of about seventy-five years. His sister, Hapula, left her husband and returned to live in her natal lineage. She was economically independent of Dubie, however; in fact, after a time he became dependent on her. He was too old to farm for himself, though he puttered with a small kitchen garden near the compound. Lineage members gave him food, but the lineage was small and all the young men had moved away except one son, Viiri. When Hapula returned she enlarged Dubie's garden and started a business selling kerosene in the village. Prior to that, kerosene had not been available except in the town of Tumu. Being the only source of kerosene for miles around, Hapula became comparatively rich, and Dubie came to depend on his sister for cash and food. After some time they quarreled over his insistent demands. She told me that she considered him to be lazy. She said, "You know that he is strong enough to go to the farm with the others, but he prefers to live off of the work of others. He is a selfish old man who even takes money from his mother."

Over a period of time the conflict between them increased as he made more and more demands on her for food and money. Finally he stopped working in the kitchen garden altogether. Hapula continued to tend the garden but told me that she had to do all the work even though he still ate out of it. Out of her anger she stopped giving him money for tobacco and incidentals, though she did continue to give him food. At this point Dubie wanted her to expand the garden to include a cash crop, which would provide him with pocket money. When she refused, he became angry, and a terrible argument ensued. Dubie shouted at her in front of the other family members, saying, "You stupid girl. Don't you know that when you leave your husband and return to your father's house, you must obey your elders?"

They became estranged over the argument, and Hapula stopped giving him food. She also abandoned his garden. This estrangement continued for several months, and then Viiri's son fell ill. Virii asked Dubie to consult a diviner on his behalf. Together they went to the diviner and determined that the illness had been caused by Hapula's not sharing her profits with the group. The divination revealed that she had to make retribution with a sheep and several chickens. Dubie informed Hapula of the outcome and instructed her to get the necessary animals immediately since the child was very ill. Hapula had to buy the animals from the town marketplace. When she had done so, she gave them to Dubie, who sacrificed them on the lineage shrine. At the sacrifice he squatted before the *lelɛɛ* shrine and, clutching the rope of the sheep in his hand, said: "Basi, you sat here before me. If you are there, hear the voice of this sheep. It is for you. It is the sheep of your daughter. Hapula has taken the wrong path, and the shrines have caught her. When one is selfish, the shrines and medicines protect us from such evil. Let this sheep end the trouble. Let all the evil persons hear the sheep's bleat."

Throughout the sacrifice, Hapula sat off to the side in a submissive manner. At several points in the rite, Dubie reprimanded her for her misdeeds, and he used the occasion to extol the virtues of proper family unity and sharing. While Hapula, who was a forceful woman, did not speak, her lack of overt opposition to the performance implied her submission to the authority of her elder brother. Nevertheless, after the sacrifice, she continued to sell kerosene, and garden alone, and she did not significantly alter her ways. She had been required, however, to share some of those profits with her elder brother and other family members through divinatory directive and sacrifice. Dubie could make such a public accusation through divinatory means because it conformed to and expressed public opinion within the lineage. Such a ritual, however, may conform in general to public opinion but still be a mask for private motivations on the part of an individual or group faction.

Divination thus can be used to label a deviant who has personally offended the headman. It also is frequently used when the case is ambiguous and difficult, as in the following case.

CASE 15.

Isaka had two wives and produced three sons by his senior wife, Halu, and four by his junior wife, Hatong. In his compound each wife had a separate house and yard. As the children grew to maturity, all played and worked together, but there was a recognized difference between the two groups of siblings. Until Isaka died, all his sons worked together on his farm. From that farm Isaka supported his two wives and the children. But as the boys grew to manhood, Halu's sons began to cultivate another farm in addition to that of their father, and the sons of Hatong did the same.

When Isaka died, his eldest son, Batong, the son of his eldest wife, succeeded him. The following farming season, all the sons continued to work together on the family farm while working separate plots as well. In the next year, however, Hatong's sons enlarged their own farm and spent very little time helping the other brothers on the main family farm, yet when it came time for the distribution of the harvest, they disputed the distribution of food. Batong became angry over this, but the matter was settled without a major argument. Grumbling and gossip followed. In the following year relations between the two groups became even more strained. This tension especially manifested itself between Batong and Chuong, the eldest son of Hatong. Through the years several arguments broke out between them over the allocation of work and the distribution of farm produce.

When Chuong's wife fell ill, he tried herbs and medicines, but she grew steadily worse and finally was confined to bed. It was then that Chuong consulted a diviner on his own. He received the vague message that "trouble in the family" had resulted in his wife's illness. He was instructed to sacrifice to his father, Isaka, upon the lineage ancestor shrine. To do this he had to approach the lineage elder, Batong, who performed the ceremony. At the sacrifice, Batong reprimanded Chuong for his deviant ways. He went on at length about how their father was angry over their negligence of their farm duties. He exorted Chuong and his brothers to mend their ways, lest more misfortunes befall the group.

This case illustrates how a contradiction between the principle of lineage unity and that of polygyny can lead to conflict within the group. Conformity to the ideal of polygynous marriage led to the creation of two maternal sibling groups within the patrilineage. This structural contradiction is so fundamental to the Sisala social order that a lineage headman, even if he were to understand it as such, would be powerless to alter it. Instead, he inherits a cultural code positing that conflict is due to personal deviation, and he controls the social institutions to label such persons as deviant. Therefore, blame is deflected away from the actual source of conflict and is affixed to the misdeeds of an individual or group. As long as legitimacy in system authority is maintained from generation to generation, each one is able to bypass structural revolution. Instead, each generation inherits a nearly identical social order, with identical structural strains and contradictions, as well as the cosmology and institutions to deal in a personalized way with conflicts generated by the system.

VII   I have defined the divinatory process in Sisala-land as a process of labeling deviance, but it is also a delabeling process: that is, it is a symbolic means of legitimizing the elders' authority by penalizing the labeled deviant in a major way and then permitting him to continue as a member of the group. Divinatory consultation is an inquiry that focuses the support available from the community for the condemnation of a coresident. If persons who live in close proximity are able to continue to do so after an accusation is made, there must be some way to depersonalize the accusation of deviance.

This delabeling and depersonalizing of deviance is legitimized by etiological beliefs. While misfortune is thought to be caused by personal anger, hatred, or misdeed, the person is not thought to be extraordinary by becoming angry, by hating, or by deviating. This behavior is normal because people are seen as weak and prone to break rules—hence the need for divination and the ancestor cult to keep them on the true path (*woŋbiing titi*). These ritual institutions are viewed as means of reminding the living of their obligations to the dead and to each other. They allow the labeling of deviants to occur in such a way that the deviant is not permanently labeled or ostracized from the group and the accuser is not thought to be malicious in making the accusation. It is thought, rather, that the righteous anger of the ancestors maintains group harmony and unity. The elder is seen merely as performing his dutiful role as an officer of the group when he is required to accuse a fellow member of the family with deviance.

Divination lends legitimacy to the labeling process because it is an integral part of ancestor cult ritual and involves a lengthy process of sifting through information about the relationship between a delict and misfortune before a public accusation is made against the deviant. Ideally, various consultations should be performed, along with a variety of checks and tests upon the verdict. Ultimately the decision is announced by the elders to the community, which indicates its acceptance and legitimacy by performance of postdivinatory piacular rites. It is important to note that if the accused is unable to carry out these rites for any reason, they will be conducted by another kinsman on his behalf.

In the context of the descent group, where kinship ties are thought to be inalienable and form the basis of citizenship, disputes must be settled so as to preserve these ties and the unity of the descent group. The divinatory process provides an institutionalized means of settling disputes and reintegrating the accused. Moreover, such institutions have socialization functions. They are ways of communicating the values and rules to the younger generation and to those who violate them. As with ritual in general, this communication may be subtle. The repeated ritual display of principles may communicate both the system's stated axiomatic quality and its structural contradictions, thereby providing a latent source of understanding. It is difficult to confirm such an hypothesis empirically, but the ritual symbols of the divinatory process are polysemous and metaphoric in quality. They have the capacity to convey multiple messages about phenomena. Thus, it may be that this process of labeling and delabeling deviants provides a ritual drama in which structural problems come to light. To this extent it can be seen as a ritual of realignment which labels deviants while at the same time, through ritual metaphor, acknowledging that the individual deviant has deviated because of system conflicts. Such a theory must remain tentative, but what is clear is that the divinatory process does provide for both the labeling and the delabeling of individuals. The deviant is "hooked" and then let off the hook in a ritual drama that may highlight several levels of human problems.

VIII In this chapter I have characterized the divinatory process as a labeling process and as a set of social institutions that are thought to have social control functions. The Sisala recognize the labeling aspect of this process but see it as a minor part of social control. To them, the social control functions are more important because the continued existence of society depends on the continued use of wisdom (*wu-jimiŋ*) to govern social affairs. Youth are thought to lack such wisdom, though they can gain it through experience (*siaa*). The divinatory labeling of deviance, and its linkage with misfortune, is seen as part of that experience. *Wu-jimiŋ* is believed to reside in three major loci: with society at large or public opinion, with authority (*hiesaŋ*), and with the ancestors (*lelɛɛ*). The process of aging is thought to provide experience and wisdom. *Siaa* literally means "to have eyes, experience, or wisdom"; hence the Sisala have institutionalized the status of the *nihiaŋ nihiaŋ*, the eldest man in the *jaŋ*, as one who can mediate disputes. Disrespectful behavior on the part of a subordinate toward an elder is called *siiduoŋ*, literally "eye-strongedness," and is taken as a sign of general disregard for the authority of elders and society in general. Elders are thought to have the capacity to govern because they are office holders in the gerontocracy, represent the ancestors and society at large, and are the eldest men in their respective groups.

The main weapons of the elders in their struggle with subordinates are public opinion and shame (*hiisiŋ*). When a deviant is ritually accused, he is drawn into a sequence of events that demand public confession and retribution through sacrifice to the community, both the living and the dead. The right to disgrace someone publicly (*biise*) is a common means of social control which rests with an office holder, but he is also constrained in his abuse of that right by public opinion. In short, while I have shown that the elder can, at times, interject private feelings into the public accusation of deviance, ultimately the accusation is a reflection of public sentiment because it is clothed in undeniable symbolism.

While the divinatory rites are seen emically as coercive, three etic factors can be viewed as influencing the outcome of the process. First, the principles of the moral order contradict each other. When a dispute involves such contradictions, it can be resolved only temporarily and only through ritual means, and the disputants may be caught up in structural relations that eventually create interpersonal tensions and cause the group to split. Second, structural position in the group and the relationship of the elder and the accused affect how the subordinate responds to accusation over a long period of time. In the short run, accused deviants may appear to respond in the same way; but those with a chance to inherit the patrimony are more likely to conform over a longer period. Thus, it would seem that in evaluating his options within and beyond the group, the subordinate takes his structural position into account when making a decision about farming for his lineage, farming for himself, or emigrating. And third, a subordinate is influenced by his perception of opportunities beyond the boundaries of his group. This perception may reflect actual historical opportunities or a misreading of the situation brought on by historical processes. The youth, for example, who identifies with sophisticated city dwellers because he received enough education to change his self-concept but not enough to acquire that life-style, may leave the group in search of that life.

The politics of divination is a struggle for the minds of the group's youth. Elders lose that struggle when internal structural factors militate against long-term conformity by subordinates or when external conditions change, thereby providing them with new behavioral options. Both internal contradictions and external options are products of historical change. I view Sisala culture and social structure as products of a historical process whereby principles and rules are added over time without resulting in a homogeneous moral order. Likewise, external options, such as the chance to migrate or to become educated, occurred in Sisala-land because of historical events in the world order, such as colonialism. I have tried to show that thought and behavior are dynamically influenced by the dialectics within social structure and between the social order and the real and perceived realities that occur over time.

In the introductory chapter I raised some questions about the nature of action and structure—for example: Does action within the institutional context of divination restore impaired social relations? For how long? What percentage of cases have this result? If impaired social relations are not repaired, what happens? The thrust of my argument has been that divination is largely ineffective as a social control mechanism as defined by the emic model, and by consensus theory. The emic view of the functions of divinatory process is that it constrains behavior and acts as a socialization mechanism to create and recreate values within persons. Furthermore, ritual action is supposed to restore impaired social relations and group harmony. These ideas are also the main concepts of consensus theory.

While I agree that, at times, such functions are accomplished by the divinatory process, I view divination as having three main functions relative to dispute settlement. First, it is an institutional framework that provides incentives and constraints while masking facts that are denied or condemned by the dominant ideology. Second, it provides a focusing mechanism, allowing people to cope with the conflictual and indeterminate nature of social life. Third, divination functions to update or rework the rules of the social order.

As I said, divination can be viewed as institutional framework that provides incentives and constraints to the disputing parties. At the same time it masks three facts that are denied or condemned by the dominant ideology. The first of these three facts is that there is significant difference between ideology and practice. While I submit that actors are aware of this difference and use it to their advantage, they must explain it away as a temporary and personal deviation from a sacred moral order. The second fact is that the divinatory process masks the contradictory nature of the premises of that ideology and the rules of the social order. I would say that actors are less aware of this than they are of the discrepancy between ideology and behavior, but contradictions are symbolically highlighted through ritual means, and actors may derive moments of insight from these performances. And the third fact is that the divinatory process masks the personalistic nature of political struggle within the general framework of its institutions. To the Sisala, their ideology and universalistic rules are in perfect harmony and function to prevent personalistic behavior. In my view, because divination serves a masking function, it provides an institutional arena for settling disputes which is safe, the decisions of which are beyond question, and which permits minor adjustments to the pattern of relations in society without disrupting the general form of the ideology by which people should live their lives.

The second main function is that divination also allows people to cope with the indeterminate and conflictual nature of social life by focusing attention in crisis situations on one set of system principles and procedures. The oracle's pile of divinatory symbols eliminates other possible explanations and directs public attention toward a specific ritual solution to the crisis. In so doing, it segregates other rule sets and makes life understandable and manageable. This focusing function may have therapeutic value for the patient, as I described in chapter 5, and may legitimize the authority structure in spite of action that runs counter to structural principles, because that action is defined as a temporary deviation and the myth of group harmony is perpetuated. Also, the divisive results of dispute may occur much later, and thus parties to the dispute do not necessarily make the connection between political struggles in the divinatory process and resulting rule violation (e.g., fission of the descent group). In this way, divination and ancestral sacrifice bridge the gaps between contradictory sets of principles in the moral order, allowing actors to make decisions and settle disputes in spite of system imperfections.

Like any institution, divination can be used by those who occupy its offices for whatever purposes they deem fit, as long as that use does not openly threaten the premises of the institution. But why is a ritual institution used for dispute settlement and the labeling of deviance? My answer is that situations arise in life which present difficult, even insoluble, problems, and authorities cannot deal with those problems directly and openly (see, for example, case 15). Some problems are better dealt with in secrecy or under the cloak of an unquestionable authority structure. These difficult problems arise not only out of conflicts in systems principles but out of greed and desire on the part of actors who are in a position to use the institution for their own purposes (as in case 14). Thus, authorities *know* that they can operate better behind the sanctity of ritual institutions and can *consciously* use them as protection against accusations of favoritism when dealing with life crises and disputes.

The third main function is that divination updates or reworks the rules of the social order. The labeling theory of deviance I have presented in this work assumes that to a certain extent authorities create definitions of the situation as they selectively apply system rules in different situations. This model views structure as a body of rules that are put to use by thinking, goal-oriented individuals, and thus structure is not seen as fixed or as acting mechanically to produce conformity. Murphy (1972:238) has said that "structure is not fixity and harmony, but an abstraction from movement." Man does not live *by* rules so much as in spite of them. The complexity of human behavior is given order and made meaningful by the creation, maintenance, and application of rules. Actors do this by communicating with each other symbolically. In this process, rules are reworked and applied situationally. It is difficult to ground the exact results of the reformulation of norms empirically, but I have tried in this work to provide some evidence about how it is done within the framework of the divinatory process. Assuming that this reworking process does take place, deductively we can hypothesize that each time an institution is "put to work," it may be changed by that use. As external factors change, divination may function to update the cultural traditions, making them applicable to contemporary concerns.

Within this interactionist perspective, I see three main causes of deviance. First, to a certain extent, deviance is caused by the selection process, or, put another way, a social definition of deviance is created through social interaction. Second, the principles and rules of the social order are not arranged, not harmoniously in a unified whole, but in a variety of sets that may have internal harmony but that stand in contradiction to each other in the larger moral order. A negotiated definition of deviance is achieved in the divinatory process by elders when they select one rule set and ignore others, even though the labeled deviant may have deviated from one rule because he was conforming to another. And third, deviance is social defined when elders misuse their authority to label a personal enemy as a deviant by personalistic criteria (case 14).

Goal-oriented actors *understand* the contradictory nature of system norms and the difference between ideology and practice and use this understanding to influence the outcome of divination and ancestral sacrifice. They are aware that the coterminous application of system rules may produce inconsistent results, and therefore they select rules that explain and pattern the situation at hand in a desired fashion. This goal may be social or personal, but it must always be couched in system terms and portrayed as a system goal.

IX   I maintain that a social theory of deviance correctly begins by locating the causes of deviance in the social structure, though we must also be aware of the influence of external factors. By "social sructure" I mean a set of norms about human behavior and the subsequent recognized relationships that link persons together. Such structural norms list rights and duties that are inherent in roles, and they define relationships between persons who occupy given statuses. Throughout this book I have stressed a view of the social order which assumes that societal rules are not absolutely coercive, that they are not in harmony with one another, and that they change as people use them in symbolic interaction. The important implication of this approach for the study of deviance is that if rules are not fixed and are not in harmony, then authorities may be faced with choices about which rules to use to label deviants, and interaction may act to change the rules or add another layer of rules to the existing corpus.

A clear understanding of societal rules is necessary before we can understand deviations from such rules. It has been demonstrated by social scientists that there are two major levels of norms, jural and behavioral (Blau 1955; Blumberg 1967; Homans 1950). The former tells people how they should behave, and the latter forms the actual behavior patterns of the members of society. Jural norms are rules or guides to behavior. Nutini (1965:719) has pointed out, "To assert, on practical and historical grounds, that jural rules [ideal behavior] are secondary to statistical norms [actual behavior] either chronologically or in importance is as nonsensical as to ask whether the chicken or the egg came first." Rather, a dialectic exists between them which leads to the alteration of rules as they are used in behavior, including the labeling of deviance and dispute settlement. The dialectic is created because a discrepancy always exists between jural rules and their implementation, and this discrepancy may lead to a critical point at which behavior is very different from the ideal model of it. This dialectic is a force for change as persons interact in situations of dispute and conflict to discuss deviance and redress, because, I submit, many actors are aware of the dialectic, or discrepancy between ideology and events, and use it to their advantage. This dialectical force for change produces changes in rules in use in the first instance and may change the ideal model in the long run.

It seems clear that man is a typifying animal who creates internal mental abstractions and external codes and that these explanatory models allow people to deal effectively with an ambiguous environment and give directions to concrete actions because "the typical is rendered homogeneous, nonproblematical and, therefore, taken for granted" (Cicourel 1972:255). That man creates such explanatory models and formalizes them into socially accepted rules does not mean that such rules are perfectly coercive or effective as guides to action, but there is a taken-for-granted aspect in human interaction which, to some extent, limits that interaction, as the ethnomethodologists, following Garfinkel, have pointed out. If one asks the question, What kinds of rule violation lead to the divinatory labeling of deviance? it is important to understand that there are more than merely jural rules and behavioral norms. Norms are generally viewed as commonly held expectations (Goffman 1963; Blake and Davis 1964), which I take to be culturally learned codes. Such expectations derive from formal rules of organizations, or they may be informal rules, such as the polite interactional rules of ceremony, civil propriety, deference, and demeanor involved in face-to-face interaction (Denzin 1970; Goffman 1971). Deviation from these rules may influence the decision of authorities to select a deviant for punishment under a formal set of rules, or their violation may increase the severity of punishment. Such informal rules are not usually directly cited as reasons for labeling deviants but are "background expectancies" taken for granted by people who share a common culture in a given situation. They are rules that are usually acknowledged through their violation (Garfinkel 1963; Scheff 1966).

I assume that such cultural expectations are created within individuals and derive from the a priori cultural ideas and social codes they encounter during their lives. The interactionist, however, says that these exist only as subjective phenomena, that is, either as the different views of individuals or as one person's evaluation of the social patterns he encounters. To the extent that the consciousness of these individuals varies, the moral order will exhibit inconsistencies (Leach 1954; Moore 1975, 1978). The nature of this sociocultural reality is critical to a proper understanding of the labeling of deviants. How harmonious is it? Is it a logical integration of cultural rules and premises (Bateson 1936)? Or is it a patchwork quilt of contradictory premises (Murphy 1972)?

In this book I have presented data that would seem to support the latter view—for example, case 15 in this chapter. Three ideals are evident in this case: polygynous marriage, unity of the patrilineal lineage, and, more generally, unity by descent. Isaka was conforming when he married two women and when he produced children by both. Likewise, he was conforming when he kept the whole family together during his lifetime and when he stressed the importance of this unity to his children. Moreover, he was conforming when he created a separate set of living quarters for each wife and her children within the lineage, thereby acknowledging the distinct maternal descent of each sibling group. That the children of each sibling group slept with their mother, ate apart from the siblings of the other wife, and were disciplined by their mother apart from the others was seen as natural, even necessary for the maintenance of peace within the family. All of this, in fact, is seen as natural and understood in Sisala-land, *yet the result of this conformity now is deviance later.*

Case 15 shows that tension and conflict between the two groups existed throughout Isaka's life and after his death. This structural separation of the sibling groups and the cultural expectation that children by one mother have greater inherent unity eventually led to fission of the group when Chuong led his group to build a separate house and to farm apart from Batong's group. The tension and conflict between the two sibling groups and the fission, emically defined as deviant behavior, are the result of contradictions between sets of ideals. The Sisala see it as natural in everyday life to marry more than one wife if possible and to have children; it is also natural for the two sibling groups to be treated differently and for them to feel a greater sense of unity within the sibling group than within the larger lineage. The formal rules of the ancestor cult, however, state otherwise, to wit: Sibling groups should not fight and should always live and farm together and worship a single group of ancestors upon one *lelɛ* shrine.

When we analyze the locus of deviance in this case, etically and according to a structural model, we see that the deviance is generated by the social structure itself because it is not a unified, harmonious set of principles and because it contains contradictory segregates or sets of principles. *Yet this is the very kind of analysis the Sisala most avoid because they have a theory that postulates a perfect moral order and a personalistic theory of deviance.* To avoid coming to this conclusion, they use the divinatory process to mask the structural source of conflict. Social integration is enhanced when institutions serve as bridges between sets of principles which are inherently conflictual. These sets are not logically integrated or harmonious but are operationally and behaviorally separated in institutional settings so as to allow the principles to exist in spite of their contradictory nature and to provide the appearance that such principles serve as guides for moral behavior.

In apparent reaction to the extremes of consensus theorists' claim that structural principles are in harmony and function to regulate behavior, Moore (1975:237) has said that life is indeterminate because "the processes of regularization and processes of situational adjustment may have the effect of stabilising *or* changing an existing social situation or order." An adequate theory of social life must take such indeterminacy into account while explaining how actors use their social structure to accomplish their ends in spite of the limits set by that structure and the indeterminacy created by change. If we view the moral order as a body of generalized universalistic principles that provide only broad incentives and constraints to behavior, and if we view the social order as composed of contradictory sets of more specific rules, and if the processes of regularization and situational adjustment provide a certain degree of indeterminacy to any given situation, then actors are faced with real life situations wherein they must steer a course between the structural constraints on the one hand and the horrific threat of chaos on the other.

I submit that institutions, like divination, allow people to operate in spite of the contradictory nature of the social order or the inherent indeterminacy of social life. They provide legitimate cloaks for action and processes that produce results that conflict with the sociomoral order. As disputes are handled within institutional frames, results are legitimized by universalistic criteria, regardless of the political nature of struggles by actors who operate within these frames. Use of the institution of divination as a mechanism of dispute settlement, for example, presents actors with the opportunity to manipulate each other while at the same time appearing to conform. This is true both of the labelers, who manipulate universalistic criteria for personalistic reasons, and of the labeled, who temporarily submit to the authorities but whose long-term behavior may not conform with the rules (see, for example, cases 6, 9, and 12); or events may turn out in such a way that the institutions appear to function as they should, as in case 11, where the death of Baadi, the headman who opposed planting cotton, allowed the new headman to reinterpret the situation for the group, thereby permitting cotton farming. Here the institution acts to legitimize change that had previously been opposed by an elder who used the same institution to legitimize a position against change. Such social institutions serve a bridging function: thinking people can use them to their advantage while upholding the general principles of the institutional order.

X In the discussion of the structure of divination and sacrifice in relation to the exercise of power within that structural arena, I have been concerned to show that, on the one hand, processual theories of power and, on the other, theories of integration, or consensus theory, are not competing theories of social organization. It has become a truism in political anthropology that all social relations have a power component and that when we talk of social organization, we are talking of the organization of power (Cohen 1976). I have focused on one process, the divinatory process, to show how interacting persons influence one another in an institutional framework. That such influence occurs in heterogeneous societies has been documented and accepted (see Cohen 1976; Van den Berghe 1973). While Van den Berghe talks about the highly diffuse structure of academic politics in Nigeria and Cohen discusses the nature of interest groups in complex societies, I have tried to show that such political manipulation as they describe also occurs in highly institutionalized settings. The example I have focused on is that of divination and ancestral sacrifice in a segmentary lineage system in a society that most anthropologists would agree is less diffuse and less complex than the ethnographic settings described by these two scholars.

The exercise of power in both heterogeneous and homogeneous settings appears to involve conscious manipulation of symbols by those struggling for system rewards. The data from Sisala-land show how the exercise of power in institutional settings can introduce change, be used to deal with conflict generated by the system itself, and also function to preserve the overall institutional framework of society. Thus, conflict and change, though they may also come from external factors, are generated within the social system by the processes of institutionalization and system maintenance.

I take power to be the ability to affect social situations. As such, there are four major categories of power criteria in Sisala society: authority, age, wealth, and sex. Of course, these criteria overlap each other in certain cases; for example, those who succeed to office are the eldest men in line for the position. On the basis of these criteria, we can identify five power categories in Sisala-land: chiefs and government officials, pagan authorities, big men, the educated elite, and youth. Generally speaking, power stems from three sources: numbers of people, social organization, and resources (for a theoretical discussion of these concepts, see Bierstedt 1950). In Sisala-land, each estate derives its power from a different source. The chiefs get power from the state, which rests on the ultimate power, force. Pagan authorities derive their power from the symbolic formation we call the ancestor cult. Big men acquire power mainly through acquisition of wealth and the maintenance of ties with other wealthy men who understand how to operate in the wider marketplace. The educated elite derive their power from their schooling and their knowledge of the "modern world," principally the bureaucracy. Finally, the youth derive their power from health, physical strength, and opportunities to work outside the control of their natal lineages.

These are categories that apply to potential power. Actual power is exercised in social relationships (Emerson 1962). In daily social intercourse persons from each of these categories interact with persons from others. Networks of persons from each category overlap and interpenetrate. Office holders of the authority structure interact with and are influenced by persons from each category, just as they try to influence others. I have chosen to concentrate on intralineage power struggles, but this is a heuristic necessity only. The politico-jural domain and the domestic domain impinge on each other in real life situations. Authorities who attempt to influence others through use of ritual symbolism are themselves influenced by considerations of the power of nonauthorities.

I have tried to show that in Sisala-land, the symbolic formation of authority is a balance to the potential power of youth. Authoritative power inheres in social, kinship, and ritual formations. The political structure is an arrangement of roles endowed with expectations of domination and subjection. Within the lineage system, this structure is dichotomous: there are office-holders and non-officeholders. It is the function of the officeholders to use kinship and ritual symbols to organize their subordinates. At the most fundamental level of ideology, this authority rests on the etiological theory that postulates that disrespect of authority causes misfortune. Thus, relations of power and dependence are symbolically portrayed in the twin institutions of divination and ancestral sacrifice as people try to solve problems in life-crisis situations. In other words, kinship and ritual symbols express power relations in the lineage system. The political power of elders stems from their understanding, control, and manipulation of ritual symbols that inform family members about their kinship obligations and rights relative to other family members. This manipulation, or its results, may lead to action that contradicts system principles, but what is important is that, symbolically, it does not appear to do so. Case 16 is an example.

CASE 16.

Nenkani was a strong youth who worked on his father's farm along with his elder brother and other siblings. He was headstrong, always getting into trouble. He frequently quarreled with his father and siblings. When he was seventeen years old, divination revealed that he had caused the death of a child of the lineage through his disrespectful behavior. He was required to confess his sin and make ritual retribution through ancestral sacrifice. He did so, but as he later told me, he was enraged by the verdict and had felt himself wronged by his father and the lineage elders. The following year he left the lineage to live with his mother's brother, who raised him. Twice more during his life, he was required to return to his natal lineage to make sacrifices of submission. At first he didn't want to, but he told me that his mother's brother had counseled him to do so. He feared that failure to perform the piacular rites might result in his mother's illness or death, he said. At the time of my fieldwork, Nenkani was an old man; in fact, he had become the *nihiaŋ nihiaŋ* (village senior male) of his maternal village. Even though he lived his life apart from his natal kin and never contributed to natal production after his early youth, he maintained proper symbolic ties with his kin through periodic ritual means. His actions never openly denied the legitimacy of the authority of his natal elders.

Lineage authorities are faced with the problem of controlling the behavior of subordinates, who can withdraw from their sphere of influence, as in the above case. As yet in Sisala-land, there are no major differences in ideology which separate authorities from subordinates, though the youth appear to be more open to economic innovation and ideas stemming from culture contact. The problem of distinctiveness of the lineage group and of the authoritative control of the behavior, especially economic and residential, of subordinates remains a central one for elders, however, because youth can leave the lineage legitimately, as in the case above, by citing their right to exploit their matrilineal kin. Elders can control the behavior of subordinates only to the extent that they can symbolically manipulate them through the use of kinship and ritual institutions. I submit that such manipulation brings to the surface tension and ambivalence that are inherent in the relationship between authorities and nonauthorities. This tension can lead to deviant behavior—for example, fission—when social relations are conducive to such action. When it is not—for example, in the case of the holder-heir relation—the ambivalence of the authority relation is expressed in avoidance taboos and in the etiological theory that the elders' and ancestors' righteous anger toward disrespectful youth leads to misfortune.

Elders are numerically and physically the weakest category of persons in Sisala society, yet their control of younger subordinates is buttressed by the weight of tradition and public opinion and, more specifically, by the authority of office. Though they are more than this, kinship relations are also relations of production. Elders use their vested authority to control the economic processes of production, distribution, and consumption. Some anthropologists have recently tried to reduce the control of the symbols of kinship to the control of skills and knowledge. For example, Meillassoux (1978:137) says, "The acquisition of technical *skills* provides those who possess them with genuine authority over the layman since the continuation of the group depends on this knowledge." This, to my mind, is a feeble attempt to account for authority relations. Since we do not have empirical access to a primal society wherein such authority is in the initial stages of emergence, such analysis remains a "just-so" story. However it may have been in that primeval time, skills certainly do not provide authority for elders nowadays, though they do provide power for subordinates who wish to leave the group. This is the crux of the elders' dilemma: How can they, being weak, control those who are strong, since the means of production are free goods, and since economic skills are easily acquired by small boys as they grow up? Authority stands as a counterweight to that power. It is a set of symbols and institutions which provides the aging elders with power over the powerful. Meillassoux (1978:139) says, "As knowledge is slowly acquired by the juniors, the seniors are gradually losing it." In Sisala-land, by the time the senior generation has reached the point where it becomes economically dependent upon the youth of the next descending generation, they have taken over the symbols of authority from their senior generation. The skills acquired by the youth do not give them authority, only power. Then why don't they break away from the authority of elders who, as some Marxists claim, are exploiting them? Some do, others do not. The difference lies in their opportunities and their structural relations to authority. Those who will eventually gain positions of authority tend to remain within the bounds of that authority; those who will not, and those who have outside options, are more likely to leave. The results of tension in authority relations are neither automatic nor uniform. Most subordinates, both male and female, have sufficient skills to leave the group by the time they are in their early twenties, but they do not because their *interests* are the same as those of authorities.

As I have elsewhere (Mendonsa 1977*b*) shown, adults clearly see that their future security lies in reproducing the authority structure so that they may be supported in their old age by their children. Remember, as the Sisala do, that it is not only the elders who are aging—it is everyone. The interests of youth to support their elders stem, not from coercion, but from their legitimation of the symbolic formation of kinship and ritual, which is the basis of Sisala political organization.

The case of women clearly points out that authority, which they do not have, is not based on the possession of valued skills. Women have skills that men do not, skills that are just as important to the continuation of the group as farming skills. This includes knowledge about where to find bush products and how to transform them into food. It is also the knowledge of the proper preparation of the products of male labor, as well as the fact of childbirth and possession of child-rearing skills. Men are very much dependent on women because of these skills, yet women are excluded from positions of authority. Meillassoux (1978:155*n*) says of women: "Women play an important role as guardians of vital knowledge (agriculture, food-gathering and food preparation). While the group is small in size the women's skills are up to its needs, giving them authority which they will lose in a more integrated group where the problems of political organization exceed the domestic and agricultural domain to which they will be restricted."

In my view, Meillassoux confuses power with authority. Power is the ability to influence others, whereas authority is the jural right to do so. In Sisala culture we can see that these rights inhere in descent relations and in the offices of the patriclan, looking at the larger political domain, or within the patrilineage, looking at the domestic domain. Women possess valuable and functional skills, yet they cannot hold office in the kinship structure, and even when one is called by illness to be a diviner, a position of power, she does not have the authority to sacrifice at her inherited shrines, which must be done by a man. Skill and knowledge may be the sources of interpersonal power, but they are not the sources of social power or authority: they do not automatically confer legitimate rights. Such rights stem from the control of the symbolic formations we call kinship and ritual.

Food production is a major concern for the Sisala, but not all food is alike, symbolically. Control of millet is a right vested in authority positions, which are ranked within the limits of the corporate patrilineage. Millet, not yams, maize, or cassava, is considered to be the food of the ancestors, and it is the agricultural product used as an offering to accompany blood sacrifice. It is food par excellence. Control of millet is the right of the lineage headman. Millet can be grown only on the lineage farm under his direction, which is nominal if he is too old to walk to the farm. Most actual work allocation and direction is done by a vigorous, older, knowledgeable farmer. Nevertheless, the harvest will be brought to the elder and placed in the lineage granary (*virebaliŋ*), and the surplus will be redistributed by him to the household heads under his leadership. They, in turn, will redistribute it to fathers in their households. The headman physically keeps just a small portion of the millet harvest, which symbolizes his authority and which may be used in time of emergency or famine. Only he can allocate this surplus. The bulk of the millet and all of the other types of food grown will physically be held by the individual families of the lineage. While some Marxists claim that the headmen control the products of the labor of their subordinates, it would be more correct to say that they have the right to do so, though much of the actual daily economic activity is very flexible. Thus, authority rests with the control of rights and symbols, not with the illegal control of the physical goods themselves. Not only does the headman—or the elders in general—not siphon off a surplus to be used for his own good at the expense of an exploited group of subordinates, but often he only symbolically and nominally controls economic processes himself. What is more important than actually doing so is the symbolic affirmation that control lies in his hands.

The Marxists are correct in pointing out that kinship relations are relations of production in societies like that of the Sisala, but they reify these relations. What we are dealing with here is the control of symbols that make up those relations. Rather than control goods, the elders control symbols. Control of economic processes, marriage, and residence rests with the lineage headman because of his legitimate rights, at one level of analysis, and, more fundamentally, because of his knowledge of the symbolic formation and the use of kinship and ritual symbols. The economic surplus is not siphoned off. There is no material surplus to speak of. The surplus is *symbolic*. If elders guard anything, they guard their right of access to kinship and ritual institutions, such as the granary or *vugun* divination to cure illness. I am not saying that they do not use these institutions as political weapons or that there isn't conflict between elders and their subordinates. The thrust of this work has been to show that *the ritual process of divination is a political process*, but the political power lies in the manipulation of symbols, not of food or goods.

Broadly speaking, the most scarce economic good in Sisala-land is labor. Authority justifies the elders' control of the products of the labor of subordinates. Millet distribution is a symbolic instrument of social relations. The fact that the headman controls the right of access to the lineage millet granary (*virebalin*) symbolizes his position at the head of the lineage hierarchy. The *virebalin* is the head granary in a rank order of millet granaries kept in each house of the various family heads under his authority. After the harvest, millet trickles down through the hands of the lineage headman and his subordinate headmen into the hands of women, who possess the skills to transform it into food. This hierarchy of granaries is also a ritual hierarchy. Each granary is a shrine (*vene*) for the social unit that eats from it. Access to the granary contents is regulated by strict ritual norms. Just as ritual symbolizes the right of headmen to control access to millet, ritual symbols dramatize the right of elders to control the labor of subordinates.

It is not the control of the millet in the granary that gives power, it is the right to control the granary *as a social symbol*. As granaries age they are repaired, physically and symbolically. The latter type of repair is done by the elders as ritual authorities. The group agrees that the headman has the right and duty to perform such rites in order to protect the contents of the granary but also to ensure the bounty of future harvests. The control of subordinate labor is also buttressed by ritual authority. No farm can be cleared, planted, or harvested without the ritual permission of the headman. While land is physically a free good, all land and economic processes come under the ritual authority of headmen at every level of segmentation up to the level of the clan.

It is thought correct that subordinates, male and female, should be dependent on the authority of elders, though physically they are not. This mystification is ultimately reinforced by the right of the authorities to control access to supernatural powers and to cure illness. If elders rule because they control anything, they do so because they have a monopoly on the transmission of ritual symbols. That this is not a perfect monopoly, I have discussed elsewhere (Mendonsa 1979). Some groups break away from the lineage and reproduce the two most important ritual symbols of a lineage, the *lelɛɛ* shrine and the *virebaliŋ*. They can do so only when the headman of their segment has attained social adulthood, that is, when he has people dependent on him. All farmers over the age of twenty have sufficient skills to farm alone, and all help build houses, so they have the skills to build a new house, which is made out of naturally free goods. What prevents most men from breaking the ties with their parental lineage is the fact that they do not possess the ritual symbols necessary to protect the economic well-being and physical health of those dependent upon them; yet as a man acquires dependents he also acquires the *nadima* bracelets they wear on their wrists which, when piled together on the earth, constitute the ancestor shrine, the major ritual symbol of a lineage. The other major shrine, the *virebaliŋ*, is built by the new headman after he plants his first separate millet harvest.

Meillassoux (1978:139) claims that in the final analysis, control by the elders depends on their control of women. He says, "The strengthening of the seniors' authority over the juniors depends on their capacity to control access to nubile women." He claims to show the alliance of groups through the circulation of goods and girls (see his figure reproduced here as figure 6.1). Meillassoux's theory, while it has merits, is incomplete because he concentrates on the transfer of goods and women, behind which lies the all-important need for labor. Thus, his analysis is curiously non-Marxian in that he focuses on the social structure of exchange—a "superstructural" formation—rather than showing the underpinning causal functions that determine it. In Sisala-land marriage goods are perishable goods that can be had by anyone for very little money. Elders do not control access to nubile girls so much as they *use* girls to control access to labor. They control the right to legitimize a marriage, *which gives the girl's lineage the right to demand labor from the groom's lineage.* Young men nowadays can get enough cash to obtain the initial marriage prestations. What

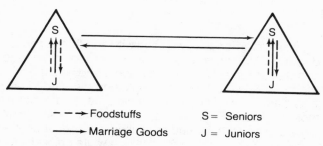

FIGURE 6.1   Alliance of Groups

they lack, and what prevents more such marriages from taking place, is enough labor potential to make the marriage worthwhile to the lineage of the girl. The right to call on the labor of one's sons-in-law is a crucial norm that makes a critical labor reserve available to the lineage. A boy who wishes to marry a girl without his father's permission is not prevented from doing so by the inability to get the marriage payments, which involve a small sum. He may do so if the bride's lineage agrees, but her elders are caught up in the same economic system and have, therefore, the same interests as other lineages—in this case, an interest in acquiring the right to call on affinal labor reserves. Control of nubile women occurs because of the limited productive capacity of the horticultural economic mode of production. Again, this control is symbolic. From the point of view of the groom's lineage, it is not the control of access to marriage goods that is important but the right to *call* those goods paid out *legitimate* marriage payments. From the point of view of the bride's lineage, what is important is that the goods received are paid by the groom's lineage so that the bride's headman has the legitimate right to call on members of the groom's lineage to weed the family's farms and perform other economic tasks. Marriage is a social affair and involves an alliance between between two lineages, both of which are in need of labor during the critical periods after the rains, when weeds threaten to choke off the growth of the crops (Mendonsa 1981).

Meillassoux raises the point about a second marriage. Why is it that the married man can pay his own bridewealth for a second wife? In Sisala-land he—and even an unmarried male, if he has the wealth—can pay the actual marriage payments, but he will do so *through the auspices* of the lineage as a social unit. He does not pay as an individual, but rather as a *representative* of the corporate lineage on whose labor the bride's lineage may call. The following case illustrates this point.

CASE 17.

Sangkuong was a married man with one wife and three children. His father was dead, but his father's younger brother headed the lineage. Relations were good between them. Sangkuong's father had paid the bridewealth for his first wife before he died. When Sangkuong decided to take a second wife, he approached his lineage headman, Tie, to ask permission. This request took the form of presenting the headman with a white chicken. Sangkuong explained that he had consulted a diviner about the proposed marriage and had been instructed to take a white chicken "to the ancestors." As the representative of the ancestors Tie received the chicken. Along with the other family heads they sacrificed the chicken on the lineage ancestor shrine. It died on its back, a sign of acceptance by the ancestors. (It must be said that this procedure is open to manipulation and interpretation. If the elder wants the marriage to go ahead, he can prod the dying chicken until it rests in the proper position. If he does not want the man to marry, he can interpret the manner in which the chicken dies as inauspicious and consult further diviners on the matter.) In this case, all was well between Sangkuong and Tie, and the rite confirmed Sangkuong's right to proceed with the marriage. Later that week he gathered several small sacks of kola nuts, a small amount of cash, two gourds of tobacco, and a piece of cloth for the girl's mother and set off for the girl's village with several of his brothers and friends. When they arrived they were treated to a special fish stew prepared especially for the occasion by the girl's mother. They presented the marriage gifts to the girl's brother, who accepted them as a *representative* of the lineage. The father does not act in this role. The next day they went to work on the father's farm. They did this bride service for three days and then begged off, claiming to have pressing work of their own back home. Throughout the next year Sangkuong made three more such visits, the last of which was slightly more elaborate in that he paid for a large quantity of beer to be drunk by the members of the girl's lineage. All expenditures were paid by Sangkuong. He received his wife and had lived with her for less than a year at the time I recorded the case. As is the custom, the initial prestations, the *haala-kiaa*, were paid as a symbol of the establishment of an affinal relationship between the two lineages. Who actually puts up the money is sociologically unimportant. What is important is that it is paid with the ritual blessing of the ancestors and the lineage headman and that these ritual acts are witnessed by representatives from both lineages. Much later, after the woman has born several children, her lineage may ask for the *ha-jaari-kiaa*, the marriage cow, which symbolizes the transfer of rights *in genetricem* (Mendonsa 1976*b*). This cow is paid, usually from the lineage herd, but again, it may be paid by Sangkuong or by anyone in the lineage, for that matter. In fact, theoretically it can be paid by anyone in the patriclan; but what is crucial is that it be paid through *legal* channels.

Meillassoux (1978:145) says that the elders are concerned "to *set the bridewealth* at a level inaccessible to the junior," but this is done symbolically, not monetarily. Elders do not control wealth or special elite goods that can be used only for bridewealth payments. They control symbols, the right to symbolically label a given good or payment as legitimate. This right is backed by ritual sanctions. Should a man marry without this backing, he stands to suffer the wrath of his ancestors, as is illustrated in the following case.

CASE 18.

Ahuno was a troublesome youth of twenty-two who wanted to marry his sweetheart. His father was against the marriage. Furthermore, the girl's father would not entertain the commencement of marriage prestations until Ahuno's father agreed to the marriage. Ahuno was a good friend of the girl's brother. He pressed his friend to lobby with the father, and finally the father consented to accept the first payment. The lineage of the girl was very prosperous and had sufficient labor reserves, while Ahuno's lineage was poor. It was not a good match for the girl's father to make, but he gave in to pressure from his son, who had been Ahuno's schoolmate in primary school. Ahuno took the first payment and performed three days of bride service, as is the custom, but his father refused to allow any of his brothers to accompany the marriage party, so Ahuno collected friends for that purpose. Ahuno paid for everything out of the proceeds of his cotton farm. Shortly after the second payment had been made, Ahuno's father learned through divination that these marriage arrangements had angered the paternal ancestors, causing the death of a small child in the lineage. The elders summoned Ahuno and confronted him with the verdict. He was required to sacrifice several chickens and a sheep, a costly animal, on the lineage ancestor shrine. As it turned out, the lineage elders later convinced Ahuno's father to sanction the marriage after he had made the piacular sacrifice. The lineage headman sent word to the girl's father about the events that had transpired and informed him that the payments were henceforth to be considered *legal*. All subsequent trips to the bride's lineage included a representative of Ahuno's lineage.

Any industrious youth can come up with the initial marriage goods. What he cannot manufacture is the legitimate sanctioning of the marriage by the legal representatives of his patrilineage. If those representatives choose to ignore the illegal payment of the marriage prestations, the marriage can proceed, though there are many ritual roles that will be difficult for the young groom to carry out without the consent of his father and the lineage authorities.

The point is that the symbolic formations, or ritual institutions, serve as checkpoints or blocks to deviant behavior. At any point, *if the authorities choose to make an issue of it,* the deviant can be labeled through divination as one who has violated customary procedure. Control of symbols and institutions gives the lineage elders the authority to make those marriage alliances that are thought advantageous for the whole lineage. The chief consideration from an economic standpoint—which is their major concern—is how much labor such an alliance will involve.

Control of social institutions provides the numerically and physically weak elders with the symbolic means to control the behavior of their subordinates. This control ultimately rests on socialization and the force of social pressure. It is not always effective, and its effectiveness is affected by the push-pull factors I have discussed in this book. The divinatory process is a symbolic arena in which elders attempt to manipulate symbols for both private and public causes in order to influence the behavior of subordinates. This set of procedures has its socializing and social control functions, but it is also an arena for the exercise of power. The weapons wielded are emotionally charged ritual symbols connected with life-and-death matters. Through symbolic bombardment the elders try to keep their juniors in line. Structure *is* power. Knowledge of and manipulation of symbols provides the ability to influence the course of action. As I have tried to show, however, the politics of divination are not isolated from influence by external pressures, such as manipulation by big men or the pull of outside economic opportunities.

Throughout this work I have stressed the instrumental nature of social structure. Authority relations are not automatically and mechanically administered, nor are they always passively accepted. Authorities manipulate structure, and those lacking authority fight back. Man, as actor, is creative and inventive when confronting the constraints placed on his actions by social structure. He both is influenced by symbolic formations and influences them. In short, rules are followed when it is in the interest of those interpreting them to do so. These interests stem primarily from one's position in the social order, but they may also be of a personal or factional nature. When authorities and nonauthorities hold common interests, they likely hold similar structural positions or have the potential to do so, as in the case of holders and heirs. Dissimilar interests are introduced by both the individual's capacity to perceive divergent opportunities and by system cleavages produced by contradictory principles.

Such factions in Sisala-land are called segments within the contexts of the lineage system, though there are other kinds of factions in society at large.

Sisala ideology postulates unity over divisiveness. The emic model hypothe-sizes that the ritual control of *doluη* (power) by kinship authorities provides the unifying force of society. The ability of elders to collect *doluη* and use it in ritual action is the key to the maintenance of social order. Competing and quarreling factions also have access to the collection and control of *doluη*, however. This can be done through magical means and is centered around the institution of medicine shrines (*daalunoo*). The power of medicine can be utilized for good or evil. Used passively and openly to protect one's family or cure illness, medici-nal power is a social good. Used aggressively and secretly to further factional ends at the expense of the larger group, it is a social evil. The emic theory of the dual use of *doluη* indicates the inherently dichotomous distribution of power in society. The ritual symbolism reflects the conflict between the power of each segment of the lineage system and the power of its subsegments. Whereas elders openly marshal *doluη* at *vesiη* (social shrines), leaders of factions within the group may secretly marshal *doluη* at *daalunoo* (medicinal shrines). As Simmel (1950:345) has pointed out, "The purpose of secrecy is, above all, *protection*. Of all the protective measures, the most radical is to make oneself invisible." Medicine shrines kept and sacrificed in public are socially accept-able. Those kept in secret, or sacrificed in private, are thought to be malevo-lent. Some men and segments keep such shrines, which they say they keep for the protection of their families, but it is always thought possible that such men can use them aggressively to cause trouble in the lineage.

Where interests between authorities and nonauthorities diverge, conflict and factionalism are generated. Dahrendorf (1959) has noted that the forma-tion of conflict groups in society is ultimately caused by the dichotomous distribution of power in society. Some men have it, others do not. Some men have access to legitimate institutions, others do not. The struggle for power in society becomes focused on its legitimate and illegitimate exercise. But in Sisala society this is not a simple dichotomy between elders and nonelders or seniors and juniors, as some Marxists have tried to portray it; rather, the illegitimate exercise of power occurs both within legitimate institutions, by authorities, and outside these structures, by competing factions. The exercise of power by authorities has both organizational functions and functions that create further conflict or exacerbate existing cleavages within the lineage group. In my view, the very processes thought to resolve conflict are partly responsible for it. The enforcement of system rules generates conflict and represents an attempt to resolve it, and in this dialectical process the symbolic formation is altered as it is renewed. In the very exercise of authority, and in its clash with other types of power, change proceeds dialectically.

Every accepted symbolic formation, once created through interaction, becomes a force in social life. I have tried to show that this is not merely a mechanical process but operates on dialectical principles as people interact with each other and attempt to use their symbols to influence each other. Symbols are used, reused, combined, recombined, altered, supplanted, and created to solve old problems as well as new ones. The sociodrama of divination is only one such institutional arena where the ideology is reformulated in a life-crisis situation and is both renewed and altered in the process, through the symbolic interaction of parties with varied interests.

By understanding better the symbolic means by which deviants are labeled, the anthropologist can investigate deviance and its implications for the social order. Deviation remains hidden from our view much of the time. It surfaces through gossip. But deviance is public knowledge; it is activity that has been labeled as deviance by societal authorities, through accepted institutional means, and therefore becomes available to the researcher. By comparing the similarities and differences in labeling procedures cross-culturally, we may find that deviance, like conflict, is a socially created fact that is inherent in the universal process of institutionalization. William Faulkner in *As I Lay Dying* had one of his characters say it nicely: "Sometimes I ain't so sho who's got ere a right to say when a man is crazy and when he ain't. Sometimes I think it ain't none of us pure crazy and ain't none of us pure sane until the balance of us talks him that-a-way. It's like it ain't so much what a fellow does, but it's the way the majority of folks is looking at him when he does it."

7
Deviance, Structure, and Process

I   During the short history of social anthropology, anthropologists have been concerned primarily with explicating the nature of the social order. In this final chapter I am interested in exploring the relationship of deviance and structure. How does deviance occur within structure? Or, put another way, why doesn't structure totally dominate man's consciousness and behavior? If there are deviations from ideology and structure, what are the implications of such? What form should our theoretical model take in order to account for both deviation and structure?

I see two major structural models of the social order, the consensus and the conflict perspectives. Standing in opposition to these structuralist perspectives is Weberian action theory (see Cohen 1968). I shall attempt to show that these points of view can be linked into a more unified theoretical model through the use of concepts from symbolic interactionism and, moreover, that such a unification is necessary if we are to understand both stability and change. Action theorists have reacted against the Durkheimian tradition by stressing the use of power by individuals and factions (Barth 1966*a*; Boissevain 1968; Mayer 1966; Nicholas 1965). Their theories are also useful, but one needs to avoid the extreme positions taken by some, such as, for instance, Boissevain (1968), who advocates a shift from the study of the group to that of the individual. Their shift of emphasis toward a more processual view of social life is welcome, but I feel that it is necessary to retain concepts that account for culturally instilled, standardized expectations, which are a vital part of any society. Individuals do not intend and act in a normative vacuum; the position

I am advocating attempts to show, rather, how conscious and active individuals take structure into account and with forethought use symbols in the pursuit of their goals.

Many sociologists have assumed that it is man's nature to conform (Harre and Secord 1973). In this view, man is thought to behave correctly for two reasons: he internalizes culture, and he seeks the self-esteem of his fellow men. These basic propensities lead man to interact with others, and thus the social order emerges out of the interaction of persons as they develop personal patterns of behavior which conform to the expectations of others. These expectations are eventually codified into cultural patterns. Deviance is viewed as abnormal because it is a departure from man's natural state of conformity, yet, since it exists, these theorists have attempted to explain its existence with theories of social strain, subcultural conflict, psychological deference or commitment, biological defects, and human nature (Edgerton 1976:18). In general, these are nonstructural explanations of deviation.

The consensus model stresses that each culture has certain basic premises about the nature of relations, both between man and nature and between men in society. These premises constitute the moral order, or value system, of a society. From the general moral order more specific rules logically follow that define and instill "expectations of behavior between actors in concrete situations" (Van den Berghe 1973). Since, as this model hypothesizes, there is consensus about such values and rules among the members of society, interaction is regulated and patterned by them. The communality of basic premises, values, and rules is the integrative force operative in society. Moreover, man codifies these assumptions into legitimate codes that are passed on from generation to generation, giving culture and society continuity.

I view this structural paradigm, found in the works of Parsons (1951), Radcliffe-Brown (1952), and Fortes (1969), and Durkheim (1964), to cite only a few, as grounded in the assumption of equilibrium and harmony in the moral order, that is, the principles that govern social behavior; and this harmony is thought to be translated, for the most part, to the actual behavior of people. The result is an ongoing social system. Radcliffe-Brown (1952:53), for example, postulates a functional consistency among the parts of a social system. He says that while this may not always be achieved in empirical reality, there is a strain toward consistency and equilibrium. He saw unilineal descent systems, such as those in Sisala-land, as social mechanisms that function to prevent conflict and maintain social solidarity. The functional consistency engendered by descent rules maintains equilibrium (Radcliffe-Brown 1952:32−48). Not only is there harmony at the level of principles, but there is a strain toward the establishment of fit between rules and behavior. This strain stems from the dual function of the social system wherein some institutions provide the means by which authorities can implement rules to control deviance when other institutions fail to socialize persons adequately. Many institutions are seen as having both socialization and social control functions, especially in "mechanical" or "primitive" societies.

Most structural-functionalists have viewed deviance as dysfunctional and as a threat to equilibrium and the security of the system. Deviance is seen as a temporary aberration that must be put right if order and stability are to be maintained. Some theorists of this camp have tried to illustrate its positive contributions to the social order (see Cohen 1966; Dentler and Erikson 1959; Erikson 1966). These theorists view deviance as a means of redrawing group boundaries and clarifying rules, and they point out that the deviant may actually serve the same function as aliens or out-groups by solidifying the group in reaction to deviance. Dentler and Erikson (1959:102) go so far as to put forth a formal proposition that *"Deviant behavior functions in enduring groups to help maintain group equilibrium"* (italics are theirs). In general, functionalists agree that there must be a close fit between rules and behavior if social order is to be maintained. In order to maintain order, authorities punish deviance, thereby controlling its incidence, and at the same time they highlight necessary rules.

These theorists postulate the existence of a universal tendency in interaction toward the establishment and maintenance of rules and institutions. Deviation from such structure is thought to come from nonsocial forces that run counter to the social good, such as individual peculiarities, alien cultural contact, or demographic or ecological factors, but such deviations are minimized by most consensus theorists. In this theoretical paradigm there is an overwhelming interest in the maintenance of the social order through the establishment of conformity. As Radcliffe-Brown (1952:10) says, "Any relationship is one in which the conduct of persons in their interactions with each other is controlled by norms, rules, or patterns." Structure is a normative order that patterns the behavior of people and prevents deviance. The maintenance of structure is clearly tied to conformity to rules.

Kelly (1977:28) has noted that structure, conceived as a set of harmonious jural rules, cannot account for behavior that deviates from such rules. One attempt to cope with this apparent discrepancy is evident in the work of Sahlins (1965). In his view, there is little relation among ideology, structure, and events, but he rejects theories that engage in reductionist explanations. Rather, he says that rule violations occur as a result of demographic or ecological factors, which he views as factors external to the social system. Such forces cause people to deviate from ideals and rules, but institutions create the appearance, after the fact, of providing redress. Societal institutions that deal with deviance merely cover up the discrepancy between rule and violation by making it look as though the deviant has been rehabilitated and/or other violations have been prevented. The discrepancy between structure and event is caused by a dialectic between the internal pressure to maintain structural unity and such external factors as migration opportunities for Sisala youth. These conflicting factors pull the individual in opposite directions simultaneously. In the Sisala case, authorities are unable to alter the external pull factors, but they do try to control behavior through institutional means. Nevertheless, the institutions fail as social control devices, leaving them no recourse but to mask, ritually and symbolically, the discrepancy between ideology and reality. I see merit in Sahlin's view with respect to the Sisala case, but Kelly rightly points out that Sahlin's theory can explain only the discrepancy, not the occurrence and patterning of such events in structural terms. For Sahlins, structure impinges on the events only by way of interpretation after the fact. As such, structure is not causal. It has only masking and social control functions. My view partially corresponds to that of Sahlins, but while I see an attempt to create social order through the systematic creation of normative rules that are formally enforced, I also see this tendency to be consistently countered by conflicting interests and multiplex social linkages that put persons, factions, and groups at cross-purposes. In this view, the causes of deviance, in addition to selfism and external factors, are grounded in the diverse and contradictory nature of social rules and relationships.

II The problem of choice has plagued sociologists who have emphasized the influential nature of structure on human thought and action. Some have attempted to solve this problem through reductionism—Homans (1958, 1961), for example, who has developed a view of social behavior as influenced by individual choices about the exchange of value, both material and non-material, in human interaction. He does not rule out the chance that such choices result in social equilibrium, but he postulates a practical equilibrium when he says:

> I do not mean that all real-life groups are in equilibrium. I certainly do not mean that all groups must tend to equilibrium. I do not mean that groups have built-in antidotes to change: there is no homeostasis here. I do not mean that we assume equilibrium. I mean only that we sometimes *observe* it, that for the time

we are with the group—and it is often short—there is no great change in the values of the variables we choose to measure. (Homans 1958:600)

This view is founded on the behavioral psychology of Skinner (1953), wherein individuals are seen as altering their perceptions and behavior on the basis of rewards and costs as they interact with others. Norms and patterns are less enduring than in the structuralist paradigm because they emerge in response to situational needs, they may persist for a while, and then they fade away. A social situation is a unique mixture of variables and as such is always in flux. An extreme interpretation of this view sees individual choice as being dictated solely by the actor's subjective perception of shifting situational needs.

Homans is not willing to go quite that far, however, because he agrees with the structuralists that norms and patterns do tend to endure and may even persist for very long periods of time. Norms are seen as an influence on the individual when he perceives their existence in the patterned behavior of his fellows. Furthermore, norms can be used by group members to influence others. Homans cites the work of Festinger et al. (1950), who found, through experimental studies of small groups, that the greater the cohesiveness of the group, the more the members of that group were able to alter the behavior of other group members. Cohesiveness derives from the relative uniformity of values of group members. It rests upon their mutual agreement about what is valuable to want and to exchange. Homans finds that there is usually group cohesiveness, or, in other words, that there is a tendency toward a certain proportionality between group values and individual values, and most people conform most of the time. He puts forth the tautologous proposition that "the more cohesive a group is, the larger the number of members that conform to its norms" (Homans 1958:600).

In most groups, then, deviants will come under social pressure to get into line. This is supported by small-group research. Schachter (1951), for instance, found that when the group perceived a person to be deviant, the members stepped up their interaction with him in an effort to get him to conform. If he continued to deviate, they began to withdraw social approval. At the end of the experimental period, recalcitrant deviants were totally rejected by conformers. Thus, it would seem that norms and definitions of deviance are partially social products of symbolic interaction, that is, emergent properties of interaction in which persons make decisions about their own behavior and the behavior of others. In Homans's view, individuals always try to maximize their profit, and minimize their costs, but profit and cost are *socially* defined. Homans (1958: 601) says that "a person stabilizes his behavior at a point where he is doing the best he can for himself under the circumstances." Personal profit is always at the mercy of others, and power struggles are played out in institutional arenas and according to social rules. Bailey (1969:xiii) puts this point nicely when he says, "The edge of anarchy is fenced off by rules." Conformers are people whose activity others find valuable, and deviants are those whose behavior is not valued; but these evaluations do not emerge out of a vacuum and are not purely situational. Rather, they are made by group members who share common rules and expectations. These emerge out of prior social interaction, but become, through time, social facts.

Anthropologists also have called into question the structuralist assumptions about equilibrium (Barth 1966*a*; Firth 1951, 1964; Leach 1954, 1960; Moore 1978; Murdock 1971). They complain that the concept of social structure is too abstract as an explanatory device, since it is a residual abstraction that results from events and thus cannot be used as a sole explanation of such events. Each has turned partly to individual choice and decision making to explain behavior and the emergence of sociocultural forms. For example, Leach (1960:124) says that in some cases social structure may be considered to be "the statistical outcome of multiple individual choices rather than a direct reflection of jural rules." Murdock (1971:22) says that the concepts of culture and social structure are epiphenomena of events. They are "the results of the interaction of individual human beings; as reified abstractions they can never be the causes or operant factors in behavior."

In his classic article, Fredrick Barth (1966*b*) initiated a new era in anthropology. He pioneered a shift from a structural-functional view of social order to an interactionist perspective (see also Bailey 1969; Kapferer 1976, 1979). Barth's beginning was important because he was concerned with how social order is generated, maintained, and changed. Barth seems to have been influenced by other anthropologists, mentioned above, who were leaning toward explaining social forms in terms of individual behavior (e.g., Firth 1954; Leach 1961) and exchange theorists from sociology (e.g., Homans 1958). He came to define social form as the regularity in individual behavior. Form, in this view, was the general feature of social process, the result of the repetitive nature of acts.

If an individual has choice, what are the constraints and incentives that influence that choice? In asking this question he rejected the consensus view of social order and claimed that social form depends on the human capacity to evaluate rules and anticipate outcomes. This does not, however, lead to completely random behavior. He claimed that nonrandom frequency distributions (patterns) do occur in human behavior and can be discovered through ethnographic fieldwork. These are the result of institutional influence on human thought and action. Barth complained that most ethnographies give only a description of patterns of regularity. Individual choice is influenced by social institutions, but what are the processes that *make* the patterns?

Like Homans, Barth claimed that individuals conform to rules because of rewards and punishments they receive from others within the system. In his approach, however, interpersonal relations, rather than abstract moral rules or highly socialized individuals, are brought to center stage. People are constrained or directed not so much by rules as they are by the actions of other people, especially those with whom they interact. In this interaction, rules are put to use, and abstract principles are used by sentient actors who communicate with others through cultural means, thereby influencing them. Thus, interpersonal relations are seen as transactional; that is, they involve reciprocal exchanges. Individuals also *decide* what is appropriate for a given situation and *negotiate* to achieve an acceptable outcome. Barth saw sequences of interaction as governed by the principle of reciprocity, which I assume he takes to be a panhuman factor. He does not, however, claim that all relations are transactional, but only that transactional relations exist in all societies. Like Goffman, Barth stresses two points: People are influenced to behave or alter their behavior mainly by other people rather than by a blind faith in abstract rules, and people also perceive cues and patterns in the events of everyday life and evaluate their own behavior in terms of these perceptions. Rules themselves are not so much the cause of conformity as is the fact that others *demonstrate* rules in patterned behavior.

Barth did not deny that values and structures exist or that they affect thought and action. Cultural values are seen as generalized incentives and constraints on choice. Social rules also act in the same manner. But how does structure limit choice? Barth answered that values and rules influence action because people evaluate the profit and loss of any proposed activity. In doing so, they take into account more than material profit or loss; they also take into account moral values and rules. Definitions about profit and loss are *socially* determined, at least partially. Decision making occurs in a cultural and social context. Thus, people are seen as calculating, though Barth said that exact ledgers are not kept by real people involved in transactions. Since many social exchanges involve no transfer of *tangible* value and transactions sometimes consist only of *token* presentations, people place meaning on them on the basis of their cultural values or their evaluation of whether the activity has occurred in the appropriate social context. Thus, social and cultural rules and principles affect decisions and interaction.

Barth seems to have been unfamiliar with the writings of the symbolic interactionists G. H. Mead, W. I. Thomas, and C. H. Cooley, some of the founding fathers of American sociology. Nonetheless, both their theories and his are saying that social exchanges involve a transfer of *meanings*. Meaning is the key concept that, in my opinion, ties together the writings of social exchange theorists, who emphasize process and individual choice, and social order theorists, who claim that cultural and social structures act as moral influences on thought and action. It also saves the abstract structuralism of Radcliffe-Brown from complete alienation from the mainstream of cultural anthropology in that cultural meaning is reintroduced as a central concept.

In symbolic interactionist theory all *"things"* (Blumer's term) in the world have equal existential status. A tree, the concept of liberty, or the status of herring-boat skipper are regarded as *things*. Any thing may be interpreted by any person; that is, human beings can apply an infinite variety of meanings to any thing. These meanings influence action toward the thing. For example, in Sisala-land, a tree can be considered a sentient being capable of harming a human being. A European missionary might consider it merely a thing of beauty. The meaning one applies influences how one behaves toward the thing.

The concept of subjective meaning can help us bridge the theoretical gap between social order and interactionist theories, but there is a significant difference to be remembered: social order theorists believe that meaning derives from a priori sociocultural structures. To them, people are socialized and therefore conform; or they are constrained in their actions by sanctions appied by legitimate authorities. Interactionists see a priori structures as only one type of factor that thinking human beings must take into account in any given social situation. While they agree that socialization and social control processes are real and effective to a degree, they also claim that one cannot assume they are always and equally effective, because people are also influenced by multiple situational factors. One must use theoretical constructs that enable one to take all such factors into account.

In the symbolic interactionist perspective, the outcome of a situation is determined by the meanings individuals hold and share relative to that situation. Such meanings may be cultural in that they derive from an inherited body of agreed-upon knowledge. They may also emerge or become refined in the process of symbolic exchange among participants. A person may be influenced by a moral principle, a social position, another person, or even a false belief that a spaceship is coming to save a frustrated religious sect. Meanings are both social facts, in Durkheim's sense of the term, and emergent properties of action.

Three concepts have been used so far: exchange, transaction, and inter-action. Exchange theories in anthropology have noted how natives exchange items, such as shells, beads, or pigs. Barth's transactional theory added that some exchanges are tangible and others are not. According to Blumer, what is important, in any case, is that persons must symbolically apply meanings to exchange tangibles or intangibles. Therefore, we need to be concerned with determining how symbols and meanings emerge and are used by people in interaction.

One important advance in interactionist theory has been the stress on *intention*. Human beings are seen as goal-seeking, deciding, and negotiating beings. It is true that a person is born into a cultural system of rules and principles that are presented to him as a set of moral imperatives, but the universal presence of conflict and deviance seem to indicate that socialization of individuals is less than perfect (Edgerton 1976). An individual has latitude to make choices, communicate them to others, revise their meanings, and engage in a variety of other intervening processes before an action is completed. Nonrandom patterns of behavior result from both an a priori system and the willful activity of goal-oriented beings.

If moral imperatives exist and the resulting pattern of behavior does not conform exactly to them, then we need to analyze the processes that mediate between them. These processes involve a series of decisions and operations leading to an end or ends. In other words, what are the operations that result in observed social patterns? In this book I have shown that the divinatory process is one such link in Sisala-land. It involves both institutionalized operations and allows for individual maneuver. It performs a connective function in that it permits willful individuals to negotiate their social order in dispute situations. Goal-oriented actors may use divination to work out their problems, and since they work within the framework of a shared cultural system, and since they communicate with each other about things, the result of their interaction is not random or chaotic, but it is less predictable than mechanistic social order theories imply.

The perspective of symbolic interactionism, coming as it does from sociology, has much to offer anthropology. Both have a common interest in exchange and meaning. Heretofore, however, anthropology has lacked an adequate theoretical construct to bring these two concepts together to analyze action. In my opinion symbolic interactionism helps us do this. It has three basic axioms: (1) human beings act toward things according to the meanings the things have for them; (2) these meanings arise out of the social interaction one has with one's fellows; and (3) meanings are handled in and modified through a process of interpretation used by an individual as he deals with things (Blumer 1969).

Central to this theory is the concept of interaction. Meaning emerges from interaction. It is an emergent property, but this does not negate the structuralist's emphasis on socialization. Children have both structured and unstructured interactions, and the formation of their personalities is influenced by both. Meanings formulated by the child are also codes derived from previously held societal beliefs and those that arise from unique situations and personal interactions with specific others. Both culture and idiosyncratic meaning are acquired and passed on in the same way: through interaction with others wherein meaning is exchanged. This theory also accounts for change because as children interact with societal members to learn their cultural codes, such codes are modified by the interactive process. Cultural meaning is mixed with personal meaning and transmitted to others, who interpret it and pass it on to others. By communicating and interpreting meaning, people alter codes imperceptably in everyday life. This process may also be organized, as in the institutions of the divinatory process described in this book.

The importance of this view for our understanding of social change is not limited to socialization of children; rather, it also adequately explains how gradual or even rapid change occurs in society as that society is influenced by external factors or as people respond to the pressures of multiplex and conflicting social relations. The point is that people are influenced not only by their knowledge of structure directly but, more importantly, by how structure is daily enacted by others. The interactionist stresses that the individual takes cues from others and thus alters his behavior to conform to behavioral patterns, even if they are at odds with abstract structure. Put concisely, people are influenced more by what others do than by what they ought to be doing.

Meaning arises out of interaction with others *and* with other phenomena. Blumer purposefully calls these phenomena "things." A thing is an object plus the meaning applied to it. Application implies the conscious action of a sentient being. One advantage of this theory is that it takes into account the thought process. An individual interacts with many kinds of things, including self. After all, an individual thinks or engages in "head talk," and unless we are willing to take a racist stance and consider tribal peoples as significantly different in this regard, we must assume that all men evaluate their culture cognitively as well as in symbolic communication with others. For all human beings, new meanings arise out of both the cognitive process of evaluation and interaction with others. As individuals interact with and think about their total real life world (*lebenswelt*; see Husserl 1931; Schutz 1967), they formulate meanings. Through the process of symbolic interaction with others, they pass on these altered meanings. Others accept, reject, or alter these new meanings. Though there are not yet many, anthropologists are becoming interested in interaction (Evens 1977; Kapferer 1976, 1979). This promises to provide us with a new theoretical perspective on culture and action and the relation between them.

III In the introductory chapter I raised the general question of the nature of the social order. In this work I have tried to show that an interactionist view of that order as a negotiated one presents a better theoretical model than the social order model and one by which we can study the statics and dynamics of social life. But it is not a simple matter of consensus versus interactionist theory or of the coercive nature of norms versus the influence of symbolic interaction on behavior. If we are to understand adequately how people make choices, we must understand how individuals are influenced by all external phenomena—physical, social, and cultural. Structural phenomena are part of that influential environment. The individual is certainly influenced by sociocultural phenomena about which he is unaware, but the individual is not a passive receptor of culture; he also contemplates, communicates and interacts with others over matters, and acts upon meanings and conclusions he arrives at by these processes.

I have also stressed the need to view normative constraints and incentives as a body of inherently contradictory principles, principles about which there is very little consensus except at a very abstract and ideal level. When people actually come into conflict with one another, consensus is less important in determining their behavior than are their knowledge of rules, their skill in using them advantageously and effectively in symbolic interaction with others, and the influence of that interaction. The contradictory nature of the social order is, in part, created by this goal-oriented behavior in symbolic interaction. As I see it, each rule set, once it comes into existence, creates its own antithesis, a contradictory rule set; hence the need to bridge the gap between them institutionally. This happens, not in any mystical manner, but because of man's capacity to have different views and interests and because of the existence of factionalism in all societies. Individuals and factions, having interests and goals that conflict with those of others, select one set of principles by which to achieve their goals, thus creating the necessity of a contrary explanation on the part of a group with different goals.

Theorists stressing choice seem to be inclined to discount the controlling and directing influence of social norms in favor of an emphasis on individual decision making, but in so doing they sometimes lead us into reductionism.

Such decisions are not made anew and from nothing in each situation; social constructions of reality are made out preexisting social facts. I would stress the selective nature of the decision-making process within the institutional context: individuals decide to select some social facts, and thus ignore others, in order to achieve their goals in specific situations. The institutions, such as divination and the ancestor cult, provide guides and boundaries to personal choice, but within those boundaries, individuals are free to choose and struggle with one another in pursuit of their goals. Kelly (1977:282) points out that the reductionists "do not elucidate the relationship between structure and empirical events," but rather their framework attempts to explain "events at the individual level in nonstructural terms." He pronounces a welcome, though I fear not a final, epitaph on such reductionism when he says, "A reductionist hypothesis charts its own developmental career whereby theoretical advance requires further reduction. The endpoint is a cul de sac."

My view does not ignore the influence of social structure, but I reject the "oversocialized view of man," which Wrong (1961) defines as the structuralist assumption that socialization works well in most cases and with most rules. This view states that deviance will not occur if people are properly trained and internalize society's rules. Instead, I see social structure as only one of the influences on choice, decision making, and action. According to my perspective, people use power to foster their view of the situation. Power can derive from authority and position in a structure, or it can derive from other factors—wealth, prestige, or a comprehensive knowledge of society's rules and the contradictions contained in the rules, for instance. Any attempt to label a deviant will entail a political struggle between labelers and the labeled, who act as strategists, using whatever acceptable means of power they can muster in a given situation to influence the outcome of the labeling process. They use their power, from whatever source it derives, to foster a situational view that they define as the best view in order to achieve their goals. To do this they attempt to get the group to select some structural principles but to ignore others as the basis of the collective definition of the situation. Rather than acting as passive receptors of structure, they attempt to manipulate it and use it to their advantage. Law is worked out in social relationships and becomes expressed through a political struggle. Not only does social structure provide the social setting for this struggle, but rules and roles are intentionally used to counter other forms of power in the struggle to define an individual, faction or group as deviant.

Bailey (1969:5) has pointed out that political struggle has a public face and its private wisdom, that is, there are universalistic rules by which the game is played and covert pragmatic procedures. Universalistic rules provide a framework of constraints and guides that are used by actors in a creative way to construct their social reality through symbolic interaction with others; but not all actors are equal in their comprehension of universalistic rules, nor are they equally competent in their use. Following Van den Berghe (1973), I see three types of actors in this regard. There are, on the one hand, those who honestly believe in the universalistic rules and who attempt to use them as guides to their interaction with others. On the other hand, there are those actors who do not believe in such rules. These cynics consciously manipulate the rules for their own particularistic ends. In between these two polar types are those actors, probably in the majority, who believe that they or the members of their faction would follow the rules if they could, but since they assume that others will not, they are forced to engage in game playing. While they honestly believe that they attempt to behave impartially within the framework provided by universalistic rules and procedures, they do little more than mask their manipulative attempts to obtain their own goals at any cost. They reason that since others are going to cheat, they have to do it too in order to win, though they would like it otherwise.

In any case of dispute, institutionalized rules and procedures provide the universalistic criteria within which the struggle takes place. Those actors, of whatever ilk, with the best chance of winning are those who know these rules and procedures. Knowledge of them is necessary in order to engage in battle with opponents, because disputes overtly invoke universalistic criteria. Any overt deviation from the formal rules is a bad tactic because an opponent can use this as a power lever against you. Effective fighting requires a knowledge of the rules because the opponent's procedural mistakes are the most potent weapons to be used against him. Rules are tools that are used creatively by actors engaged in political struggle. In addition to being used to attack an opponent, rules are also a shield to one's own intentions and goals. One who knows the rules well can effectively use them to disguise one's own prejudices or the dishonorable aims of one's faction.

The basic assumption of most actors is that others will deviate from the universalistic criteria, if given the chance, in order to attain their goals. They are aware of the discrepancy between ideology and events, and they use this knowledge to their advantage. Thus, most disputes involve actors with zero-sum assumptions about conflict situations. But merely assuming that others will deviate does not permit open deviation. In fact, there is general agreement to abide by the rules, but the real skill comes in using the rules to mask one's own prejudices and illicit goals while tripping up an opponent on procedural grounds. Direct attack is not possible, lest the universalistic criteria be defined as invalid; therefore, one must use the rules to catch an opponent in a weak position, in order to further one's own particularistic interests.

No consensus theory assumption of internalization of rules is necessary to an understanding of the politics of divination. However much the actors have been socialized to the rules and have internalized them, they are *cognitively* aware of the rules and procedures that are the agreed-upon constraints to the conflict. Most actors at least partially abide by the rules in order to protect their own positions and to catch an opponent in a weak position through the clever use of legalisms. Since the universalistic criteria do not form a unified body of premises and norms, a thorough knowledge of them provides the actor with ample scope for particularism in that he can maneuver among rule sets, selecting those that further his cause or those that damage his opponent when that opponent makes a procedural error or is insufficiently informed of all the rules.

I do not completely ignore the fact that societies develop ideals emphasizing unity and that these principles provide a moral framework to action. The Sisala come to any dispute with abstract cultural values that lead them to assume it will result in compromise and peace. The ambiguity of the normative system, however, allows political interests to select and foster a certain mix of less abstract rules which suits them on any given occasion. Opposing interests, if they lose the battle of the day, concede and compromise, leaving the abstract principles intact. Compromise is a culturally desirable end enhanced by the inconsistency of the rules. A formal set of consistently ordered rules would render one party right and another wrong, with less room for political manipulation. A set of formal rules only provides an overt framework, behind which goal-oriented actors and factions can operate to achieve the best possible outcome in a given dispute. Conflict and struggle also occur through a set of unacknowledged, though known, covert procedures, under the guise of such axiomatic, institutionalized principles and procedures as divination and ancestral sacrifice. Thus, because actors use known covert procedures and rules and means of goal attainment, the general value system is protected, leaving ample room for manipulation of the rules and opponents. All Sisala would openly admit that it is correct for an insubordinate youth to apologize to an elder when he has done wrong, for this is an untouchable principle; but for the youth the question becomes this: How can I reduce the severity of this sentence on me, given the circumstances? The Sisala also understand the appropriateness of the youth's attempt to avoid being labeled as a deviant. Within the institutional context of divination, he is *expected* to try to do so.

The question of order arises. How does a society maintain order if such political and creative use of contradictory universalistic norms occurs with a high degree of frequency? There are two points to be made here. First, the vast majority of the actors, no matter how cynical they may be, have an interest in the perpetuation of the system. They support conflict, even devious strategies, only insofar as these procedures do not threaten the universal structural framework within which the game is played. For example, in a football game the players have an interest in playing within the limits of the rules, lest they be suspended or thrown out of the game and fined. The officials have an interest as well because they make their living from the existence and enforcement of rules. The team owners also benefit from the structure, as do the fans, who would lose a recreational opportunity if the rules were violated to the point where the game was canceled. Actors can focus on more than the present situation; they can foresee future events, even hypothetical ones, and take these events into account when engaged in interaction with others. Likewise, in the context of dispute and divination, actors have an interest in the maintenance of the institutions of divination and the ancestor cult, but they also have ample scope for the pursuit of particularistic goals through an educated manipulation of ritual procedures. Without the game of football, all types of participants would lose. Without ritual means to cure illness and resolve conflict, the Sisala would also be worse off. *Actors know this, and they take this fact into account when making decisions.*

The second point to be made is that systems are given perpetuation by the crisscrossing lines of cleavage and conflict which shift with the passage of time. If alignments among individuals and groups keep shifting according to a variety of changes in circumstances, the integrity of the system is not threatened. This shifting is facilitated by the contradictory nature of the moral order and universalistic norms and by the fact that they are segregated into recognizable sets that can be used to explain a given situation from different points of view. For example, elsewhere (Mendonsa 1979) I have shown that Sisala patrilineages undergo fission in spite of the fact that this is a violation of fundamental norms about the unity of the patrilineage through time. These norms are not taken lightly and form the core of authority in Sisala society. Nevertheless, fission occurs, and the system is not destroyed; in fact, through fission the form of the domestic group is reproduced, and the system is preserved because this process is defined as an expansion of the descent group rather than as a destruction of domestic group unity. The validity of patrilineal descent as *the* critical unifying principle is untouched by the ugly fact of fission. Why? How do people explain this apparent discrepancy? When the lineage undergoes fission, the split is characterized, not as a negation, but as an extension of kinship, a retention of amity within another level of family. The new group is not cast off; rather, it is incorporated into the more inclusive *jaŋ*, the next highest level of the segmentary lineage system. When confronted with the fact that his younger brothers had left the realm of his authority, the lineage, one informant said, "Is it not good for the *jaŋ* to grow?" What can be viewed as disunity at one level is viewed as unity at another. Actors redefine fission as segmentation, or the development of a wider network of kinship through the proliferation of lineages.

Actors accomplish this through the process of secondary elaboration (Horton 1967), which is the use of one principle in the ideology to explain the violation of another. Sisala ideology emphasizes the primacy of descent as a principle of social organization, yet polygynous marriage introduces structural cleavages into the fabric of the patrilineage. Sibling sets by different mothers are united by patrilineal descent but divided by matrilineal descent. When a set of siblings by one mother (*naaŋbiiriŋ*) separates from the natal lineage to live, farm, and sacrifice apart, actors select a principle other than unity of patrilineal descent to rationalize the accomplished fact. Filiation is set aside as an explanatory principle, and the break is explained as being due to the expansion of fraternal relations, another axiomatic value in Sisala ideology. The new group, once it attains the status of a *jachikiŋ*, is drawn back into a relationship with the original group, but it is a new type of relationship, not filial, but fraternal. The Sisala see the relationship between the members of the lineage authority structure, especially the headman, and the component compounds as analogous to the father-son relationship. Compounds proliferate like children under the protection of a father, and this is good. If we see it from a different perspective, however—that is, using a different definitional principle—proliferating lineages are good because they are regarded as standing in fraternal relations within the larger structural framework of the *jaŋ*. The principle of descent remains untouched because the level of analysis has been shifted from the lineage to the *jaŋ* level. The *jaŋ* also has a single apical paternal ancestor—a father figure, if you will—who unites the group into a corporate group for ritual purposes. Thus, conflict divides at one level but unites at another, ultimately leaving the abused principle intact.

I submit the continuity of the social order is facilitated by the fact that the moral order is composed of highly abstract, segregated sets of contradictory principles and rules and also by the fact that these principles and rules are used creatively to explain apparent rule violations. This is done by actors who maintain an interest in the continuity of the social system, which to them is the ultimate reality. Endemic conflicts between individuals and factions do not lead to a revolutionary change of the general structure of society because of the creative use of principles and rules to explain it *in terms of the axiomatic values of the system*. Depending on situational interests and actors' intentions to ignore some rules and use others to their advantage, alliances form and are dissolved. Factionalism and power struggles do not threaten the social whole because they can be explained by particularistic deviation from system principles, and the lines of cleavage change in covariation with the interests of actors and alliances between them.

IV   As I have indicated, I do not advocate replacing the structuralist model with another one. Rather, I suggest that we need to use concepts from a number of perspectives in order to understand human behavior and the nature of the social order properly—for example, those to be found in the conflict or tension-management model (Edgerton 1976; Etzioni 1968; Moore 1963; Moore 1978; Murphy 1972. Socialization, in this view, is always an incomplete process, and man is never perfectly socialized; thus, there is always tension within individual personalities and between persons. Furthermore, society has conflicting rules and principles; hence, social order is difficult to achieve through either socialization or mechanisms of social control. Deviance derives from the inherently conflictual nature of the social order itself and the way this conflict is transmitted to society's members, and a societal reaction to such deviance does not necessarily restore balance but may lead only to a new state of tension management.

Conflict theorists have also had an interest in integration. Some have argued that social systems are integrated through crisscrossing lines of cleavage, which shift as alliances between individuals and factions shift. Since the lines of cleavage shift, no rigid split occurs to tear society apart because of differences of values and interests, which are seen by some conflict theorists as inevitable in every society. Conflict theorists have written mainly about modern societies (see Coser 1956; Dahrendorf 1959), but Evans-Pritchard (1940), in his classic work on the Nuer, a tribal society in the southern Sudan, noted that their society was filled with cleavage and conflict yet remained a recognized and recognizable entity. He postulated that conflict is the binding force uniting the various factions of Nuer society into one system. The historical flow of Nuer society is one of fission and fusion of groups wherein conflict divides people at one level but unites them at another. Since these lines of cleavage change over time as a result of a complex variety of social, historical, and environmental changes, the integrity of Nuer society is not threatened.

In this view, social order is maintained, not by consensus or by a harmonious moral order, but through conflict among competing social groups, none of which has enough power to dominate the others. The norms they use to support different goals are also in conflict because they have been established over time under varying conditions, and the accumulative process does not result in harmonious ideology and social structure. Moreover, since the social order is filled with contradictory principles and a variety of rule sets, or segregates, authorities may select different principles or sets to deal with particular cases and situations that arise in the everyday life. Competing factions may, however, use their power to select alternative principles and sets to explain the situation. The process of labeling deviance through divination, seen in this light, thus becomes a struggle between powerful persons and factions with opposing goals, each of which tries to force a different set of principles on the situation so that they can control the outcome. Thus, like the interactionist model, this view emphasizes decision making by individuals and groups, who make choices about the best course of action in a given social situation. Actors are seen as attempting to manage the situation in order to effect a solution to problems.

Gluckman has also taken a view of the social order as a normative structure, but one with inherent contradictions that, from time to time, erupt in social conflict. He sees the social order as containing symbolic statements and institutions that express these contradictions—for example, rituals of rebellion—or ones that mask them—for example, the divinatory process (Gluckman 1965, 1973). Specifically, with regard to divination, he has pointed out that the diviner exaggerates the wickedness of individuals and holds them responsible for misfortunes that arise from struggles rooted in the social structure itself (Gluckman 1972:5). Throughout his writings he demonstrates that he realizes norms are neither entirely fixed nor absolutely coercive. He rebelled against the overdeterministic view of the Durkheimians, who have taken norms to be largely determinative of action. He understood that norms are built up into a complex arrangement of overlapping sets, which sometimes are mutually contradictory. Different normative sets pertain to different domains of social life. Disputants refer to those normative sets that enhance their position in a dispute. This dialectical view of the relation between the ideal order and situational adjustments led him to conclude that the social order is worked out and altered in everyday interaction. Yet throughout his career he remained committed to the structural perspective, trying to salvage the concept of equilibrium (Gluckman 1968).

Kelly (1977:3) also deals with the apparent incongruity between a view of the social order filled with contradictions and the fact that it endures over time as a recognizable system. He says:

> The organization of contradictions is the essence of social structure, [and] cultural perception of the social order expresses an ideological denial of its dialectical basis. There is a conscious contextual segregation of rule systems at the surface level, while at a deeper level, the relationship between them is contradictory. These fundamental contradictions are empirically manifested in the totality of observed behavior—which includes both conformity and deviance. The patterning of deviance is thus a product of the structure itself, not of forces external to it.

Note the similarity of this position to that of Murphy (1972:240) when he says: "It is the very incongruence of our conscious models and guides for conduct to the phenomena of social life that makes life possible." And again, Turner (1967:196) puts it this way:

> From the point of view of social dynamics, a social system is not a harmonious configuration governed by mutually compatible and logically inter-related principles. It is rather a set of loosely integrated processes, with some patterned aspects, some persistencies of form, but controlled by discrepant principles of action expressed in rules of custom that are often situationally incompatible with one another.

This conflict view has been around in social anthropology for a long time, sprinkled throughout the writings of various scholars. In the 1960s, in both sociology and anthropology, the writings of some began to reflect an increasing interest in trying to deal with inconsistencies, process, and the differences between ideal norms and real behavior, and there has since been a shift to the study of specific situations and specific sequences of events. Murphy (1972:117) stresses the need to use the dialectical methodology of questioning and examining social life to evaluate the nature of oppositions and contradictions in social life—to look beyond content and surface structure, even to go beyond the apparent dissonance and contradiction to determine the underlying order.

Where is that order to be found? I submit that the basic assumption of structuralism—that it is found at the level of moral imperatives and behavior in the form of patterns—is still a valid working hypothesis. Two kinds of mistakes have marred structural analysis in this regard, however. First, there has been too much emphasis on the unity or homogeneity of cultural values and rules. The second mistake is that one is left with the impression that the moral imperatives *cause* the behavioral patterns, the regularities in action, and, furthermore, that this causation is pervasive and functional. We must resist the urge to react against such determinism. What we need to do is develop a model that both classifies and explains the apparent order in culture and social organization and also takes into account the flux of everyday life. Moore (1978:39) offers a useful direction when she says: "How can one analyze such order and regularity as there is while fully taking into account the innumerable changes, gaps, and contradictions? I propose that one useful way is to look at social processes in terms of the inter-relationship of three components: the process of *regularization*, the process of *situational adjustment*, and the factor of *indeterminancy*."

She goes on to point out that the conditions to which she refers are ubiquitous in social life and that there appears to be a continuous dialectic between the tendency toward order and that toward disorder. Within a conflictual and tension-filled social reality, the individual is rarely totally committed to conformity; rather, he tries to manipulate others to define the situation in his favor. Seeing himself or his faction as a "special case" with regard to the rules, he struggles to adjust the structure in that specific situation. Against this action there may be others who support an opposing interpretation of the rules. In other words, rarely is structure automatically enforced in real life situations, nor do the results of the enforcement effort always coincide with the ideal. Furthermore, in the enforcement process the structure may be altered by competing actions of opposing individuals and groups.

In a footnote Moore (1978:53) clarifies that by "determinacy" she does not mean "cause and effect" but rather "that which is culturally or socially regulated or regularized." She is dealing with sentient beings who think, plan, intend, develop strategies, and take rules as well as other things, options, and potentialities into account. She does not want to discard a study of socio-cultural order but rather stresses that all symbolic and social formations exist in conjunction with indeterminacy, ambiguity, uncertainty, and manipulability. She says: "Order never fully takes over, nor could it. The cultural, contractual, and technical imperatives always leave gaps, require adjustments and inter-pretations to be applicable to particular situations, and are themselves full of ambiguities, inconsistencies, and often contradictions" (Moore 1978:39).

What we must do, then, is construct a model that accounts, first, for deviance and change, because any situation or encounter always involves a range of options for individuals who select from that range, and, second, for the fact that *there are background rules of a cultural nature which order the situation beyond the consciousness or choice of the individuals in the situation.* We must not forget that the individuals in any social situation may have different levels of awareness about the nature and effect of cultural and social uniformities. Such uniformities may determine the situation for some participants or may be used and manipulated by others who understand their political function. I have in mind the kinds of hidden cultural patterns, such as time and space concepts discussed by Hall (1959, 1966), that can subliminally regulate or disrupt human interaction or the "hidden persuaders" used by advertising agencies to motivate the public (Packard 1957). For a more complete understanding of social life we must develop a theoretical model that accounts for this range of consciousness and the resulting differential manipulation of cultural realities by various individuals, factions, or groups in any given social situation. I submit that there is a dialectic between structure and consciousness and that individuals may change their behavior only to the extent that they become *aware*, or *conscious*, of the hidden patterns, the deep structures, that rule their lives. On the one hand, options are not unlimited but are bounded by cultural and structural expectations; on the other hand, the individual is not totally dominated by structure but is free to the extent that he becomes aware of the structural forces that influence his life.

I assume that sociocultural order exists because people need order and consciously strive to create and maintain it. Such need may derive from deep-seated psychological realities, about which I feel ill equipped to comment at length, but I have observed behavioral patterning in the absence of explicit rules in a variety of situations in a number of countries in which I have lived. Closer to home, I have noted through years of teaching classes that though I never assign a seating arrangement for my students, they invariably arrange themselves into a more or less fixed seating pattern. Yet there is also ample evidence from the observation of social life that such patterning does not always work, or if it does, it does not last. I have come to view social life as accomplished by people working out their problems within the dialectic between the tendency toward order and the tendency toward randomness. Neither tendency attains ascendency, and there forever remains a dialectic that provides, on a microscale, the processes of competition and cooperation which may occur within institutional frames—for example, manipulation of the divinatory seance by elders and juniors or plea bargaining in the American judicial system—and, at the macrolevel, historical processes, fission of domestic groups in Sisala-land, for instance, or industrialization and urbanization in Western Europe over the last few centuries. The trick is to link the two levels of analysis with one theoretical model containing concepts that account for the conscious attempts of individuals to regularize their fortunes and for historical movement.

I see social life as a mixture of human thought and action which results in social processes of regularization and situational adjustment of structural rules. Both forces for order and forces for change are at work in the actions of persons in any social field or situation. We need to account not only for continuity but also for indeterminacy. As persons and factions struggle for perceived rewards, they often do so within the context of societal rules, which provide a general backdrop to the social drama. Some rules, and certainly the general form of society in most cases, are not open to questioning and manipulation. As Moore puts it, "An adequate study of what is negotiable in situations cannot be made without attention to what is not negotiable in the same situation."

V   I have presented my view of the processual and dialectical nature of the social order. In this last section I want to explore some important questions for political anthropology raised by Godelier (1978). He struggles with the problem of order versus change and also concludes that man's efforts to stabilize social life result in social change as well. How is it, he wonders, that sociocultural formations do not completely dominate man's consciousness, and what are the implications of this lack of domination for social change? In his reply to critic's comments, Godelier (1979:109) says: "The problem at the heart of my paper is how we are to distinguish between the ideological and nonideological." How is it that anti-Establishment thoughts and counter-ideologies develop within a society? Bloch (1978:768), in response to Godelier, says that "*all* societies have some completely nonideological concepts, formed through the interaction of man and the world at a given historical conjuncture." He goes on to comment that Godelier makes a distinction between ideas that legitimate power, or ideology, and the process of concept formation. In his Malinowski Memorial Address, Bloch (1977:289) notes that static notions of time contained in institutionalized ideologies are at odds with the experience of everyday life where such order does not prevail, except as they are created through ritual and other social institutions. While he doesn't present any analytical concepts to explain how this happens, he is on the right track. Thus, he notes that people can think nonideological thoughts, ones that don't legitimate the sociopolitical formation. Bloch claims that Godelier posits a total domination of man's consciousness by structure. Godelier (1979) replies that Bloch had misread him because it is clear that people can hold anti-Establishment views, as, for example, the Marxist minority in a capitalist society does. Furthermore, all historic charters are to some extent *false* consciousness in that they postulate that *a* social order is the *only* possible solution to the organization of resources (Godelier 1978:766). In a footnote he goes on to say:

> The fact that kinship, for example, is dominant in a given society means that every problem or event is going to take the form of a problem of kinship; where politics dominates, every problem will inevitably assume a "political" form in order to become thinkable. Thus, depending on the locus and the form of relations of production, history's actors, on each occasion, develop a *specific form of illusion* regarding their own conditions of existence. Each mode of production thus spontaneously engenders a specific mode of screening, of occultation—in the *spontaneous* consciousness of the members of a society—of the content and foundations of their social relations. (Godelier 1978:768*n*).

Thus it seems that any structure can be dominating in a way that is taken as legitimate, but if ideology and institutions are illusory forms that lend legitimacy, what do they legitimate and for whom? Are all legitimizing ideas illusory, and if so, for whom? In this work I have said that illusion is not the same for all members of society. Godelier (1979:109) says that consciousness about domination may undergo a sequence of transformations, as in the continuum of active consent, passive dissent, passive resistance, active resistance, open rebellion, social revolution. Any of these forms of consciousness may or may not change society, but clearly they can arise in an ideology within which they are in conflict.

What is the main determinant of ideas? The structuralist answers: position in the social order. Right. The symbolic interactionist answers: the nature of the interaction between the individual and "things." Right again. Are these contradictory statements? Not to my mind. I see them as focusing on two aspects of the same process of domination. Ideas and interests do situationally emerge from the individual's interaction with "things," but that interaction in society is not totally random—it is patterned, it depends on membership in diffuse aggregates, such as social class, in structured groups, such as corporations, in loosely organized relations, such as networks, coalitions, and reference groups, and in arenas of transaction or competition, such as neighborhoods. Thus consciousness and action within a society will have a social form, an ideology and structure, as well as a specific configuration depending on the individual's exact interactions, which, while following the general pattern of his class or group, will not reproduce it exactly. Within ideology there are contradictory ideas; within social structure there are divergent actions.

But if systems are piecemeal and are built up by incremental accretion over time, how do systems gain legitimacy in the eyes of the public—how do rules come to bear the mantle of legitimate customs? Moore (1978:9), speaking specifically about legal systems of states, provides the answer when she says: "Making the bits and pieces 'systematic' is the after-the-fact work of professional specialists, or the before-the-fact work of political ideologues in complex societies." She goes on to note that in prestate societies there is less need to rationalize the legal system—to present it to a public as a coherent whole. Why is this? She relies on Durkheim's thesis that in such "mechanical" societies there is an emphasis on maintaining relations between like units that have like normative orders. She says: "This may act as a brake on significant normative changes within individual subunits since innovations might cut off important relationships. The commitment to maintaining connections among units might account for some of the putative stability of 'customary law.' " This stability can be seen in the fact that "the proportion of newly constructed rules to received rules is much greater in modern societies" (Moore 1978:13).

I disagree. Moore is on the right track when she notes the creation of legitimate orders by specialists, but she fails to deal with the problem of interests. Why do specialists have an interest in doing this? Why do Sisala elders have an interest in reproducing the social order? To my mind, the answer is the same for both state societies and nonstates: certain persons have an interest in maintaining the social order because they perceive that order will benefit them. Put another way, interest derives from social position in a *functional* order. By this I mean that certain categories of actors define given orders as beneficial to them, and they act to support and reproduce them. In Sisala-land, those persons who hold authority in the formal structure are old because that structure is a gerontocracy. If youth and women are allowed to leave the group at will, or if they stay but engage in independent economic activities, the security of the elders is threatened. I submit that an interactionist perspective that focuses our attention on the actor's perception of the situation leads us to a form of functional analysis not unlike that of Malinowski (1960), who saw the need to stress that *real people evaluate their security in social life and act accordingly.* Furthermore, their evaluation of the situation is influenced by their membership in groups, position in the social order, and perceived membership in social categories, such as social class or elderhood. There is no need to resort to mystifications based on Durkheimian tautologies concerning "mechanical" societies. As in states, elites in Sisala-land are those who benefit in the reproduction of the social order. Their interest in reproducing it is grounded in their like social positions, which afford them such benefit.

In Sisala-land, when fission of the lineage occurs, the lineage structure is reproduced exactly by the new group because there is no perceived need to construct a new structure—the relation of the new elder to producers and his definition of security are exactly the same as before the split occurred. When new opportunities for security arise which do not seriously threaten basic conceptions of reality, new lineages adopt them because the elder defines this as in his best interest. For example, in the 1960s some progressive elders chose a bright lad from the family to attend the newly established government schools. Their reasoning was this: While it means a loss of one child's labor on the farm now, it will mean an employed family member with a secure cash income later on. Later, when the opportunities dried up for such educated boys, elders refused to send them to school, and many schools closed throughout Sisala-land.

The thrust of Moore's work is that in states a rational code does not exist either in the form of core principles or as an integrated body of rules, but that *the very idea that it does exist* is what the state fosters through the use of specialists who manipulate public symbols to do so. The case materials in this book have shown that also in Sisala-land, through the institutionalized procedures of the divinatory process, elders foster the idea that a unified body of axiomatic principles and rules exists and that all should use such universalistic norms as guidelines to thought and behavior. I have shown that they may do this while pursuing particularistic interests under the protective cloak of authority. The rules of the social order provide them not only with material and social rewards but also with a camouflage for the pursuit of particularistic, asocial goals. The elders foster the idea that the ancestor cult exists an an unchangeable ideology just as state specialists present the state ideology. In both cases the motivation is essentially the same: actors in certain positions in specified sets of social relations define their interests in patterned ways.

Godelier questions how the state could have gained legitimate domination over its citizens. How could, for example, state institutions come to replace the domination of the ritual system controlled by kinship officials? The answer lies in the slow, accretionary nature of change. No single generation perceives a loss of political control over its own lives—elders do not notice the process by which their authority is eroded, or they choose to live with the erosion; and hence, in time, the *idea* that the state is legitimate parallels the fact of its monopoly of weapons or the means of destruction. The state doesn't need to exercise force frequently because of its monopoly of ideology. Yet within states, the dominated also develop anti-Establishment ideas and organizations. History is full of underground movements and revolts against domination (see Wolf 1969). The key question becomes, Why do most people in most places and at most times *consent* to domination? What is the social basis of that "consent/domination syndrome"? When does it break down, and when do the rulers need to resort to violence? Godelier (1979:109) says: "I have emphasized the idea that, from its beginnings, any kind of domination between sexes, orders, castes, or classes is based on a specific *combination* of violence *and consent* and that this combination evolves as the contradictions involved in these relations of domination and subordination develop."

Then how do illegitimate ideas become part of the dominant ideology without radically altering the control of dominant structures? The answer is that elites attempt to *manage* such emergent ideas by incorporating them into the dominant ideology and structure, or they attempt to stamp them out. As new symbols emerge, elites attempt to use them for their purposes, but again it must be remembered that this is never a perfect management because contradictions emerge from their attempts to organize society through information management, and such organizational practices result in unintended consequences. The powerful are in a better position to manage information, but they cannot do so perfectly or indefinitely.

But how do these nonideological thoughts change ideology or become part of it? The symbolic interactionist viewpoint is that change is embedded in institutional processes manifestly designed to maintain the social order and uphold the interests of those who control the dominant institutions of society, whether those institutions be kinship among the Sisala or multinational corporations in the world economy. Nonideology becomes interjected into ideology, and new social values and rules emerge because individuals operating within institutional contexts interpret and misinterpret complex social situations and communicate or miscommunicate their impressions and personal views to others, who then must evaluate such views and act on the basis of their own interpretation of events they do not clearly comprehend. Hence there can be unanticipated consequences of social action (Merton 1936). It is important to remember that structures must always be mediated by individuals who act according to self-interest and an imperfect awareness of the long-range ramifications of their action.

There is, however, another reason why form is not routinely reproduced: there is always a conflict of interests in society. Marx said that interest derives from social position, especially class position, while others have talked of different interest groups (Cohen 1976). Individuals as members of different categories or groups may have conflicting interests and therefore interpret situations in light of those structurally produced interests.

If ideology doesn't completely dominate the thought processes of the individual, and if subgroups holding variant interests and ideas can form within the larger social order, precisely how do anti-Establishment, nonlegitimizing ideas, organizations, and actions occur? The symbolic interactionist answers that interacting human beings think and derive meanings based on legitimate or institutionalized interactions, but these meanings are not *automatically* determined by those interactions *equally* for all actors. Actors perceive situations and symbols differently. Thus, while actors operate within institutions that are legitimate in that they support the status quo, not all actors perceive such institutions in the same way, nor do they communicate their ideas to others in the same manner. Godelier (1978:766) gets close to this when he says that: "all social relations *arise and exist simultaneously both in thought and outside of it*—that all social relations contain, from the outset, an *ideal* element which is not an a posteriori reflection of it, but a condition for its emergence and ultimately an essential component."

This exists in both the content and the form of thought. He goes on to say, "Thought does not passively 'reflect' reality, but rather interprets it actively" (Godelier 1978:766). And again: "Thought not only interprets reality, but actually *organizes* every kind of social *practice* on the basis of this reality, thereby contributing to the production of new social realities" (Godelier 1978:766). Thus, change is to be seen as embedded in the processes by which actors carry out their roles and by which institutions are reproduced on a daily basis.

Godelier seems to be saying that ideas have force and can transform society and that they are as "material" as the mode of production in that they have real material consequences in nature and in man's transformation of nature into culture. He implies that individual meanings as well as social meanings are part and parcel of the reproduction of the social order. He says, "We cannot really understand the logic of a society without explaining the meanings and institutions this society has for its members, meaningfully producing and reproducing their social relationships" (Godelier 1979:109—110). That is, as people work together within institutional settings, they reproduce and change those settings imperceptably in a piecemeal fashion through their symbolic interaction with things, including structure, self, and others.

One reason why most structuralists have trouble understanding how individuals can both create structure and be influenced by it lies in the fact that they lack a dynamic theory of the relation between the individual and structure. It is my contention that a processual theory, which accepts a partial influence of structure on the individual as well as the influence of the individual on structure, better allows us to understand the complexity of social life and temper structuralism's propensity toward synchronic explanations and the tendency to overemphasize the domination of the individual by social formations and ideology.

I take it that systems of domination are built up in an evolutionary process of accretion and that this piecemeal process results in forms of domination which are presented as taken-for-granted, legitimate charters of action by those in power. Furthermore, such systems only partially dominate the consciousness of societal members because this accretionary process causes the development of contradictory institutions and conflicting organizational bases of power, and *deviant* views may arise within the system at the level of both the individual and subgroup.

According to Popisil (1971:107), and viewed from the perspective of the individual, a person is subject to contradictory rules at several *legal levels* simultaneously, and even rules within a level may vary from one subgroup to another. Moore (1978:28) goes even further to state that the individual in any event or situation will be confronted with conflicting rules and possibilities of action. She says:

> If the form of an organization is to continue as it was, persons must work actively to reproduce it in succeeding generations (or cohorts). They must prevent slippage or resist pressure in any transforming direction. The pressure may emanate from inside the organization or from the outside. It may accompany a substantive change in activities, but need not. The possibility of alteration and shift is always there.

This view is one of tension management, or of actors attempting to plan, control, make rules, dominate, organize; but contradictions arise as unintended consequences of their very efforts to stabilize society and prevent change. A contradictory rule, rule set, or structure may come into existence because of the perceptions and actions of an individual or group of individuals. This contradiction may be the result of a willful effort to create an alternative to existing structures, or it may merely be a consequence of conflicting perceptions of what is functionally necessary to reproduce the social order. Because of such contradictions, individuals in succeeding generations must take into account further rule sets and possibilities and must try to organize their everyday world accordingly. The conclusion of such a dynamic view of society is that domination is tenuous, that control is only temporary, and that organization may be only incompletely ordered synchronically for any given social situation. Diachronically, any group attempting absolute control will face thorny organizational problems because its efforts to regularize social life will also produce contradictions, which lead to change. Moore (1978:26) goes to the state: "It can be postulated that there are certain contradictory principles which must be addressed in all corporate organizations, and in the ordering of higher level relations, the organization of organizations." Such contradictions include, for example, hierarchy versus "the tendency toward equivalence, or equality"; another is the "struggle between elements pushing toward greater and greater rationalization of centralized direction, and elements pulling away toward subunit autonomy." To these I would add the contradiction between universal rules and particular interests of individuals operating within institutions, as well as that between purposive action and its unintended consequences; furthermore, there are presumably many other contradictions and levels of contradiction based on the fact that individuals subjectively perceive that institutions and rules can be put to many purposes.

Firth (1969) has noted that a major contradiction runs through society: that between social structure and social organization. The former is the ideal set of rules and relations, while the latter is the "process in which *choice* is exercised in a field of available alternatives, resources are mobilized and decisions are taken in light of probable social costs and benefits" (Firth 1969:17). Firth notes the inherent tension between individual meaning and society's ideology but provides no linking concepts to help us understand how individuals in social situations go about constructing their social order and how that process of ordering leads to change. We are left with the impression that domination, whether we are talking about that between groups, between individuals, or between an individual and a group, is a tenuous affair. But why is it tenuous and partial? How can we explain theoretically why consciousness and action are not totally subordinated to the ideology of the kinship or the state? Going back to my presentation of the concepts of symbolic interactionism, we may find the answer in the fact that all things, including the symbols and constructed orders of the elites, must be apprehended and subjectively evaluated by individuals, and therefore no external symbol, ideology, or structure is going to impress the individual in the same way, nor will he be able to communicate with others in absolute terms about his understandings. In this misapprehension and miscommunication about ideology and structure lie the seeds of the continual construction and reconstruction of society. That is not to say, however, that apprehension (or misapprehension) is random, for we must remember that structuralists and phenomenologists agree that consciousness derives from position in the social order, or, said another way, from the nature of one's patterned interactions with others. We can now explain the uniformity of "false" consciousness that appears in dominated classes of people. Different networks and groups of persons who interact with each other and develop shared meanings will perceive the whole differently, but those in whose perceived interests it is to support the social system will perpetrate and perpetuate an ideology that supports those interests.

If new, even anti-Establishment ideas are constantly being interjected into the social order, why doesn't it change rapidly in form? From my perspective, domination is as much an acceptance of an ideology by the dominated, as it is a means of control for the ruling elites. The ruled come to legitimize the ideology and social formations of the ruling elites. This is a much more insidious form of domination than simply holding onto the means of production by violence. Legitimation takes place because, as symbolic interactionism states, when deciding to act people take into account what they think other people will think about their actions; that is, they are influenced by their knowledge of the patterned cultural expectations of the members of their society, class, and network of friends. We all *assume* that any act that we perform will not be apprehended randomly, but that "they" (society) will usually respond in an ordered, structured fashion. People are influenced both by what others do and by what they *think* others will do in any given situation.

Marx (1932) said that internal contradictions build up to a point where the form of society and the mode of production are qualitatively changed. Consciousness of individuals may transcend the form, but it is difficult (impossible?) to change it until it is prepared to be changed. Why don't slaves overthrow rulers, or South African blacks overthrow whites, or young men revolt against the elders of Sisala-land? These are possibilities, but not probabilities. As Godelier (1978:768) puts it, "The thinkable and the do-able thus reach out beyond thought, but they cannot escape the nature of the relations of production and the productive forces existing in a given society."

Persons who reject the dominant ideology, either partially or completely, sometimes stimulate conflict within the dominant order, but as Firth (1969:25) shows, it is important to distinguish between *conflict*—empirically observable behavioral opposition between persons and groups—and *contradiction*—inference from the logic of cultural systems. Conflict may be resolved while leaving the social structure intact; but contradictions may lead to increased consciousness and change of system form.

To conclude, I have tried to show that structures cannot completely and forever dominate the consciousness and action of the individual and that this makes society an ongoing, dynamic process. This is so because structures are socially constructed artifices that must be apprehended and actively reconstructed daily and through time. In this process of reconstruction, institutions and structures are changed because people apprehend them differently. Furthermore, they communicate their subjective evaluations to others in situations and arenas wherein actors must interpret the communication of others as a "thing" to be evaluated also. Each situation is, to some extent, a bounded unique event, though the actors obviously bring taken-for-granted rules to the situation; but it is in the daily life within institutions that people symbolically communicate with each other and reorder their world in the process. This is because their apprehension of "things" is never equivalent, nor is their communication of their ideas to others.

Viewed from my perspective, all *things*, whether a new tool, a new rule, a new corporate group, or even a new situation, must be apprehended and acted upon by individuals whose actions are based on taken-for-granted assumptions and on ideas and interests that may conflict with such cultural patterns. But there are two facts that prevent all perceptions from having equal causal status in social life. First, the perceptions of the powerful are systematically put forth as legitimate. Second, those things perceived to give greater economic security are given preference by most actors. Marx also understood that personal and cultural perceptions often dominate thought and action synchronically, but he pointed out that ultimately, in the long run, it is the changes within the mode of production that cause qualitative shifts in the social and ideological superstructure as people adjust their social arrangements to accommodate economic and material changes.

Tension exists in society between the synchronic tendency toward order and the diachronic tendency toward change because all *things* are perceived as functional or useful, but that functionality is multifaceted in nature because it is a subjective evaluation by the individual and by individuals in groups. Thus the uses people decide to apply to the *things* of everyday life are variable and will necessarily come into conflict with functions perceived by others. Marx saw that in the flux of everyday life wherein people pursue their own interests and those of their groups, some persons, groups, and classes of persons will necessarily accommodate some things for themselves—be they the means of production or information—and they will organize their lives around the reproduction of a system that perpetuates their self-interests by attempting to dominate others without such *things*. His theory postulates that they will succeed for a while, but eventually the unintended consequences of their organizational efforts will create slippage, or change, the basis of which is the rise of a new consciousness among the have-nots—a process that is constantly at work in the everyday construction of social reality.

In this work I have tried to show that as people seek to satisfy their needs and pursue their interests, they regularize procedures for doing so, codify them, and pass them on to future generations as social formations. What starts out as particularism becomes universalism as individual or subgroup strategies are transformed into legitimate procedures for society at large. Absolute particularism is impossible because no generation or cohort of persons exists in a rule-free social field—they always inherit and face the weight of custom; equally, absolute universalism is made impossible by the ever-present realities of conscious, goal-oriented, symbol-interpreting human beings who, as individuals and as members of subgroups, must interpret symbolic and social formations fostered by authorities. Most frequently they choose to operate within the legitimate framework of society, not seeking revolution, but only attempting to operate according to and in spite of the rules. Mostly they consent, but they need not, and they do not once they become conscious of the social forces negatively affecting their lives.

The implication of this view is that as authorities apply ideology and enforce rules in a piecemeal fashion, and as members of the public partially comprehend the nature of the imposed ideology and structure, and as they attempt to live their private lives within system boundaries, unintended forces are set in motion which alter the system through the very processes of reglementation and system renewal. Order and change are both inherent in the processes of institutionalization and social control. They *must* always be, in that ideology and structure exist as imperfectly perceived formations, and intended action never perfectly reproduces moral imperatives. In this contradiction and the unintended consequences that result from it lie man's potential for increased consciousness about the influence of structure in his life and the results of his action in the real world. It is that potential for consciousness that is partially obscured by the institutions of divination and the ancestor cult in Sisala-land, and the masking function of such institutions permits, to a limited degree only, the continued domination of subordinates by the elders.

This work has attempted to show that rather than structure acting directly in a coercive manner on human beings' minds and actions, it is used by them to create and recreate their order. Order is an emergent product of social processes by which people try to fix social reality, but never quite succeed. Deviance, when viewed from this tension-management perspective, is seen as structurally produced by the contradictory nature of the social order and socially defined by persons engaged in incomplete processes of systematization and political struggle.

References

ACKERKNECHT, E., ed. 1971. *Medicine and Ethnology: Selected Essays*. Baltimore: Johns Hopkins Press.

ALEXANDRE, P. 1970. "Chiefs, Commandants, and Clerks: Their Relationship from Conquest to Decolonialisation in French West Africa." In *West African Chiefs: Their Changing Status under Colonial Rule and Independence*, ed. M. Crowder and O. Ikime, pp. 2–13. Ile-Ife: University of Ife Press.

ALLAND, A. 1970. *Adaptation in Cultural Evolution: An Approach to Medical Anthropology*. New York: Columbia University Press.

BAILEY, F. 1969. *Strategems and Spoils: A Social Anthropology of Politics*. Oxford: Blackwell.

BALLARD, J. 1972. "Pagan Administration and Political Development in Northern Nigeria." *Savanna* 1:1–14.

BARTH, F. 1966a. "Anthropological Models and Social Reality." *Proceedings of the Royal Society*. Series B, Biological Sciences, July, pp. 20–34.

———. 1966b. *Models of Social Organization*. London: Royal Anthropological Association.

BASCOM, W. 1969. *Ifa Divination: Communication between God and Men in West Africa*. Bloomington: Indiana University Press.

BATESON, G. 1936. *Naven*. Cambridge: Cambridge University Press.

———. 1949. "Bali: The Value System of a Steady State." In *Social Structure: Studies Presented to A. R. Radcliffe-Brown*, ed. M. Fortes, pp. 35–53. London: Oxford University Press.

BECKER, H. 1963. *Outsiders: Studies in the Sociology of Deviance*. New York: Free Press.

BERGER, P., and T. LUCKMANN. 1967. *The Social Construction of Reality*. New York: Anchor Books.

245

BIDNEY, D. 1963. "So-called Primitive Medicine and Religion." In *Man's Image in Medicine and Anthropology*, ed. I. Galdston, pp. 141–56. New York: International University Press.

BIERSTEDT, R. 1950. "An Analysis of Social Power." *American Sociological Review* 15:730–745.

BLAKE, J., and K. DAVIS. 1964. "Norms, Values, and Sanctions." In *Handbook of Modern Sociology*, ed. R. Faris. Chicago: Rand McNally.

BLASS, R. 1975. *Sisaala-English English-Sisaala Dictionary*. Kumasi: Institute of Linguistics.

BLAU, P. 1955. *The Dynamics of Bureaucracy*. Chicago: University of Chicago Press.

BLOCH, M. 1977. "The Past and the Present in the Present." *Man* 12:278–292.

———. 1978. "Comments on: On Infrastructures, Societies, and History." *Current Anthropology* 19:768–769.

BLUMBERG, A. 1967. *Criminal Justice*. Chicago: Quadrangle Books.

BLUMER, H. 1969. *Symbolic Interactionism: Perspective and Method*. Englewood Cliffs, N.J.: Prentice-Hall.

———. 1972. "Symbolic Interaction." In *Culture and Cognition: Rules, Maps, and Plans*, ed. J. Spradley, pp. 65–83. San Francisco: Chandler.

BOATENG, E. 1959. *A Geography of Ghana*. Cambridge: Cambridge University Press.

BOHANNAN, P., and L. BOHANNAN. 1968. *Tiv Economy*. London: Longmans.

BOISSEVAIN, J. 1968. "The Place of Non-groups in the Social Sciences." *Man* 3:542–556.

BRAVMANN, R. 1974. *Islam and Tribal Art in West Africa*. London: Cambridge University Press.

CARDINAL, A. 1925. *The Natives of the Northern Territories of the Gold Coast*. London: George Rourtledge and Sons.

CHISHOLM, M. 1970. *Rural Settlement and Land Use*. Chicago: Aldine.

CICOUREL, A. 1972. "Basic and Normative Rules in the Negotiation of Status and Role." In *Studies in Social Interaction*, ed. D. Sudnow. New York: Free Press.

COHEN, A. 1969. *Custom and Politics in Urban Africa*. Berkeley and Los Angeles: University of California Press.

———. 1976. *Two-Dimensional Man: An Essay on the Anthropology of Power and Symbolism in Complex Society*. Los Angeles, Berkeley, London: University of California Press.

———. 1979. "Political Symbolism." *Annual Review of Anthropology* 8:87–113.

COHEN, A. K. 1966. *Deviance and Control*. Englewood Cliffs, N.J.: Prentice-Hall.

COHEN, P. 1968. *Modern Social Theory*. London: Heinemann.

COR. n.d. *Colonial Office Records*. Accra: Ghana National Archives.

COSER, L. 1956. *The Functions of Social Conflict*. New York: Free Press.

DAHRENDORF, R. 1959. *Class and Class Conflict in Industrial Society*. Stanford: Stanford University Press.

DAVIES, O. 1961. "The Invaders of Northern Ghana: What Archaeologists Are Teaching the Historians." *Universitas* (Accra) 4:134–136.

DENTLER, R., and K. ERIKSON. 1959. "The Functions of Deviance in Groups." *Social Problems* 7:98–107.

DENZIN, N. 1970. "Rules of Conduct and the Study of Deviant Behavior: Some Notes on Social Relationships." In *Deviance and Respectability*, ed. J. Douglas. New York Basic Books.

DOUGLAS, J. 1971. *American Social Order*. New York: Free Press.

DRAKEFORD, J. 1967. "Integrity Therapy." In *Religion and Medicine*, ed. D. Belgum, pp. 304–308. Ames: Iowa State University Press.

DURKHEIM, E. 1964. *The Rules of the Sociological Method*. New York: Free Press.

EASTON, D. 1969. "Political Anthropology." *Biennial Review of Anthropology*. Stanford: Stanford University Press.

EDGERTON, R. 1976. *Deviance: A Cross-Cultural Perspective*. Menlo Park, Calif.: Cummings.

EMERSON, R. 1962. "Power-Dependence Relations." *American Sociological Review* 27:31–41.

ERIKSON, K. 1966. *Wayward Puritans: A Study of the Sociology of Deviance*. New York: Wiley.

ETZIONI, A. 1968. *The Active Society*. New York: Free Press.

EVANS-PRITCHARD, E. 1937. *Witchcraft, Oracles, and Magic among the Azande*. Oxford: Oxford University Press.

———. 1940. *The Nuer*. Oxford: Oxford University Press.

———. 1954. "The Meaning of Sacrifice among the Nuer." *Journal of the Royal Anthropological Institute* 84:21–33.

EVENS, T. 1977. "The Prediction of the Individual in Anthropological Interactionism." *American Anthropologist* 79:579–597.

FABREGA, H., JR. 1972. "Medical Anthropology." In *Biennial Review of Anthropology, 1971*, ed. B. Siegel. Stanford: Stanford University Press.

FERGUSON, P., and I. WILKS. 1970. "Chiefs, Constitutions, and the British in Northern Ghana." In *West African Chiefs*, eds. M. Crowder and O. Ikeme, pp. 326–369. Ile-Ife: University of Ife Press.

FESTINGER, L., et al. 1950. *Social Pressure in Informal Groups*. New York: Harper and Brothers.

FIRTH, R. 1951. *Elements of Social Organization*. Boston: Beacon Press.

———. 1954. "Social Organization and Social Change." *Journal of the Royal Anthropological Institute* 84:567–578.

———. 1959. "Acculturation in Relations to Concepts of Health and Disease." In *Medicine and Anthropology*, ed. I. Galdston, pp. 129–165. Freeport, N.Y.: Books for the Libraries Press, 129–165.

———. 1963. *Elements of Social Organization*. Boston: MIT Press.

———. 1964. *Essays on Social Organization and Values*. London: Athlone Press.

————. 1969. "Comment on 'Dynamic Theory' in Social Anthropology." In *Essays on Social Organization and Values* by R. Firth, pp. 7—29. New York: Humanities Press.

FORTES, M. 1945. *Dynamics of Clanship among the Tallensi*. London: Oxford University Press.

————. 1949. *The Web of Kinship Among the Tallensi*. London: Oxford University Press.

————. 1958. Introduction to *Developmental Cycle in Domestic Groups*, ed. J. Goody, pp. 1—14. Cambridge Paper in Social Anthropology no. 1. Cambridge: Cambridge University Press.

————. 1959. *Oedipus and Job in West African Religion*. Cambridge: Cambridge University Press.

————. 1966. "Religious Premises and Logical Technique in Divinatory Ritual." *Philosophical Transactions of the Royal Society of London*, Series B, 251:409—422.

————. 1969. *Kinship and the Social Order*. Chicago: Aldine.

————. 1970. "Descent, Filiation, and Affinity." In *Time and Social Structure and Other Essays*, ed. M. Fortes. London: Athlone Press.

————. 1975. "Tallensi Prayer." In *Studies in Social Anthropology*, ed. J. Beattie and R. Lienhardt, pp. 132—148. London: Oxford University Press.

FORTES, M., and E. EVANS-PRITCHARD, eds. 1940. *African Political Systems*. London: Oxford University Press.

FOSTER, G. 1976. "Disease Etiologies in Non-Western Medical Systems." *American Anthropologist* 78:773—782.

FRANK, J. 1961. *Persuasion and Healing*. Baltimore: Johns Hopkins Press.

————. 1965. "The Role of Cognition in Illness and Healing." In *Research in Psychotherapy*, ed. H. Strupp and L. Lubovsky, vol. 2. Washington, D.C.: American Psychological Association.

FRAZER, J. 1922. *The Golden Bough*, abridged ed. New York: St. Martin's Press.

GARFINKEL, H. 1963. "A Conception of, and Experiments with, 'Trust' as a Condition of Stable Concerted Actions." In *Motivation and Social Interaction*, ed. O. Harvey. New York: Ronald Press.

GENNEP, A. VAN 1960. *The Rites of Passage*. London: Routledge and Kegan Paul.

GLUCKMAN, M. 1955. *The Judicial Process among the Barotse of Northern Rhodesia*. Manchester: Manchester University Press.

————. 1962. "Les Rites de passage." In *Essays on the Ritual of Social Relations*, ed. M. Gluckman. Manchester: Manchester University Press.

————. 1965. *Politics, Law, and Ritual in Tribal Society*. Chicago: Aldine.

————. 1968. "The Utility of the Equilibrium Model in the Study of Social Change." *American Anthropologist* 70:219—237.

————. 1972. "Moral Crises: Magical and Secular Solutions." In *The Allocation of Responsibility*, ed. M. Gluckman, pp. 1—50. Manchester: Manchester University Press.

————. 1973. *Custom and Conflict in Africa*. New York: Harper and Row.

GODELIER, M. 1978. "Infrastructures, Societies, and History." *Current Anthropology* 19:763—768.

————. 1979. "On Infrastructures, Societies and History: Reply." *Current Anthroplogy* 20:108—111.

GOFFMAN, E. 1963. *Stigma: Notes on the Management of Spoiled Identity*. Englewood Cliffs, N.J.: Prentice-Hall.

————. 1971. *Relations in Public*. New York: Basic Books.

GOODY, J. 1958. "The Fission of Domestic Groups among the Lo Dagaba." In *Developmental Cycle in Domestic Groups*, ed. J. Goody, pp. 53—91. Cambridge: Cambridge University Press.

————. 1962. *Death, Property, and Ancestors*. London: Tavistock.

————. 1970. "Sideways or Downwards? Lateral or Vertical Succession, Inheritance, and Descent in Africa and Eurasia." *Man* 5:627—638.

————. 1972. *The Myth of the Bagre*. London: Oxford University Press.

GRINDAL, B. 1972. *Growing Up in Two Worlds: Education and Transition among the Sisala of Northern Ghana*. New York: Holt, Rinehart and Winston.

————. 1973. "Islamic Affiliation and Urban Adaptation: The Migrant in Accra, Ghana." *Africa* 63:333—346.

HALL, E. 1959. *The Silent Language*. Garden City, N.Y.: Doubleday.

————. 1966. *The Hidden Dimension*. Garden City, N.Y.: Doubleday.

HARRE, H., and P. SECORD. 1973. *The Explanation of Social Behavior*. Totowa, N.J.: Littlefield, Adams.

HARRIS, G. 1978. *Casting Out Anger: Religion among the Taita of Kenya*. Cambridge: Cambridge University Press.

HARWOOD, A. 1970. *Witchcraft, Sorcery, and Social Categories among the Safwa*. London: Oxford University Press.

HAWKINS, R., and G. TIEDEMAN. 1975. *The Creation of Deviance: Interpersonal and Organizational Determinants*. Columbus, Ohio: Charles E. Merrill.

HILTON, T. 1968. "The Settlement Pattern of the Tumu District of Northern Ghana." *Bulletin de l'Institut Fondamental d'Afrique Noire* 30:868—883.

HOLDEN, J. 1965. "The Zabarima Conquest of North-west Ghana, Part I." *Transactions of the Historical Society of Ghana* 3:60—86.

HOMANS, G. 1950. *The Human Group*. New York: Harcourt.

————. 1958. "Social Behavior as Exchange." *American Journal of Sociology* 63:597—606.

————. 1961. *Social Behavior as Exchange: Its Elementary Forms*. New York: Harcourt, Brace and World.

HORTON, R. 1967. "African Traditional Thought and Western Science." *Africa* 68:50—71, 155—187.

HUNTER, J. 1967. "The Social Roots of Dispersed Settlement in Northern Ghana." *Annals of the Association of American Geographers* 57:338—349.

HUSSERL, E. 1931. *Ideas: Pure Phenomenology*. London: George Allen and Unwin.

KAPFERER, B. 1976. "Introduction: Transactional Models Reconsidered." In *Transaction and Meaning*, ed. B. Kapferer, pp. 1—22. Philadelphia: ISHI Press.

————. 1979. "Mind, Self, and Other in Demonic Illness: The Negation and Reconstruction of Self." *American Ethnologist* 6:110—113.

KELLY, R. 1977. *Etoro Social Structure: A Study in Structural Contradiction*. Ann Arbor: University of Michigan Press.

KENNEDY, J. 1974. "Cultural Psychiatry." In *Handbook of Social and Cultural Anthropology*, ed. J. Honigmann. Chicago: Rand McNally.

KIEV, A. 1964. "The Study of Folk Psychiatry." In *Magic, Faith, and Healing: Studies in Primitive Psychiatry Today*, ed. A. Kier, pp. 3—35. Glencoe: Free Press.

KOPYTOFF, I. 1971. "Ancestors and Elders in Africa." *Africa* 31:129—142.

LAMBO, T. 1969. "Traditional African Cultures and Western Medicine: A Critical Review." In *Medicine and Culture*, ed. F. Poynter, pp. 201—210. London: Welcome Institute of the History of Medicine.

LAUGHLIN, W. 1963. "Primitive Theory of Medicine: Empirical Knowledge." In *Man's Image in Medicine and Anthropology*, ed. I. Gladstone, pp. 116—140. New York: International University Press.

LEACH, E. 1954. *Political Systems of Highland Burma*. Boston: Beacon Press.

————. 1961. *Rethinking Anthropology*. LSE Monograph on Social Anthropology no. 22. London: Athlone.

————. 1962. "On Certain Unconsidered Aspects of Double Descent Systems." *Man* 62:130—134.

LEVITZION, N. 1968. *Muslems and Chiefs in West Africa*. London: Oxford University Press.

LEWIS, I. 1961. "Force and Fission in Northern Somali Lineage Structure." *American Anthropologist* 63:94—112.

————. 1971. *Ecstatic Religion: An Anthropological Study of Spirit Possession and Shaminism*. Harmondsworth, United Kingdom: Penguin.

LIENHARDT, G. 1961. *Divinity and Experience: The Religion of the Dinka*. London: Oxford University Press.

LUGARD, L. 1970. *Political Memoranda*, 1913—1918. 3d ed. Memorandum 7, paragraph 34.

MALINOWSKI, B. 1960. *A Scientific Theory of Culture and Other Essays*. New York: Oxford University Press.

MARWICK, M. 1965. *Sorcery in Its Social Setting: A Study of the Northern Rhodesian Cewa*. Manchester: Manchester University Press.

MARX, K. 1932. *Capital, The Communist Manifesto, and Other Writings*, ed. M. Eastman. New York: Modern Library.

MAYER, P. 1966. "The Significance of Quasi-groups in the Study of Society." In *The Social Anthropology of Complex Societies*, ed. M. Banton, pp. 97—122. London: Tavistock.

MBITI, J. 1969. *African Religions and Philosophy*. New York: Praeger.

MEILLASSOUX, C. 1972. "From Production to Reproduction: A Marxist Approach to Economic Anthropology." *Economy and Society* 1:93–105.

——. 1978. "The Economy in Agricultural Self-sustaining Societies: A Preliminary Analysis." In *Relations of Production: Marxist Approaches to Economic Anthropology*, ed. D. Seddon, pp. 127–158. London: Frank Cass.

MENDONSA, E. 1973. "Divination among the Sisala of Northern Ghana." Ph.D. thesis, Cambridge University.

——. 1975*a*. "The Journey of the Soul in Sisala Cosmology." *Journal of Religion in Africa* 7:1–9.

——. 1975*b*. "Traditional and Imposed Political Systems among the Sisala of Northern Ghana." *Savanna* 4:103–115.

——. 1976*a*. "Elders, Office-Holders, and Ancestors among the Sisala of Northern Ghana." *Africa* 46:57–64.

——. 1976*b*. "Aspects of Sisala Marriage Prestations." *Research Review* (Ghana) 9:23–56.

——. 1977*a*. "The Soul and Sacrifice among the Sisala." *Journal of Religion in Africa* 8:1–17.

——. 1977*b*. "The Explanation of High Fertility among the Sisala of Northern Ghana." In *The Persistence of High Fertility: Population Prospects in the Third World*, ed. J. Caldwell, pp. 225–258. Canberra: Australian National University Press.

——. 1978*a*. "The Position of Women in the Sisala Divination Cult." In *The New Religions of Africa*, ed. B. Jules-Rossette, pp. 57–66. Norwood, N.J.: Ablex Press.

——. 1978*b*. "Sacrifice in Sisala-land: A Test of an Economic Hypothesis." *Savanna* 6:129–140.

——. 1978*c*. "Etiology and Divination among the Sisala of Northern Ghana." *Journal of Religion in Africa* 9:33–50.

——. 1979. "Economic, Residential, and Ritual Fission of Sisala Domestic Groups." *Africa* 49:61–79.

——. 1980. "The Failure of Modern Farming in Sisala-land, northern Ghana." *Human Organization* 39:275–279.

——. 1981. "The Status of Women in Sisala Society." *Sex Roles: A Journal of Research* 7:607–625.

MERTON, R. 1936. "The Unanticipated Consequences of Purposive Social Action." *American Sociological Review* 1:894–904.

MIDDLETON, J. 1960. *Lugbara Religion: Ritual and Authority among an East African People*. London: Oxford University Press.

MIDDLETON, J., and D. TAIT, eds. 1958. *Tribes without Rulers*. London: Routledge and Kegan Paul.

MIDDLETON, J. and E. WINTER, eds. 1963. Introduction to *Witchcraft and Sorcery in East Africa*. London: Routledge and Kegan Paul.

MOORE, S. 1975. "Epilogue: Uncertainties in Situations, Indeterminacies in

Culture." In *Symbol and Politics in Communal Ideology*, ed. S. Moore and B. Meyerhoff, pp. 210—240. Ithaca: Cornell University Press.

————. 1978. *Law as Process: An Anthropological Approach*. London: Routledge and Kegan Paul.

MOORE, W. 1963. *Social Change*. Englewood Cliffs, N.J.: Prentice-Hall.

MURDOCK, G. 1971. "Anthropology's Mythology." *Proceedings of the Royal Anthropological Society for 1971*, pp. 17—24. London: Royal Anthropological Institute.

MURPHY, R. 1972. *The Dialectics of Social Life*. New York: Basic Books.

NADEL, S. 1952. "Witchcraft in Four African Societies." *American Anthropologist* 54:20—45.

NASH, M. 1966. *Primitive and Peasant Economic Systems*. San Francisco: Chandler.

NGUBANE, H. 1976. "Some Aspects of Treatment among the Zulu." In *Social Anthropology and Medicine*. ed. J. Loudon, pp. 318—357. New York: Academic Press.

NICHOLAS, R. 1965. "Factions: A Comparative Analysis." In *Political Systems and the Distribution of Power*, ed. M. Banton, pp. 21—61. London: Tavistock.

NUTINI, H. 1965. "Some Considerations on the Nature of Social Structure and Model Building: A Critique of Claude Levi-Strauss and Edmund Leach." *American Anthropologist* 67:707—731.

ODTD. 1913—1916. *Official Diary of the Tumu District*. Accra: Ghana National Archives.

PACKHAM, E. 1950. "Notes on the Development of the Native Authorities in the Northern Territories of the Gold Coast." *Journal of African Administration* 2:26—30.

PACKARD, V. 1957. *The Hidden Persuaders*. New York: Pocket Books, Inc.

PARKIN, D. 1968. "Medicines and Men of Influence." *Man* 3:24—39.

PARSONS, T. 1951. *The Social System*. Glencoe, Ill.: Free Press.

POPISIL, L. 1971. *Anthropology of Law*. New York: Harper and Row.

PRINCE, R. 1968. "Psychotherapy without Insight: An Example from the Yoruba of Nigeria." *American Journal of Psychiatry* 124:57—62.

PRUSSIN, L. 1969. *Architecture in Northern Ghana: A Study of Forms and Functions*. Berkeley and Los Angeles: University California Press.

RADCLIFFE-BROWN, A. 1952. *Structure and Function in Primitive Society*. London: Oxford University Press.

RATTRAY, R. 1932. *The Tribes of the Ashanti Hinterland*. London: Oxford University Press.

REYNOLDS, B. 1963. *Magic, Divination, and Witchcraft among the Barotse of Northern Rhodesia*. London: Chatto and Windus.

RUEL, M. 1968. "Religion and Society among the Kuria of East Africa." In *Readings in Anthropology*, vol. 2, *Cultural Anthropology*, ed. M. Fried, pp. 636—650. New York: Thomas Y. Crowell.

SACKS, H. 1972. "An Initial Investigation of Usability of Conversational Data for Doing Sociology." In *Studies in Social Interaction*, ed. D. Sudnow. New York: Free Press.

SAGARIN, E. 1975. *Deviants and Deviance: An Introduction to the Study of Disvalued People and Behavior*. New York: Praeger.

SAHLINS, M. 1965. "On the Sociology of Primitive Exchange." In *The Relevance of Models for Social Anthropology*, ed. M. Banton, pp. 139−236. London: Tavistock.

―――. 1972. *Stone Age Economics*. Chicago: Aldine.

SCHACHTER, S. 1951. "Deviation, Rejection, and Communication." *Journal of Abnormal and Social Psychology* 46:190−207.

SCHEFF, T. 1966. *Being Mentally Ill*. Chicago: Aldine.

SCHUTZ, A. 1967. *The Phenomenology of the Social World*. Evanston: Northwestern University Press.

SELLIN, T. 1938. *Culture Conflict and Crime*. Social Science Research Council Bulletin no. 41.

SIMMEL, G. 1950. *The Sociology of George Simmel*. Translated and with an introduction by Kurt H. Wolff. Chicago: Free Press.

SKINNER, B. 1953. *Science and Human Behavior*. New York: Macmillan.

SMITH, M. 1956. "On the Nature of Segmentary Lineage Systems." *Journal of the Royal Anthropological Institute* 86:39−80.

TAUXIER, L. 1912. *Le Noir du Soudan*. Paris: Emile Larose.

TDRB. 1912−1919. *Tumu District Record Book*. Accra: Ghana National Archives.

THOMAS, W. 1928. *The Child in America*. New York: Knopf.

TNA. 1918−1939. *Tumu Native Affairs*. Accra: Ghana National Archives.

TREWARTHA, G. 1972. *The Less Developed Realm: A Geography of its Population*. New York: Wiley.

TURNER, R., ed. 1974. *Ethnomethodology: Selected Readings*. Harmondsworth, United Kingdom: Penguin.

TURNER, V. 1957. *Schism and Continuity in African Society*. Manchester: Manchester University Press.

―――. 1961. *Ndembu Divination: Its Symbolism and Techniques*. Rhodes-Livingston Paper no. 31. Manchester: Manchester University Press.

―――. 1963. *Lunda Medicine and the Treatment of Disease*. Occasional Paper of the Rhodes-Livingston Museum, no. 15. Lusaka: University of Lusaka Press.

―――. 1967. "Aspects of Saora Ritual and Shamanism: An Approach to the Data of Ritual." In *The Craft of Social Anthropology*, ed. A. L. Epstein, pp. 181−204. London: Tavistock.

―――. 1968. *Drums of Application: A Study of Religious Processes among the Ndembu of Zambia*. Oxford: Clarendon Press and the International African Institute.

―――. 1974. *Dramas, Fields, and Metaphors: Symbolic Action in Human Society*. Ithaca: Cornell University Press.

VAN DEN BERGHE, P. 1973. *Power and Privilege at an African University*. Cambridge, Mass.: Schenkman.

VAN DOORN, J. 1963. "Sociology and the Problem of Power." *Sociologia Neerlandica* 1:3—47.

VAN VELSEN, J. 1967. "The Extended-Case Method and Situational Analysis." In *The Craft of Social Anthropology*, ed. A. L. Epstein, pp. 129—149. London: Tavistock.

VAUGHN, J. 1964. "The World View of the Marghi." *Ethnology* 3:129—149.

WERBNER, R. 1972. "Sin, Blame, and Ritual Mediation." In *The Allocation of Responsibility*, ed. M. Gluckman, pp. 227—255. Manchester: Manchester University Press.

WILKS, I. 1975. *Asante in the Nineteenth Century: The Structure and Evolution of a Political Order*. London: Cambridge University Press.

WILLIS, R. 1968. "Changes in Mystical Concepts and Practices among the Fipa." *Ethnology* 7:139—157.

WILSON, M. 1957. *Rituals of Kinship among the Nyakyusa*. London: Oxford University Press.

WILSON, T. 1970. "Conceptions of Interaction and Forms of Sociological Explanation." *American Sociological Review* 35:697—710.

WOLF, E. 1969. *Peasant Wars of the Twentieth Century*. New York: Harper and Row.

WRONG, D. 1961. "The Oversocialized Conception of Man in Modern Society." *American Sociological Review* 26:183—193.

List of Cases

Index

Designer: Linda Robertson
Compositor: Trend Western Technical Corporation
Printer: Braun-Brumfield, Inc.
Binder: Braun-Brumfield, Inc.
Text: 11/13 Garamond Roman